CHINA IN THE NINETIES

CHINA IN THE NINETIES

Crisis Management and Beyond

Edited by

DAVID S. G. GOODMAN
and
GERALD SEGAL

CLARENDON PRESS · OXFORD
1991

Oxford University Press, Walton Street, Oxford OX2 6DP
Oxford New York Toronto
Delhi Bombay Calcutta Madras Karachi
Petaling Jaya Singapore Hong Kong Tokyo
Nairobi Dar es Salaam Cape Town
Melbourne Auckland
and associated companies in
Berlin Ibadan

Oxford is a trade mark of Oxford University Press

Published in the United States
by Oxford University Press, New York

British Library Cataloguing in Publication Data
Data available

Library of Congress Cataloging in Publication Data
China in the nineties : crisis management and beyond / edited by David S. G.
Goodman and Gerald Segal.
p.   cm.
Includes index.
1. China—Politics and government—1976- 2. China—Foreign relations—1976-
I. Goodman, David S. G.   II. Segal, Gerald, 1953-
DS779.26.C47352   1991   951.05—dc20   91-17277
ISBN 0-19-827362-2   ISBN 0-19-827363-0 (Pbk.)

Printed and bound in
Great Britain by Bookcraft (Bath) Ltd.
Midsomer Norton, Avon

PREFACE

During 1988-9 a special issue of *The Pacific Review* was prepared to commemorate the fortieth anniversary of the establishment of the People's Republic of China. The journal's publishers, Oxford University Press, decided to reproduce the original articles in a single volume under the title *China at Forty: Mid-Life Crisis?* Literally as the book was reaching the final stages of preparation the major crisis that had been signalled in its pages erupted violently in Beijing and around China.

China at Forty was published in time for National Day (1 October) 1989 and sold out almost immediately. In consequence, the publishers requested a second edition and this volume is the result. The original contributors were asked to update their chapters, or to write a completely new chapter for this volume, and in most cases the second option was preferred.

In *China in the Nineties: Crisis Management and Beyond* the intention is to address the same problems as the original volume but to look at them now in the light of 4 June 1989 and its aftermath. As before, the emphasis has been placed on the challenges facing the PRC in the foreseeable future. However, 4 June 1989 has not only made many of those challenges more acute, it has also brought them into clearer focus.

The contradiction which underlies almost all the chapters in this book, and which bedevils China's attempt to manage its current crisis, is that while there is an urgent need for reform, real fundamental change—whether it is economic, political, social, or cultural—can and will only occur slowly. Unlike the rhetoric to reform, the speed of change is necessarily more constrained. Moreover, with an ageing leadership and an uncertain future, even changes in rhetoric have less of an impact on society at large.

The line-up for *China in the Nineties* is slightly different to that provided in *China at Forty*. David Kelly has written on Marxism and its future in China; whilst Ann Kent has written on questions of human rights, a topic which was a serious omission from the earlier volume. A special acknowledgement is due to both of them for agreeing to write (and delivering) at relatively short notice.

D.S.G.G.
Murdoch University, Western Australia
19 September 1990

NOTES ON CONTRIBUTORS

MARC BLECHER is in the Department of Government, Oberlin College, Ohio.

ANITA CHAN is an Associate of the Contemporary China Centre, Australian National University.

DAVID S. G. GOODMAN is Professor of Asian Studies and Director of the Asia Research Centre at Murdoch University, Western Australia.

DAVID KELLY is a Research Fellow of the Contemporary China Centre, Australian National University.

ANN KENT is an Associate of the Contemporary China Centre, Australian National University.

HARLAN W. JENCKS is a Research Fellow at the Centre for Chinese Studies, University of California, Berkeley.

MICHÈLE LEDÍC researches China's foreign trade and energy at Birkbeck College, University of London.

GERALD SEGAL is a Senior Research Fellow at the International Institute for Strategic Studies in London, Reader in International Affairs at the University of Bristol, and editor of *The Pacific Review*.

LAWRENCE R. SULLIVAN is in the Department of Political Studies, Adelphi University, New York.

LEE LAI TO is Senior Lecturer in the Department of Political Science, National University of Singapore.

CONTENTS

FIGURES

ABBREVIATIONS

BR	*Beijing Review*
CAC	Central Advisory Committee
CCP	Chinese Communist Party
CD	*China Daily*
CMC	Central Military Commission
CPSU	Communist Party of the Soviet Union
FBIS	*Foreign Broadcast Information Service*
FEER	*Far Eastern Economic Review*
GDP	Gross Domestic Product
GNP	Gross National Product
JFJHB	*Jiefangjun Hua Bao*
JPRS	*Joint Publications Research Services*
KMT	The Nationalist Party (Kuomintang or Guomindang, the ruling party in the Republic of China on Taiwan)
NPC	National People's Congress
PLA	People's Liberation Army
PRC	People's Republic of China
RMB	Renmimbi (PRC currency)
SWB	BBC, *Summary of World Broadcasts*
ZTN	*Zhongguo Tongji Nianjian*

Introduction
The Authoritarian Outlook

DAVID S.G. GOODMAN

In the aftermath of 4 June 1989 many Western commentators have looked to the fate of the communist party state in Eastern Europe to predict radical future change in China. The general, currently fashionable argument that authoritarian political systems and economic modernization cannot coexist in the long term, and indeed that the latter ensures the transformation of the former into some form of liberal democracy, seems particularly apposite in the case of the People's Republic of China. However, the relationships between political and economic development are not so easily reduced to such a simple equation, and the parallels between China and Eastern Europe may be more superficial than appears at first sight.

This introduction to the following more detailed chapters on specific aspects of China's current crises examines the dynamics of the current authoritarian regime, to assess the prospects for its future, and against the background of recent developments in Eastern Europe in order to contribute to the wider debate. It concludes that the present political situation in the PRC is inherently unstable, but that a liberal democracy is not a likely outcome. There was no significant pressure to establish a liberal democracy of any sort before mid-1989, but rather a more pluralist (or, more accurately, corporatist) communist-party-led political system. The ideological divide which characterized the late 1980s was not one between the status quo of the Mao-dominated era and liberal democracy but rather between two different visions of an authoritarian communist party state. Paradoxically, the leadership's actions in mid-1989 are likely to have jeopardized both of those possibilities. Change is thus probable but by no means certain or radical. If there is to be change then, for structural reasons as much as because of the PRC's inherently authoritarian political culture, an authoritarian regime may still result and even one where the Chinese Communist Party (CCP) may play a role.

On the more general question of economic change and political transformation it is suggested that the management of the social reaction to economic change is a more important determinant in the transformation of authoritarianism than the drive to economic modernization itself. The articulation and management of that social reaction in the PRC has been crucially different to the experience of Eastern Europe, not least because the process of economic modernization started sooner in China than Eastern Europe and because of the difference in relationships to the USSR. In Eastern Europe the social reaction to economic change, and local leadership's response, has clearly been determined in large part by the international environment. Gorbachev's and the USSR's role as the midwife of change in Eastern Europe has been considerable, as has the lure of the West. In the PRC, by contrast, those factors are replaced by different expectations and a different state idea.

Competing Political Strategies

Although the 1980s saw the most stable period of China's politics since the early 1950s, it was a decade of intense debate within the leadership of the CCP. After 1982, though the leadership was able to agree what it did not want (the Cultural Revolution), it was unable to agree on its strategic replacement. There was general broad agreement that China needed to import foreign technology, to be part of the international economic order, to introduce market forces into the economy, to plan according to economic rather than political criteria, to institutionalize politics, and to relax controls. However, there was also considerable disagreement over the extent to which and the means by which these goals should be achieved.

Two broad notions — neither of which embraced liberal democracy[1] — informed the discussion of China's future during the 1980s. One was of a market-determined economy with an institutionalized and relatively open political system though still ruled by a communist party. The other was of a market-oriented economy, with considerably less political liberalization (liberalization here being the process of redefining and extending rights), where the communist party and the state still dominated the economy and society.

---

[1] B. Womack, 'Party-State Democracy: A Theoretical Exploration', in *Issues and Studies*, 25/3 (1989), 37.

Increasingly after 1986 the former, more liberal attitude was characterized as emphasizing the immediate need for both political and economic reform; the latter, more conservative view, as stressing a more gradualist approach to economic reform and being extremely reticent about political reform.

Although the CCP appears to have polarized in the middle of 1989 on the issue of political reform, in general the battle lines were neither clear cut nor static. Factional loyalties, ideological propensities, and policy stances are rarely dependent variables in Chinese politics.[2] As new initiatives were discussed, and new policies implemented experimentally, the debate developed its own dynamic. In general, the more liberal reform ideas, largely — or at least until the end of 1986 — with Deng Xiaoping's encouragement and support, made the running.[3] At the top of that agenda were the issues of price reform, and the separation of party and government.

However, the initiative was not always monopolized by those impatient for reform. Thus, for example, at the 1985 CCP National Conference, Chen Yun, the most senior conservative reformer, argued quite openly that the reform era had substantial achievements but political control of the economy had been relaxed too much and required readjustment. In particular he highlighted what have become key issues over the years for conservative objections to the more liberal position on reform: he argued that some economic decisions should still be taken on political grounds, such as those which affected the distribution of wealth, the production of food grains, or the extent to which the economy had become decentralized. His position has been that, whilst a socialist economy must run according to economic laws, if it is to remain socialist it requires the dual-track system where market and command sectors coexist, even when problems result.[4]

There were even periods before June 1989, though admittedly relatively few and short, when the initiative lay very firmly with the conservative reformers. Such ascendencies — which usually,

[2] See e.g. L. Pye, *The Dynamics of Chinese Politics* (Cambridge, Mass., 1981); and K. Lieberthal and M. Oksenberg, *Policy Making in China* (Princeton, NJ, 1988).

[3] T. Saich, 'Reforming the Political Structure', in R. Benewick and P. Wingrove, *Reforming the Revolution: China in Transition* (London, 1988), 27.

[4] Chen Yun, 'Speech at the National Party Conference', *BR* 39 (30 Sept. 1985), 20.

as in 1989, coincided with periods of economic contraction (as opposed to those of economic expansion when the liberal reformers tended to be in the driving seat) — led to similar policy initiatives as those promoted since June 1989, and included anti-liberalization movements of various kinds. In 1981, 1983/4, and 1987, in particular, conservative reformers promoted greater political control of the population in general, as well as of dissent, in campaigns against 'spiritual pollution' and 'bourgeois liberalization'. Individual behaviour and attitudes, the purity of Chinese tradition, and of socialism, have all been largely conservative concerns during the 1980s.

The leadership crisis which came to a head under the impact of popular demonstrations in May/June 1989 had its immediate origins during July 1988. After September 1986 the pace of reform had started to slow, experiments with political reforms being shelved when they began to be seen as leading to a threat to the CCP's monopoly on political power not only by the arch-conservatives within the party's leadership but also by other more reform-minded individuals, notably Deng Xiaoping.[5] Popular reactions, notably from student demonstrators, and the subsequent ouster of Hu Yaobang from office as general secretary in January 1987, ensured that the issue of political reform was doubly politicized. Events in 1988 repeated history for the pace of economic reform. The key issue was price reform. The introduction of market structures alongside the institutions of the command economy had led to economic dysfunctionalities not least because of price differentials between the two sectors. The reformers sought the introduction of a full market system for the determination of prices. The conservatives highlighted the political dangers which included not only the CCP's decreased ability to direct the economy, but also their concerns about the possible effects on the CCP's natural constituencies of support should (as they feared) price reform prove inflationary. Experiments with price reform were introduced in early 1988 but in late July the CCP leadership's usual summer meeting at Beidaihe postponed any further developments in that direction. By late July it had become clear that the conservatives' worst fears might be about to be realized and that China was in

---

[5] Deng Xiaoping, 'Remarks at the 6th Plenary Session of the Party's 12th Central Committee', in Deng Xiaoping, *Fundamental Issues in Present Day China* (Beijing, 1987), 154.

the middle of an inflationary economic crisis. Unauthorized price increases were mushrooming, goods were being stockpiled, consumers were going on non-stop shopping expeditions, and there were runs on Chinese banks.

Zhao Ziyang's position in particular became extremely exposed as a result of these set-backs. In 1986 Hu Yaobang and he had, at Deng Xiaoping's direction, engineered the experiments with political reform. In October/November 1987 the Thirteenth CCP Congress signalled a renewed commitment to more liberal reform through both Zhao's work report to the congress (as CCP general secretary) and through the changes it approved in the leadership of the CCP. By July 1988, Zhao had been in frequent conflict with the more conservative voices within the CCP leadership, particularly that of Prime Minister Li Peng. At the Beidaihe meeting he is reported to have lost his temper with Li Peng, and threatened resignation, offering Li the job if the latter thought he could do it better. Although Deng had supported price reform in the early part of 1988, and indeed pushed Zhao to proceed further and faster, shortly before the Beidaihe meeting he indicated that he had an open mind on the subject and saw no need to stand unreservedly behind Zhao.[6] When the CCP's Political Bureau met in August Zhao was removed from the economic policy-making process and primary responsibility handed over to Li Peng and Yao Yilin. By September, when the Third Plenum of the Thirteenth Central Committee convened there was apparently some possibility that Zhao might have been removed altogether from the CCP leadership.

The Aftermath of June 1989

Events in mid-1989 provided the opportunity for the advocates of the more conservative vision of reform to seize the upper hand for longer and more surely than at any time during the 1980s. However, it is still a vision of reform and its ascendancy does not herald an attempt to restore the status quo ante of the Mao-dominated years of PRC politics. Moreover, though at first sight it may seem otherwise, events since June 1989 have not destroyed the uneasy

---

[6] L. Dittmer, 'China in 1988: The Continuing Dilemma of Socialist Reform', *Asian Survey*, 29/1 (1989), 21.

relationship between the more liberal and more conservative visions of reform which characterized the second half of the 1980s.

Even a somewhat cursory examination of policy implementation, as opposed to the political rhetoric, suggests that though the reform programme has taken on a more conservative perspective since June 1989, the reform era as conceived in 1978 has yet to be deliberately abandoned. Most of the fundamental reforms — particularly in the economy — introduced at the third plenum remain in place. For example, although the CCP blames much of the June 'counter-revolutionary rebellion' on Western influence and Western intervention, and despite the fundamental xenophobia of much of Chinese nationalism, foreign economic relations remain the cornerstone of China's development strategy. During the 1980s the most visible symbol of this 'open policy' were the Special Economic Zones. Although these were not always as successful economically as the CCP leadership would have liked, or had hoped when they were first established, they have been retained. In the second half of 1989 their importance, as opposed to other avenues of foreign economic involvement in China, was re-emphasized, largely no doubt because they were seen as isolatable ghettos of foreign influence. They are regarded as devices whereby foreign technology and assistance can be introduced into China without the 'pollution' of foreign ideas and values.

There has been no attempt to undo the reform of the wage system. During the 1970s the work-force's lack of motivation was clearly creating problems for economic growth. The late 1970s saw the large-scale reintroduction of material incentives in order to encourage production, and during the 1980s inequalities in income largely determined by the market increased. Certainly, such inequalities and perceptions of relative deprivation were powerful factors in creating the popular disturbances of 1989. None the less, the CCP remains heavily committed to the general principles of wage reform and critical of earlier egalitarian tendencies and practices such as security of tenure for employees. The new general secretary of the CCP, Jiang Zemin, has made several public statements to the effect that, whilst inequalities should not get out of hand, they are not only generally acceptable but also are desirable: it is equality of opportunity that is considered important, not equality of wealth or income.[7]

[7] Jiang Zemin, 'Eliminate Unfair Income Distribution', *B R* 35 (28 Aug. 1989), 15.

Similarly, there has been no suggestion of a change in the pattern of land usage established during the 1980s. Decollectivization of agriculture was the cornerstone of economic reform, especially during 1979–84. There has been no attempt at recollectivization, and few suggestions that peasants should be more restricted in how they farm their land. Paradoxically, this is an urgent problem, for agricultural growth has slowed dramatically since 1984, and demand for essential foodstuffs has grown more rapidly than supply as peasants have reacted through their new economic freedom to market forces. This was precisely one reason why Chen Yun spoke out at the 1985 CCP National Conference: he was concerned that peasants were switching production from food to cash crops on too large a scale. Even the most politically controversial aspect of land usage during the last decade—land sales to foreigners—has not changed. Indeed, the purchase of a slice of Tianjin by an American company during August 1989 was trumpeted in the Chinese press as an example of the way everything was back to normal as far as foreign economic involvement in China was concerned.

Despite the conservative reformers' adherence to more orthodox versions of communism in many respects, this has not applied to the introduction of market forces. Here they remain committed to a dual-track system, with a market sector alongside the state sector. Although the CCP attacked the private sector after June 1989 and held out the virtues of the state-run economy—pointing out that the state sector had performed better than the private sector—the non-state nascent corporate sector is the collective sector. The private sector in China is comprised of small, usually very small, private businesses, often owned and run by one person, and it has an almost negligible share in economic output. Outside the state sector, corporate enterprises are almost all in the collective sector, which consistently outperformed the state sector during the 1980s.[8] However, the collective sector has not been under attack or criticism. On the contrary, though the speed of reform to introduce capital and securities markets has slowed, plans along these lines continue. For example, in late September 1989, by way of preparation and training, officials were sent abroad to gain experience in major foreign securities companies.

Two further examples of the introduction of market forces may help to illustrate the extent to which reform principles have been

[8] L. do Rosario, 'Three Years Hard Labour', *FEER* (30 Nov. 1989), 68.

pursued. One of the bolder reforms of the 1980s has been what amounts in essence to the privatization of housing. Previously most urban housing was provided by the state or the enterprise (and when most enterprises were state run there was little difference) at highly subsidized rents and on a permanent basis. Demand has consistently outstripped supply, and of course the provision of housing has been a considerable cost on the public exchequer. Small-scale experiments in different parts of China before 1989 resulted in various schemes for house purchases and higher rents. Starting in October 1989 these reforms were continued on a larger scale with everyone in Guangzhou (China's first metropolis to experience the reform *in toto*) required either to buy their dwelling or pay a market-clearing rent. Of course, housing reform of this kind also has a useful deflationary consequence. A final example of the continued recognition and introduction of market forces is the recent agreement by the State Council that pensions for cadres, intellectuals, and all state employees above a certain level should be index-linked. At a time of severe inflation such as China has suffered since 1987 this is a matter of no small importance.

The reform vision of the current leadership is then one which has much in common with the reform or 'goulash communism' of the early 1960s in the USSR and Eastern Europe. Reforms in the management of the economy, economic liberalization, and even considerable measures of consumerism are permissible, but only limited political reforms. The purpose of political reform is to ensure 'clean and honest' government, not the emergence of civil society. Unlike in the Cultural Revolution the legal system continues to flourish. However, its purpose is not so much to protect rights as to ensure the rules upon which efficient bureaucracies operate. It is certainly not intended to be depoliticized.[9] Thus, for example, not only was a new law governing demonstrations promulgated at the start of 1990, but the criteria for their permissibility were explicitly political. Generally, the 'Four Basic Principles' elaborated by Deng Xiaoping in March 1979 — accepting the leadership of the CCP, the supremacy of Marxism-Leninism-Mao Zedong Thought, the socialist road, and the dictatorship of the proletariat — are the touchstone of acceptable political behaviour.[10]

---

[9] 'Jiang Zemin Urges More Legal Learning', *CD* (8 Jan. 1990).

[10] Deng Xiaoping, 'Uphold the Four Cardinal Principles', in *Selected Works of Deng Xiaoping* (1975-82) (Beijing, 1984), 166.

The Dynamics of Change

Even without the intervention of public disorder during April, May, and June of 1989 and the subsequent leadership crisis, PRC politics were fast becoming ungovernable. Within the leadership there was little room for agreement or compromise on interest or principle. In society at large, urban and rural China seemed on a collision course: the latter wanted price reform and the introduction of a free market for their produce, the former were concerned about the inflationary effects of price reform on foodstuffs. The events of June 1989 have exacerbated these tensions and virtually ensured that in all but the immediate term the status quo cannot be maintained. PRC politics are now inherently unstable, with the leadership of the CCP under threat from the immediate consequences of its reaction to the events of May–June 1989, the socio-economic forces which led to those events, and changes in China's international environment.

In 1978 when the CCP launched the reform era it fully realized that its ability to motivate the new drive to economic modernization was severely restricted. Although the CCP had consistently sought positive support for its policies after 1949, it had always been prepared to settle for mobilization. By the late 1970s, as a result of the Cultural Revolution and the instabilities of the previous thirty years, it had exhausted even that capacity. Various leaders of the CCP, including both Deng Xiaoping and Chen Yun, recognized that a new social contract had to be created between the party and people if the CCP was to realize any of its goals. The bases of this new social contract were to be the immediate benefits of economic growth, as well as the promise of sustained modernization and political reform, and sooner rather than later.

One immediate impact of the political clampdown that has occurred since June 1989 has been a severe challenge to the existence of the social contract of 1978. The events of May/June 1989 have led the northern urban work-force in particular to question the CCP's sincerity across the board and not just with respect to political reform. In that respect Deng's attitudes may prove to be self-defeating. He wants the population to take initiatives and be self-regulating, but is not prepared to accept all the political consequences, and particularly not any discussion of liberal democracy. Sending in troops to suppress popular demonstrations of discontent, which were for the most part not originally directed against CCP authority, is unlikely to encourage the development of a proactive work-force, particularly when political controls of the economy are reasserted.

The challenge of liberal democracy is something the CCP took extremely seriously throughout the 1980s. After mid-1989 the CCP attempted to propagandize against liberal democracy and in favour of its own particular brand of authoritarianism through a very high profile appeal to nationalism. Liberal democracy has been characterized as a Western pollutant unsuited to Chinese conditions. Ironically, the current leadership has been assisted in this endeavour by Zhao Ziyang and his supporters' efforts to shore up the cause of liberal reform after August 1988. One of these was support for a highly controversial television series — *River Elegy* — which was highly critical of Chinese tradition, and argued that China needed to adopt new perspectives if it were to modernize. The new perspective which was promoted throughout the media was the concept of 'New authoritarianism'. This argued that the developing countries of East and South-East Asia have neither the capacity for nor the tradition of liberal democracy. In a era of rapid modernization they require government based on the indigenous Confucian authoritarianism if limited resources are to be used to their best effect and chaos is to be avoided. With obvious differences, the current leadership is adopting what may be regarded as the Singapore Strategy: it believes that if the economy can be righted and economic prosperity, or even its real promise, restored then demands for further democratization will decrease. There is more than a little logic to this position — corruption did not become an issue in the demonstrations of May 1989 because the practices so described were new features of the political process.

Before mid-1989 the CCP had achieved a remarkable political stability during the 1980s. In previous decades there had been a dramatic change in the PRC's politics about every four or five years. The political stability and unity of the 1980s had been based on a gradually increasing political institutionalization, a rejection of the personalist political style associated with the Cultural Revolution, and a rejection of extremism in any form. After 1978 it became accepted that it was necessary to re-establish inner-party democracy and recognized rules of political conflict that would apply to everyone equally. Political developments since June 1989 would seem to question both political stability and party unity.

In the first place, the rules of politics have suddenly and unexpectedly been changed to favour some leaders and discredit others. As in the Cultural Revolution, by being on the losing side in an inner-party debate Zhao Ziyang has become a 'counter-revolutionary' likely to be held responsible for all the CCP's recent mistakes. Zhao and other liberal reformers (all loyal CCP members) have been criticized for attempting to restore capitalism in China. Though the attacks are perhaps less extreme than in the past, similar accusations were laid at the feet of Liu Shaoqi and Deng Xiaoping during the Cultural Revolution, and Deng Xiaoping during 1976. Such actions not only undermine confidence in the CCP, but impair its efficiency by creating an atmosphere of fear and suspicion within its ranks.

In the second place, the CCP leadership was badly split over how to react both to the student demonstrations and the demands for political reform. It is far from clear that the majority within the CCP's political bureau supported the action taken by the People's Liberation Army, or the scale and nature of the political clampdown. Indeed, the evidence would appear to be to the contrary. It is reasonable to assume that the leadership remains badly split, though at the moment divisions can hardly be aired in public, for to do so would be to invite danger. None the less, the result – in a situation where politics is once again increasingly dependent on personalities – is an inherently unstable political system. Any crisis which might earlier in the 1980s have been regarded as relatively minor (as for example, Deng's death, poor food production, a shortage of foreign exchange, or a foreign debt crisis) may cause severe dislocations and sudden changes in policy and political direction.

The long-term socio-economic trends which caused the manifestations of popular discontent in May and June 1989 are necessarily an essential part of the challenge to the current leadership. For a start, the economy faced a severe crisis even before mid-1989. The successes of the early 1980s, when there had been spectacular increases in almost all the indicators of growth but particularly food output, labour productivity, and rural incomes, had been replaced by major problems as reforms focused on the urban economy and agricultural growth approached its limits. Inflation increased dramatically, as did income differentials and corruption.[11]

The post-June 1989 reaction to these economic problems has been more of the same austerity measures as were introduced in September 1988, and which in large measure were responsible for bringing people out onto the streets as demonstrators in May and June 1989. Attempts have been made to recentralize control of the economy, to supervise credit and investment more closely, and to support infrastructural projects. It is too early to assess the impact of these new measures. However, to date, all the evidence suggests that the reimposition of controls will be not only difficult but also economically unsatisfactory. Moreover, it is likely that there will be a geographical dimension to the extent of the new leadership's economic initiatives. A province such as Guangdong, which is wealthy, distant from Beijing, and with a degree of economic independence has considerable opportunity to resist newly restored controls. Despite Chen Yun's view to the contrary the overwhelming weight of non-Chinese economic expertise is that the economic crisis is largely the result of the dual-track system: the elements of neither the command nor the market economy are able to work properly, and price reform is urgently needed.[12]

As the popular demonstrations of May/June 1989 indicate only too well, one result of these economic problems is that China has experienced a severe revolution of rising expectations. Shopping sprees and runs on the bank in July 1988 were the panic reaction of an urban population faced by inflation. It is undoubtedly significant that though demonstrating students in 1986 were greeted almost universally with derision by the urban work-force, by 1989 the latter were willing to make common cause. Any CCP leadership has successfully to meet the new economic expectations which it has created.

However, the revolution of rising expectations has also given birth to new political forces. The demand for democratic reforms in the demonstrations of May/June 1989 were themselves evidence that those rights could be exercised.[13] Students, intellectuals, urban

[11] Liu Guoguan, 'A Sweet and Sour Decade', *BR* (2 Jan. 1989), 22.

[12] J. Prybyla, 'China's Economic Experiment: Back from the Market?', *Problems of Communism*, 38/1 (1989), 1.

[13] B. Womack, 'Heroes, History and Recent Chinese Politics', *CCP Research Newsletter*, 3 (Summer 1989), 55.

workers, and the new class of entrepreneurs created by the introduction of market forces into the economy had all found a new political voice. Other social groups (including cadres themselves) have also developed expectations, political as well as economc, which have not been met fast or well enough. It would even appear that the revolution in rising expectations has spread to the peasantry. Research on rural China during the late 1980s suggests that, if anything, the demand for democratization is further advanced among the peasantry than among the urban work-force. Throughout the 1980s the CCP has tried to walk the thin and difficult line between encouraging freedom and ensuring its own dominance of politics and society. Having promised economic and political reform in 1978, it is now all but impossible ten years later to restrict that offer to economic reform alone.

In addition to these problems, the CCP has to deal with significant changes in its international environment. since 1978 foreign economic involvement in China has been seen by CCP leaders, of whatever persuasion, as a *sine qua non* for modernization. Despite problems which became increasingly acute during the 1980s this desire for co-operation was reciprocated by and from the industrialized nations. However, even before June 1989 it was apparent that the prospect of business with China had lost much of its early 1980s glamour. It is unlikely that foreign economic involvement in China has been permanently jeopardized by the CCP's repressive measures, though clearly — not least because of the coverage by the international media — there was some short-term adverse reaction amongst foreign governments, potential investors, and international agencies. None the less, there have been significant changes in the rest of the world's appreciation of the China market which the CCP leadership can only ignore as a calculated risk. A measure of those changes, particularly when compared to the early 1980s, can be found in the way uncertainty about the amount of China's foreign debt became a subject of investigation in the international media during the second half of 1989.

The more serious long-term threat is likely to be posed by the dramatic changes in Eastern Europe. With democratization, the radical transformation of the communist party state, and the reunification of Germany there are new openings for Western and Japanese capital, aid, and advice. China can no longer be presented as the only last, great untapped market. Moreover, many of those in the West — particularly in Western Europe and North America — may actually prefer to do business with Eastern Europe because of familiarity, family ties, or some other source of identification. The effective end of the cold war not only reduces China's ability to play off the USA and the USSR, it also reduces its importance to the rest of the world.

1989 in Comparative Perspective

There is considerable belief in the PRC that the status quo is only temporary. As in 1976, after that year's Tiananmen Incident, there is an air of uncertainty waiting for the man in charge to pass from the scene. The difference is of course that, whereas in 1976 Mao was clearly very ill, Deng in 1990 appears to be in almost the best of health for a man of 86. None the less, in addition to the intractable socio-economic problems, it is clear that leadership politics are inherently unstable. The coalition which triumphed in June 1989 has been unable to consolidate its position. For example, Zhao Ziyang's fate remains in doubt and remarkably few leading members of the CCP have so far been implicated in 1989's events.

Undoubtedly, some of those who have been forced into exile will look to the experience of Eastern Europe for prognosis and encouragement. There clearly are parallels and lessons to be learnt. Certainly, the current CCP leadership is mindful of events in Eastern Europe. Thus, for example, on 25/6 December 1989 (Christmas Day; Boxing Day and Mao Zedong's birthday), when the Romanian revolution was bringing down Ceauşescu, several thousand additional troops were moved into Beijing to forestall any street demonstrations. The CCP has been very reticent about developments in Eastern Europe and has concentrated on shoring up its relations with the USSR and the Democratic Republic of Korea. Its support for the CPSU and the USSR — in terms of a close community of socialist nations — is somewhat ironic in the history of Sino-Soviet relations but perhaps no more surprising than Deng's own volte-face. In 1977 when he denounced the USSR he insisted that leaders of the CPSU would not come to China in his or his successors' generation.

The structures of the Stalinist state have bequeathed similar economic and political patterns, and problems, throughout Eastern Europe and East Asia. Indeed, for that reason, the PRC's economic reforms in the early 1980s were seen as a model for the communist party states of Eastern Europe. However, there are significant differences between the PRC and Eastern Europe which suggest that the transformation of authoritarianism in China may have different results.

Communist party rule in the PRC came about as the result of an indigenous communist movement, struggling for power through popular mobilization for some twenty-eight years, two civil wars, and war with a foreign invader. War was the midwife of communist party rule in Eastern Europe, but in a different way. The Red Army's advance at the end of the Second World War provided not only the legitimacy for communist party rule but also the basis for Gorbachev's fundamental reform of the USSR's relations with its Eastern European satellites in the 1980s. The CCP always had more popular support than its Eastern European counterparts, and was regarded as an inherently nationalist as opposed to an alien political force. Disenchantment may have come harder, but it has taken longer to emerge for the CCP's support has always been correspondingly less brittle.

The CCP has brought considerable tangible improvements to the daily life of the general population. In contrast, the countries of Eastern Europe have seen a long declining economic base in the period since the Second World War. There are really two distinct perspectives to be adopted here in looking at China. The first is the general rise in the standard of living since before 1949. The successes are not as great as is often claimed, yet the improvements in health care, food consumption, and housing are real enough. The other is the dramatic revolution of rising expectations which has occurred during the 1980s. In the early 1980s the Chinese workforce came to expect a rapid increase in its standard of living. Economic and political problems during the second half of the 1980s have meant that those expectations remain unfilled leading to considerable feelings of relative deprivation, particularly amongst the urban work-force. Such frustrations clearly led to demonstrations in 1989 but they are very different to those which occurred in Eastern Europe, not least because they are more likely to be directed at the regime rather than the state itself.

Western capitalism has clearly been a beacon for change in

Eastern Europe and by extension liberal democracy has been seen as the political model for emulation. This is far from the case in the PRC. Throughout the twentieth century the various causes of Chinese revolution have had a love–hate relationship with the West. There is a popular antipathy to Western capitalism: for the Chinese body politic the goal has been a distinctively Chinese modernization. This relates back to the earlier point about the nationalism of the CCP. For many Chinese, the CCP represented, and still represents, the best hope for national regeneration.

The countries of Eastern European have populations which in international terms, and certainly by comparison with the PRC, are highly educated, literate, and urbanized. They also have traditions of greater participation in politics. The concept of democracy was an essential part of that tradition, before and even during the years of communist party rule. China's intellectual and political traditions are very different. The Confucian tradition stresses duties rather than rights; there is no notion of civil society; and it is quintessentially conservative, looking back to a golden age of harmony with limited political participation. The dominant state idea in Eastern Europe may be said to be some form of democracy, or even liberal democracy, but that hardly applies to the PRC. It is hard to identify the dominant state idea precisely, but it seems more likely to be some form of authoritarianism, albeit a benevolent dictatorship.

Eastern Europe's communist leaderships at the start of 1989 were predominantly second- or third-generation revolutionaries. These were not the people who had established their communist party states. In the PRC the original revolutionaries were still in power, whatever their formal positions in the leadership, and calling the shots. The role of the CCP Central Committee's Advisory Commission in the events of June 1989 was clearly decisive and showed where real decision-making powers reside. To say that they were still in power is of course to underestimate their tenacity, for few of them had been at the top of politics throughout the period since 1949. One explanation of their tenacious control of politics lies with their experiences during the Cultural Revolution. Their desire to ensure that nothing similar recurs is exceptionally strong, for both personal and altruistic reasons. Doubtless street demonstrations of any kind are too redolent of the Cultural Revolution for many of the gerontocracy. In Eastern Europe a considerable number of communist party leaders placed themselves in the vanguard of movements for political change.

Leadership is necessarily a key factor in political change, as is organization. In Eastern Europe there was not only opposition to communist party rule but it had leadership and organization. In the PRC most of the opposition was loyal rather than systemic opposition — the original goal was reform of the existing system not radical surgery. Intellectuals such as Yan Jiaqi and others now in exile saw themselves before June 1989 as operating within the system, a position which remains a matter of considerable debate for the dissident *émigré* community. Their former strength lay precisely in their involvement in the CCP. This was a common feature not only of politics in the PRC but also of the economy. As already indicated, unlike Eastern Europe, there is no private sector of substance in the PRC even after a decade of economic reform. The collective sector is a managerial sector run by former cadres and relies heavily on its connections, formal and otherwise, with the state-administered economy and the political system, and is rightly regarded as part of the state.

Of course a historian might argue that the emergence of radical opposition in Eastern Europe and the USSR since the mid-1950s was identical. The dissidents of that time saw themselves as loyal to the regime, let alone the state, believing that they were openly being encouraged to criticize for the good of the cause. It may prove to be the case that through exile and alienation the Chinese dissident movement does develop an alternative political programme for China. However, while in exile, its ability to organize against the CCP is made considerably harder. Its ideas become too easily characterized as Western rather than Chinese, and therefore unsuitable for the PRC, and it loses its social and political base of support in China.

The Authoritarian Outlook

Before the second half of 1989 few, if any, commentators would have predicted the radical changes that have swept Eastern Europe. It is thus necessary to be very careful in attempting any evaluation of the process of transformation in the PRC. On balance, it would seem that the Chinese case is different and more likely that the current authoritarianism of the CCP will be replaced by something similar. So far it has been the regime rather than the state which has been under attack; the dominant state idea is authoritarian rather than anything else; and there is a distinct lack of an organized alternative.

During the 1980s the CCP attempted to transform the political system of the PRC, in the wake of the Cultural Revolution, in order to restore its legitimacy. Necessarily, its inability and reluctance to manage the crisis of mid-1989 without recourse to the politics of confrontation has weakened its case. However, the evidence of the not-so-distant past is that the situation is remarkably still not irretrievable for the CCP. In April 1976 it found itself similarly at odds with popular sentiment, yet by the end of the year it had already started to reharness popular support and in late 1978 completed that process. The longer the current policy line is maintained and becomes institutionalized the more difficult it will be for the CCP to distance itself at some point in the future, and the more likely that disaffection may lead to other political solutions.

At the moment there are few alternatives. The CCP is not the PRC's only political party, but the so-called democratic parties are rightly not regarded as truly autonomous. The Nationalist Party on Taiwan is not only separated from the rest of the country by the Straits of Quemoy, but also has its own problems with the transformation of authoritarianism. Clearly, the relatively large number of intellectuals currently outside the country with the ability and possibly the inclination to develop an alternative programme cannot be disregarded. However, to gain acceptance within China, such a programme requires the domestic economic situation to worsen, as well as a higher degree of organization than has been demonstrated so far.

The strength of the state and the dominant state idea both indicate an authoritarian future, if a modified form of the status quo. Almost every social, economic, and political group of any significant account is integrated into the state system. There are certainly groups who have become alienated from the current leadership and its policies, but there is as yet little evidence that they have become disaffected from the state. On the contrary, as one might expect in an inherently authoritarian political culture, they appear at least for the present to be doing their best to come to terms with current political imperatives.

1. Chinese Marxism since Tiananmen Between Evaporation and Dismemberment*

DAVID KELLY

Another issue is how to shake the commonplace view of Marxism. Even though Fang has been criticizing Marxism all this time, in China almost no one dares voice agreement with him. In the past when I read his statements, I felt that Fang was extremely courageous as a man; but he did science, so he could say this where we could not! . . . Put another way, his statements had an attraction for us, but we could not raise a real chorus of agreement; we dared not admit that what Professor Fang said was right. Something very heavy weighed on our minds, because this thing, Marxism, had already taken root among the younger generation in China and could not be shaken. When he made his criticisms of it, I felt there was reason in what he was saying, but I didn't dare let my faith be shaken . . .

Yan Jiaqi, prominent political theorist and Chairman of the Paris-based Federation for a Democratic China, made this statement in Cambridge in a discussion with the astrophysicist Fang Lizhi and his wife, Li Shuxian, shortly after their removal from the US Embassy into exile in July 1990.[1] Two lessons may be drawn from the statement. First, Marxism continues to operate as an integral part of a tension-ridden political mechanism of self-legitimation. Second, intellectuals whose task it is to maintain this mechanism are able to detach themselves from its frame of reference only with enormous effort. A third conclusion will emerge from other considerations to be pursued in this chapter: that they and many others in the wider society are likely in the end to do so, but even if the ideological apparatus were to be dismantled will retain elements of Marxist political culture.

In discussing possible post-Marxist transitions in China, one naturally looks over one's shoulder at recent developments in Eastern Europe, which have tended to weaken the view that such regimes can indefinitely sustain their authority without abandoning

* I am grateful to Chris Buckley for his comments on this paper.

[1] 'Fang Lizhi, Yan Jiaqi duitan jilu' (Record of dialogue between Fang Lizhi and Yan Jiaqi), 2 pts, *Zhongyang Ribao* (Taibei), 16–17 Aug. 1990.

Marxism. However, the relevance to China of these developments is not straightforward. Chinese Marxism was not imposed by a conquering army, but developed indigenously over a long period before the communist takeover. It successfully incorporated aspects of the traditional culture, as well as nationalism, a more recent source of identity. It came to power as the seeming fulfilment of early twentieth-century ideals of national sovereignty, democracy, and socialism. Chinese Marxism is a very specific, historically conditioned, ideological system, whose pure philosophical form continues to find true believers, despite the long-term signs of degeneration. No full account of this system, however, can be restricted to its true believers.[2] Public figures in the CCP and the intelligentsia may very well be committed to Marxism only to the extent that it serves immediate national interests, unquestionably a less full-blooded belief than that of Mao or even Deng Xiaoping.[3] But this level of commitment, if sustained, is enough to fuel the production and consumption of self-images which constitute the life cycle of the ideology.

It is useful here to distinguish between the evaporation and the dismemberment of Marxism. These outcomes are not mutually exclusive but complementary. Evaporation affects the leadership particularly: faith in the classic Marxist-Leninist teleology tends to die out with the original revolutionary generation, and avowal of such faith to become more or less tactical. Dismemberment is a process affecting the wider political culture, which may have ceased long ago to be directly driven by Marxist doctrine.[4] In this domain one finds products of ideological decay which may, to use an analogy with nuclear chemistry, have longer half-lives than the systematic doctrine from which they originated. The classic example in China would be the egalitarian ethic or 'eating out of a big pot', which continues to affect economic decisions in enterprises both state-owned and private. Less well understood, but perhaps more

---

[2] The importance of belief in the maintenance of any ideological system is open to question. See J. G. Merquior, 'Power, Ideology and Legitimacy, or, Exit Belief', in *The Veil and the Mask: Essays on Culture and Ideology* (London, 1979), 20–30.

[3] Despite his 'pragmatism', or willingness to introduce market mechanisms, Deng apparently continues to believe in the long-term workability of the Stalinist model as a vehicle of economic development.

[4] Early symptoms of this condition were noticed as long ago as 1951 by Benjamin Schwartz, who referred to it as 'decomposition'. See his *Chinese Communism and the Rise of Mao* (Harvard, 1981), 4, and *passim*.

significant, is the operation of Marxist education at major points of entry to the education system. Even at the most relaxed moments of the Zhao Ziyang era, textbooks and teaching methods were in much of their ideological content little if at all different from the Maoist period. Teachers and others with vested interests in the ideology as a concrete social institution tend to form a conservative force at the base of the system. Conversely, loss of ideological authority at this level would be an especially dangerous develop-ment for the regime.[5]

One implication of this analysis is that orthodox Marxism con-tinues to provide and propagate a discursive field, setting up the ways in which social and political reality is categorized, and thus the ways in which political problems are resolved.[6] Some party factions, and intellectuals identifying with them, may well prefer gradual dismemberment to accelerated evaporation. Many intellec-tuals, for example, have tried to identify a 'remainder' of critical theory left when the legitimating role of Marxism is subtracted.[7] To an unknown extent, however, these changes in commitment in the vanguard, making it truly revolutionary for the first time in decades, are counterbalanced by ideological conservatism at the grass roots of a state apparatus which remains in place.

Self-Legitimation

The view taken here should not be taken as a cynical reading of Marxist ideology as a façade. As Yan Jiaqi would be the first to admit, 'Marxism' in the statement quoted at the introduction of this chapter refers to the official variant in which Leninist, Stalinist, and Maoist accretions have long overwhelmed other interpretative traditions. In our book, Brugger and I have pointed out the

---

[5] Andrew J. Spano, 'Death of a Dream in Rural China', in George Hicks, ed., *The Broken Mirror: China after Tiananmen* (London, 1990), 310–19, is a striking eyewitness account of disillusionment and rebellion among students in a rural teachers' college in Taian, Shandong. The problems described give every appearance of being widespread.

[6] For a sophisticated theory of such discursive fields in history, see Robert A. Wuthnow, *Communities of Discourse* (Harvard, 1990).

[7] This theme is developed more fully in Bill Brugger and David Kelly, *Chinese Marxism in the Post-Mao Era* (Stanford, Calif., 1990). It should go without saying that 'Marxism' here means orthodox Marxism-Leninism in its major Chinese acceptances.

important tendency of humanist intellectuals to question the supportability of, first Lenin, then many aspects of Marx himself.[8] One may question their political relevance, but not the right for intellectuals to continue to identify as Marxists.

None the less, it is impossible to discount entirely the functioning of orthodox Marxism as a façade. Ann Anagnost's application to China of the views of Claude Lefort is useful here.[9] Lefort taught that the diffusion of politics throughout society — a specific feature of Leninist systems — is intended to fuse together state and civil society. But in effect it merely projects an imaginary unity, 'the image of a society at one with itself'. Anagnost finds that the power 'to create categories and . . . assign economic actors to them' rests firmly in the hands of the state; 'while the organization of production has undergone dramatic changes, these have not been accompanied by any significant change in the relations between state and society'.[10]

The common view that the CCP 'sacrificed its legitimacy' when it carried out the Beijing massacre in June 1989 is readily understandable and in some senses justifiable. There are serious problems, however, with the underlying assumption: that of a two-way flow of state actions claiming, and popular responses according, the gratifying aura with which legitimacy is associated. While signs of such a flow can always be found, it would be mistaken to treat it as a critically important pillar of the CCP's rule. Leninist parties by their nature monopolize the public sphere.[11] If anyone were to doubt the sincerity of claims of popular support they are certainly not free to say so.

This is exemplified by the congratulatory meetings of leaders with the martial law troops in the wake of 4 June, and in later extravaganzas like the Asian Games. They prove little about the legitimacy of the regime, which in any case lacked legitimacy in the journalistic sense long before 1989. And yet such a regime is

---

[8] Our argument draws on Li Zehou, 'Shitan Makesizhuyi zai Zhongguo' (Provisional discussion of Marxism in China), in *Zhongguo xiandai sixiang shi lun* (Beijing, 1987), 143–208. Liu Binyan has adopted a similar anti-Bolshevik position.

[9] 'Prosperity and Productivity: The Moral Discourse of Wealth in Post-Mao China', in Arif Dirlik and Maurice Meisner, eds., *Marxism and the Chinese Experience* (Armonk, NY, and London, 1989).

[10] Ibid. 228.

[11] Barrett L. McCormick, *Political Reform in the Post-Mao Era* (Berkeley, Calif., 1990).

sensitive to chronically sullen populations and perhaps more critically requires a minimum level of morale among its own cadres. Much as vice is prone to pay homage to virtue, rituals of legitimacy are constantly enacted, not so much because they matter but because it is uncomfortable and costly to admit, especially to outsiders, that they do not.

The real pillar of the system is the mechanism of self-legitimation, of which Marxism is an integral part. A full development of this term would have to go beyond Lefort's point that an imaginary unity is projected: the same can be said to a greater or lesser extent of many political systems, including democracy.[12] As indicated above, 'self-legitimating' is applicable to states whose autonomy from the societies they govern is maintained through the production and consumption of self-images. This production mechanism supersedes the need for belief (although it is no doubt better if people do believe). Hegemony over ideological production is regarded within the doctrine itself as evidence of legitimacy. Thus an August 1990 article in *People's Daily* argued that 'we shall be in a bad way if we do not talk about our achievements', since in fact in any society the ruling class always propagates its 'merits and virtues' in order to strengthen its ruling position.[13] The subtle point of articles such as this is that the ability to propagate a favourable image is — particularly in China — already evidence of legitimacy.[14]

The mechanism's deep-seated circularity is reflected in the many self-entailments on the doctrinal level: for instance the 'Four Basic Principles' include maintaining the socialist road, the dictatorship of the proletariat, the leading role of the CCP. Each entail aspects of the other and all are anyway comprehended in the fourth final principle, the maintenance of Marxist Leninism — Mao Zedong Thought. As a concrete behavioural example, we note the political ritual of *biaotai*. This literally means 'display one's attitude (to the Party)'. The subtext always reads 'legitimate the Party'. To *biao* any other *tai* is a politically excluded possibility, and is *always* (and this is significant) open to the charge of a deviation from Marxism. For it is Marxism that underwrites at a deep level the proposition

---

12 Barry Hindess, 'Imaginary Presuppositions of Democracy' (May, 1991).

13 'We shall be in a Bad Way if we do not Talk about Our Achievements', *Renmin Ribao* (7 Aug. 1990), 4; trans. in *FBIS* China 90-159 (16 Aug. 1990), 12–14.

14 For a useful insight into this aspect of legitimacy, see J. G. Merquior, *Rousseau and Weber: Two Studies in the Theory of Legitimacy* (London, 1980), 130–6.

that opposition to the vanguard is class treachery which will invoke the exercise of the dictatorship of the proletariat. The pressure of the self-legitimation mechanism can be raised. In China this has been classically achieved through mass movements, which, while of course serving a number of state purposes, were often invoked to handle legitimacy crises such as the failure of the Great Leap Forward. The costs of doing so were eventually regarded as too severe, and while mass campaigns certainly remained vital to the CCP's repertoire, other mechanisms were sought. The most important solution in the post-Mao period involved deriving renewed legitimacy from the formerly despised and abused intellectuals. Two steps were necessary to bring this about: a public sphere had to be reintroduced, in which intellectuals were licensed to deviate within accepted limits, establish their credentials, and build their audiences.[15] Second, the state had to develop the tools of soft authoritarianism by means of which it could, so to speak, extract surplus legitimacy from this semi-liberalized intellectual discourse. When these tools failed to work recourse had to be had to older, hard controls.

There was nothing strange and unprecedented about this. It provides the setting for the phenomena of the 'velvet prison' analysed in Eastern Europe by Míklós Haraszti and applied to China by Geremie Barmé.[16] But whereas Haraszti portrayed it as extending triumphantly into the indefinite future, George Schöpflin finds in this mechanism a root cause of the collapse of state socialism in Eastern Europe:

The supporting intellectuals sustain authoritarian regimes by acting as a mirror in which the rulers see themselves reflected. It is vital that this mirror reflects a picture that is positive for the rulers, because at the moment when some other, much more realistic picture is visible in the public sphere – and the intellectuals control the public sphere through their hegemonial control of language – the rulers become confused. This confusion is then transmitted through the hierarchy, upwards and downwards, until the ruling party loses its cohesion and becomes prey to self-doubt.[17]

---

[15] Much of this process is described in Merle Goldman, Tim Cheek, and Carol Hamrin, eds., *Chinese Intellectuals and the State: In Search of a New Relationship* (Cambridge, Mass., 1987).

[16] Míklós Haraszti, *The Velvet Prison: Artists under State Socialism* (New York, 1987). Geremie Barmé, 'The Chinese Velvet Prison: Culture in the "New Age", 1976–89', *Issues and Studies* 25/8 (Aug. 1989), 54–79.

[17] George Schöpflin, 'The End of Communism in Eastern Europe', *International Affairs* 66/1 (1990), 3–16; quote from p. 6.

The participation of the intellectuals in the 1989 democracy movement deserves to be described in such terms. Their actions — notably the defection of the media — were consciously intended as a 'breaking of the mirror' of self-legitimation. Arguably, however, their historically unprecedented protest had somewhat more ritual than immediate political significance.[18] Has the party fallen completely prey to self-doubt, or is its underlying grip still strong? Although we shall shortly turn to evidence for the former option, this must remain an open question.

The Official Line

The self-legitimating role of Marxism introduces fundamental instabilities even as it shores up the regime. Because of the subtle closed loop between theory and politics, it is impossible to undertake reform without simultaneously providing the doctrinal setting for a conservative revenge. The Four Basic Principles were introduced simultaneously with the reforms, in part to silence conservative objections. Deng Xiaoping had constantly to defend his reformist alliance with Hu Yaobang and Zhao Ziyang in the early 1980s against conservatives like Chen Yun, Peng Zhen, Deng Liqun, and Hu Qiaomu, who were inclined to play the card of Marxist orthodoxy.

Apart from the military crackdown, the central authorities' major reaction in the first year following the 1989 popular movement was an all-out renewal of ideological orthodoxy. The tone increased in stridency following the collapse of Eastern European communist regimes in the space of a few months in late 1989.

Yet once again the pendulum swung back to institutionalized revisionism, the tacit acceptance of unorthodoxy in policy-making. The current leadership is confronted with mounting problems brought about by the attempts at recentralization. Zhao's major ideological innovations — notably the notion that China is only at

---

[18] David Kelly, 'Chinese Intellectuals in the 1989 Democracy Movement', in Hicks, ed., *Broken Mirror* (see n. 5), 24–51, is written in this spirit, if not with Schöpflin's 'mirror' metaphor. It has been argued that the Tiananmen incident showed the 'complete loss of ideological control'. See Zhang Yajun, 'Deng Xiaoping luxian xia Zhonggong de yishixingtai yu shehui kongzhi' (The Communist Party's Ideological and Social Control under the Deng Xiaoping Line), *Zhongguo dalu yanjiu* (Taiwan), 32/11 (May 1990), 28–39.

the 'elementary stage of socialism' — have been left in place. Once again, Marxist doctrine has to be fenced off from the policy arena to allow pragmatic responses. The convolutions this gives rise to are well illustrated in a *People's Daily* article of 30 July 1990 devoted to refuting the claim associated with Zhao that 'socialism cannot be clearly explained'.[19]

In January 1987 Zhao (clearly identifiable but not directly named in the article) had said, 'In referring to the Four Cardinal Principles, we need only pay attention to the leadership of the Party. No one can state clearly what is the road of socialism. We should not talk too much, or at all, about it.' This position was, according to Xu Zhengfan, the article's author, widely accepted by the reformist élite. Unlike He Xin, Xu defines socialism in straightforward teleological terms: 'It is clear that Marx's understanding of future communism and its first historical stage of development — socialism . . . is in no way a rhapsody coming from his study, but a scientific observation and foresight based on reality.' However, Marx, Engels, Lenin, Mao, and Deng Xiaoping have all admitted that socialism is a changeable and reformable society. 'The practice of socialism is far from being sufficient or deep or the theory of socialism is far from being rich or developed.' Xu now attempts a clarification:

In a word, first, we will make sure that we are clear about the issue of what socialism is if we analyse and evaluate it using the Marxist world outlook and methodology. To put it precisely, we can say that we are basically clear about it. Then, we should admit that we are not clear about it. In saying that we are basically clear about it, we mean general, fundamental and essential aspects. In saying that we are not clear about it, we mean the aspects of some concrete manifestations of essential characteristics and fundamental principles, and a certain part and detail of certain levels and aspects of the economic foundation and the superstructure.

It is difficult not to see this as evidence of Schöpflin's 'confusion transmitted through the hierarchy, upwards and downwards'. If we overlook the extreme awkwardness of this formulation, the result is a position little different from that of Zhao Ziyang himself (one might argue that it actually affirms Zhao's point in the very act

---

[19] Xu Zhengfan, 'Who Says Socialism Cannot be Clearly Explained?' *Renmin Ribao* (30 July 1990); trans. in *S W B* FE/0836 (7 Aug. 1990), B2/1–4. This article contains a valuable succinct definition of the socialist system. See Willy Wo-Lap Lam's commentary in the *South China Morning Post* (8 Aug. 1990), 17; repr. in *FBIS* China 90–153 (8 Aug. 1990), 23–4.

of criticizing him). The policy settings envisaged are implicitly more tilted towards the state-owned sector. But much the same space for pragmatism has finally to be left; the pot is calling the kettle black. As Terrell Carver and Li Jun have noted, Marx may not have pronounced in detail on procedures for building socialism, but he was rather unsympathetic to market mechanisms of any kind.[20]

Dismemberment: He Xin's Apologetics[21]

Self-legitimation has an important analogy in the scientific method. Indeed, what separates Marxism from other ideologies is, in the view of Alain Besançon, its radical claim to scientific status. It differs from true science, however, in according privileged access to truth to a delimited set of agents, the revolutionary vanguard.[22] The claim to represent the supreme scientific truth must contend somehow with the fruitfulness of science carried out with no reference whatever to Marx. The need to reconcile Marxism with contemporary science offered great protection to intellectuals endeavouring to establish the public sphere as described earlier. They could lever aside the orthodox grip on a wide number of conceptual issues, previously under the sway of the reflection theory of consciousness and dialectical materialism of the Engels-Lenin variety. New claims for the individual consonant with humanism and democratic socialism could then emerge.[23]

This could happen because, among other things, the ideological system avoids open reference to its reliance on self-legitimation. Hence He Xin's open advocacy of instituting Marxism as a religion in the wake of the 1989 crisis was startling:

A genuinely revolutionary religion (like the Protestantism of the English Revolution) could, under certain historical conditions, benefit the indus-

---

[20] Terrell Carver and Li Jun, 'Marxism and Reformism', in David Goodman and Gerald Segal, eds., *China at Forty* (Oxford, 1989), 10–17.

[21] 'China's Democracy and Future: He Xin's Conversation with Guy Sorman'; 'Economic and Political Reforms: He Xin's Conversation with Barbara Alighiero', *BR* (20–6 Aug. 1990), 27–35.

[22] *The Intellectual Origins of Leninism* (Oxford, 1981).

[23] David Kelly, 'Debates on the Guiding Role of Philosophy over Science', *Australian Journal of Chinese Affairs*, 14 (July 1985), 21–35; Chris Buckley, 'Science as Politics and Politics as Science: Fang Lizhi and the Chinese Intellectuals' Uncertain Road to Dissent', *Australian Journal of Chinese Affairs*, 25 (Jan. 1991).

trial revolution and modernization. Then why are people blind to the fact that Marxism too has been an extremely important spiritual support and binding force in China's advance into modernization and industrialization?
. . . Marxism in China is not purely scholarly doctrine, it is at the same time the basis of the political theory of the state, it is the spiritual pillar of the moral and ethical beliefs and the value concepts of a billion people. It is the spiritual source of society's binding and dynamic forces. It is the intellectual guarantor of social stability and peace. In China's mega-society, with such a teeming population, so divided, so complex in ideas and even in language, and which cannot look to any other spiritual faith or religious authority as a substitute: even to demote Marxism from its authority as doctrine of the state to being merely one of a hundred schools of thought (to say nothing of abandoning it completely) must of necessity be the prelude to a great upheaval.[24]

This was, among other things, a tacit admission that the appeal of Marxism as a science could not be depended on any further.

He Xin had previously made a name for himself after publishing some strikingly realistic assessments of the crisis facing the reforms. Emerging as an apologist of the regime in the immediate wake of the massacre, he sharply attacked liberalizing intellectuals who had previously been his mentors.[25] His defence of the regime a year later, in the widely read *Beijing Review*, reveals much about the current ideological settings.[26]

Contrary to the Chinese government's critics, He Xin maintains that 'the banner of democracy has become a powerful leverage in international strategic contention'. The US in particular promotes its dreams of world empire in this way. Democracy, he concedes, is a valuable modern political culture. But transplanted to China the result would be a politically weak, lax, and extremely pro-US 'molluscan' government unable to unite the nation. China has its

---

[24] He Xin, 'Jisi zhi luan houde lengjun fansi' (Sober Reflections on the June 4 Disorder), *Zhongguo qingnian bao* (6 Dec. 1989), 3. I am grateful to Geremie Barmé for drawing my attention to this interview.

[25] He Xin, 'A Word of Advice to the Politburo', trans., annotated, and introduced by Geremie Barmé, *Australian Journal of Chinese Affairs*, 23 (Jan. 1990), 49–76. He Xin, 'Li Zehou yu dangdai Zhongguo sichao' (Li Zehou and the Contemporary Chinese Intellectual Tide), *Guangming Ribao* (16 May 1988).

[26] He Xin's Conversation with Barbara Alighiero', *Beijing Review* (20–6 Aug. 1990), 18–35. The article presumably meets with the approval of Jiang Zemin and Li Peng. The picture is complicated by the recent emergence of Li Ruihuan, responsible for propaganda, as inheritor of Zhao Ziyang's 'liberal' mantle. His interest in He Xin's article is hard to determine.

own 'substantive democratic' tradition, notably manifested in the Spring and Autumn, and Warring States periods. It is this tradition that should be built on, rather than a blind emulation of Western models. Democracy is essentially a matter of allowing the people to enjoy sovereignty over the administration of the state. Indeed, democracy is a means, not a purpose, as Mao once said. As it is expanded, the way in which political leadership is exercised will improve.[27]

Turning to Marxism, He Xin predicts that the situation in Eastern Europe is unlikely to happen in China. Marxism was carried in by a victorious national liberation war, protecting the national economy and revitalizing China's national spirit. State ownership furthered the national aims of rapid industrialization and economic resistance. Marxism's theory of social justice decreased the gap between rich and poor and helped avert the brutal deprivation characterizing earlier experiences of primitive capital accumulation elsewhere.

Noteworthy here is that He Xin's defence is essentially backward-looking. It is consonant with the nostalgia for the golden age of the 1950s of many senior conservative cadres like Hu Qiaomu. Marxism is justified pragmatically and contingently, with no reference to necessary historical progression or *telos* beyond national wealth and power. This line is, however, susceptible to many objections which point to China's poverty and weakness. He Xin glosses over the 'mistakes' of the Cultural Revolution, as if these were not squarely the fault of the Marxist-Leninist-Maoist Party itself.[28] What little is said about the increasing level of political repression needed to maintain order is attributed to foreign interference and irrationalism. The logic of self-legitimation has drawn more tightly circular: the tendency to chaos must be staved off by indoctrinating Marxist ideology. While the outside observer sees that the ideology somehow induces chaos of itself, for He this only confirms the need for more indoctrination.

---

[27] Ibid. 19–22.
[28] An important perspective here is provided by Lynn T. White III's recent study of the Cultural Revolution, which traces its causes back to the social control mechanisms serving the dictatorship of the proletariat: *Policies of Chaos: The Organizational Causes of Violence in China's Cultural Revolution* (Princeton, NJ, 1989).

Evaporation: New Authoritarianism

If one could bracket off the doctrinal requirements of self-legitimation, the pragmatic core of Chinese Marxism today is by and large a defence of the state-owned sector of the economy. Hu Qiaomu, the theoretical spokesman for Deng's original reform programme in 1978, praised the early socialist economy as a 'miracle' founded on unified economic and fiscal management conducted by the central government in the whole country, and argued that 'when the socialist economy has acquired full ruling status there can be allowed a small amount of capitalist elements'.[29] Neither he nor He Xin are prepared to point out that the non-state sector has accounted for a growing proportion of economic growth and plays a crucial role in employment. The return to Marxist doctrine cannot but make life difficult for this sector.

The belief that China's economic problems could only be addressed by wholesale retreat from the socialist road became prevalent in élite circles in the 1980s. It was no more evident than in the New Authoritarianism which emerged into the limelight in late 1988.[30] This doctrine was associated with Zhao Ziyang's intellectual supporters and included senior Party School theorists. It was the first clear non-Marxist theory to emerge from within the party. A fundamental objective of these theorists was to install a modern market economy based on private ownership. The only arguments against it which cited Marx came, significantly, from humanist intellectuals like Yu Haocheng who repudiated the anti-democratic thrust of the theory. Yu particularly objected to the theory's retention of the vulgar Marxist idea of determination of the superstructure by the base in arguing that political democracy must be preceded by economic democracy.[31] Since June 1989 it

---

[29] Hu Qiaomu, 'How China Chose Socialism in the Fifties', *Renmin Ribao* (3 Oct. 1989), trans. in *FBIS* (12 Oct. 1989), 34-7; quote from p. 37. Cf. Hu Qiaomu, 'Observe Economic Laws, Speed up the Four Modernizations', speech to State Council, 7 July 1978, *BR* 45 (10 Nov. 1978), 7-12; 46 (17 Nov. 1978), 15-23; 47 (24 Nov. 1978) 13-21.

[30] Versions of the theory had surfaced several years before. See Ma Shuyun, 'The Rise and Fall of New Authoritarianism in China', *Australian Journal of Chinese Affairs* (1991). Major writings on the topic are included in Liu Jun and Li Lin, eds., *Xin quanweizhuyi* (*New Authoritarianism*) (Beijing, 1989).

[31] Yu Haocheng, 'Zhongguo xuyao xin quanweizhuyi ma?' (Does China Need New Authoritarianism?), in Liu Jun and Li Lin, eds., *Xin quanweizhuyi* (see n. 30), 162-71. Cf. pp. 166-7.

has been repudiated on more orthodox grounds, but it gave clear evidence of the collapse of faith in Marxism among many senior cadres concerned with the economy. Their residual dogmatism of base–superstructure determinism is a good example of what may be termed 'dismemberment' of Marxism.

Reformation: The Fate of Dissident Marxism

It has been argued elsewhere that the attempts by critical intellectuals in the 1980s to rethink Marxism from within carried on important historical traditions of Chinese Marxism.[32] By the end of the 1980s, these efforts were clearly outrunning the capacity of the ideological system to adapt. One important flank of revisionist theory was intimately connected with science. Cosmology and quantum physics were used to discredit several key dogmas, first dialectics of nature, then materialism *tout court*. Similarly, humanist scholars and philosophers used the recurrent Chinese concern with cultural identity to advance sociological concepts of culture with political bearing.[33] New concepts of the autonomy of the subject of consciousness emerged from literary and aesthetic theory to challenge Maoist dogma on these matters, perhaps the most ingrown branch of the self-legitimating apparatus.

Scholars working directly with Marxist texts repeatedly provided reinforcement for these revisionist efforts. Those prepared to risk conservative backlash could exploit the proclamations of intellectual openness of the immediate post-Mao period to introduce major reinterpretations of the canon. As well as the well-known controversy on alienation and humanism, discussion of the asiatic mode of production and a range of similar topics were important for general social theory. Equally significant were the economic theorists, who had, if anything, an even clearer green light to produce 'pragmatic' readings of central dogmas like the labour theory of value.[34]

In the aftermath of the Beijing massacre the intellectual figures

---

[32] Bill Brugger and David Kelly, *Chinese Marxism in the Post-Mao Era* (Stanford, Calif., 1990).

[33] David Kelly, 'Another Face of Modernity: The Cultural Background to the Beijing Massacre', *Thesis Eleven*, 27 (Oct. 1990).

[34] Brugger and Kelly, *Chinese Marxism* (see n. 32).

driving this movement of ideas dominated the official hit-lists. Predictably, the most important of their works became targets of ideological criticism very similar in style to that of the Cultural Revolution. Jin Guantao, Liu Zaifu, Yan Jiaqi, and Li Zehou are only a few who come to mind.[35] What prospect now remains for a reformation of Marxism at the hands of such people, who had remained for the most part loyal believers or at least publicly committed to Marxism?

A large number of critical intellectuals were overseas at the time of Tiananmen or managed to escape later. This has allowed some significant writing to emerge from which their thinking can be assessed. Su Shaozhi, for example, has maintained a commitment to Marxism in exile; Jin Guantao has reaffirmed his view, first mooted in late 1988, that the history of socialism had been one of failure. Yuan Zhiming, a younger 'cultural critic' involved in the television documentary series *River Elegy*, has somewhat startlingly moved from a *Marxisant* critique of the regime as a fulfilment of Marx's mysterious asiatic mode of production, to support of New Authoritarianism.[36]

These views may all be analysed under the heading of dismemberment and evaporation. Even where an explicit Marxist commitment is affirmed, the underlying ideas involve jettisoning large parts of the identifiable core of Chinese Marxism. One should not be surprised, however, if a change in the regime sees a number of these figures returning to the mainland to resume the role of loyal critic. Nor should this be dismissed out of hand as hypocritical and self-serving. The underlying commitment to intellectual service within an ideologically unified state would for many such people be

---

[35] For criticism of Jin Guantao see He Zuoxiu, 'Why does Jin Guantao want to Negate the Objectivity of Objective Reality? Commenting on *The Philosophy of Man*', *Qiushi*, 23 (1 Dec. 1989), trans. in *FBIS* China 89–247 (27 Dec. 1989), 21–5. Wang He, 'Huiji dui Makesizhuyi weiwu shiguan de tiaozhan — bufen lishixuejia pingxi fin Guantao san ben lishi zhuzuo zuotanhui jiayao' (Rebutting the Challenge to the Marxist Historical Outlook — Notes on a Conference on Three Historical Works by Jin Guantao), *Qiushi*, 2 (Jan. 1990), 37–9. Hu Maoren, 'Weiwuzhuyi bei zhengweile ma?' (Materialism Refuted?), *Guangming Ribao* (27 Nov. 1989), 3. On criticism of Li Zehou see 'Wentan zuopai weigong Li Zehou' (Literary Leftists Lay Siege to Li Zehou), *Jiushi Niandai*, 9 (Sept. 1990), 60–1, '"Xin qimeng yundong" yiweizhe shenme?' (What Does the 'New Enlightenment' Movement mean?), *Guangming Ribao* (6 Aug. 1990), 3. Repr. in *FBIS* CHI-90-167 (28 Aug. 1990), 12–14.

[36] *Minzhu Zhongguo*, 2 (June 1990), 45. Chris Buckley, reminding me that *River Elegy* carried its fair share of proto-facism, finds this unsurprising.

essentially unchanged, and their return would be a conditional, ethical judgement of the national interest. One might say that, for such Chinese intellectuals, the judgement levelled on He Xin would not be so much for the service he has rendered but for whom he has rendered it.

Marxism genuinely devoted to the 'critical heritage', as exemplified by Wang Ruoshui, Li Zehou, Su Shaozhi, and others would seem to be a transient generational phenomenon. If we take Yan Jiaqi's earlier quoted remarks to Fang Lizhi seriously, we should expect such figures to be widely honoured but little emulated. But if Western observers with a lingering respect for Marx think it a pity that the poor and exploited of China should lose in this way a voice which might defend their interests, the sad fact is that Chinese Marxism has, overall, a bad record in backing the wretched of the earth against the state.

Conclusion

Marxism is integral to the maintenance of the regime. Since the ideological revolution of the Soviet Union under Gorbachev we cannot confidently say that it is indispensable to state socialist regimes. While China is at least a decade away from an event similar to the formal repudiation of the Leninist model in June 1990, the tensions now manifesting as side-effects in the political system are obvious.

The long-term trend under which, as Terrell Carver and Li Jun noted in 1988, 'the traditional methodological framework and substantive doctrines of Marxism are being stretched almost beyond recognition'[37] has only been temporarily halted. June 1989 and its aftermath brought in a wave of orthodoxy. But conservatism and reformism, orthodoxy and heterodoxy, have already lost what clarity they may once have had. Once dismemberment reaches the core region of Marxism, they usefully label only the transitory, tactical shifts of power. More effort might perhaps be devoted to finding some useful categories of analysis.

The very ingenuity of the remaining party faithful in shoring up nominal orthodoxy while allowing pragmatic flexibility threatens

---

[37] Carver and Li Jun, 'Marxism and Reformism' (see n. 20), 10.

to drive the process of dismemberment of Marxist ideology to its limit. The needs of pragmatic policy-making are making themselves felt in yet another cycle of CCP-sanctioned revisionism. Looking over their shoulders at what was once the Eastern bloc, the party's leaders have decided that self-legitimation must be driven harder rather than abandoned. Are they correct in their faith in China's ability to withstand more of it than any previous socialist society? If this is so, one very unattractive outcome may be the installation of a New Authoritarian regime which dispenses with Marxist state ownership and its attendant social welfare functions, such as they are, but which maintains the self-legitimating apparatus of Marxist ideology.

2. Sounds of Silence and Distant Thunder: The Crisis of Economic and Political Administration

MARC BLECHER

At the core of China's programme of comprehensive reform since 1978 has been a redefinition of the role of the state *vis-à-vis* the economy. This has included the organization and activities of state administration.[1] Two directions may be distinguished analytically, although they need not be mutually exclusive. Indeed, in theory they may be complementary, and in practice they may overlap. One is the *separation* of state administrative structures and activities from the economy, the other the *reorientation* of such administration in ways more consistent with effective management of the economy. The former has included administrative streamlining, increasing enterprise managers' authority and independence from other state officials, reducing state agencies' financial leverage over enterprises, allowing enterprises to be dissolved through bankruptcy, and reform of investment finance through creation of an independent banking system. The latter has included meritocratic personnel reform (so state officials will be better qualified to run the economy), the separation of party from the government, and the effort to reorient the role of state officials in the economy.

Various policy offensives, directions, and experiments were undertaken in the decade from the end of 1978 (when the landmark Third Plenum of the Eleventh Party Central Committee met) through the middle of 1989. They are sketched in this chapter. In 1989 the popular movement for political change — itself a product of the multiple crises and exhaustion of the reformist juggernaut — was accompanied by a predictable, comprehensive, and potentially damaging stall and even reversal of the various reforms, a phenomenon we shall also examine.

---

[1] To be consistent with conceptual usage in comparative politics, the term 'state' is used here to refer to the totality of political institutions, including the CCP, the government, and the mass organizations associated with them. This differs from a common usage in comparative communist or socialist studies, in which the term 'state' refers to the government, and is therefore differentiated from the CCP.

Separation of State and Economy

Administrative Streamlining

Of course China's state administrative apparatus expanded during the Maoist period as part and parcel of the socialist transformation of the economy. Contrary to what one might expect, though, the retreat from centralized control during the reformist decade has actually fuelled even faster growth in the size of the state administration. From 1952 to 1978 state personnel rolls increased 61 per cent, for an average annual rate of 1.85 per cent.[2] But in the decade after 1978 it nearly doubled from 4,300,000 to 8,420,000, and the average annual rate of increase almost quadrupled to 6.95 per cent (while population was rising 1.3 per cent per year). This acceleration occurred despite all the steps towards privatization, expanded market relations, decentralization, and deregulation.[3] A CCP circular issued in May 1988 continued to urge 'government streamlining', an indication that the problem of administrative bloat is ongoing.[4] In Xinji municipality, a rural but rapidly industrializing county in the hinterlands of the North China Plain,[5] the number

[2] Calculated from State Statistical Bureau, *Statistical Yearbook of China, 1986* (Oxford, 1986), 97.

[3] Calculated from State Statistical Bureau, *China Statistical Yearbook, 1989* (Beijing, 1989), 63, 81.

[4] 'Party Promotes Enterprise Law', *BR* 31/21 (23–9 May 1988), 11.

[5] Xinji municipality is the site of an ongoing research project conducted since 1979 by Professors Vivienne Shue, Wang Shaoguang, Mitch Meisner, Phyllis Andors, Stephen Andors, and myself. It is a rural county located approximately 70 km. east of Shijiazhuang city (the capital of Hebei province), to which it is connected by paved road and by railway. It is a rural rather than suburban area. With its agriculture engaged primarily in production of maize, winter wheat, and cotton, it is about average for its area in rural development. But it is relatively advanced industrially; in fact, it is the most industrially advanced county in the prefecture. In 1978, gross value of industrial output (GVIO) made up 55% of total output value by official count, and by 1986 the figure was 63%. Per capita income was Y88 in 1978, well below the national average though above average for Shijiazhuang prefecture; in 1986 it was up to Y522. Still, in 1978 only 4% of the county's population was classified as 'non-rural householders', and by 1986 this figure had risen only to 6%. With 537 persons per km.[2] and 5.4 persons per cultivated hectare in 1978, it is densely populated. It had never been a national model of economic development, either in the Maoist or post-Maoist periods. In May 1986, as part of a national policy of elevating more economically advanced rural localities to an administrative status that reflected their regional centrality, Shulu county was redesignated Xinji municipality (*shi*), after the name of the town (*zhen*) that had served as the county seat. In this chapter it is referred to technically inaccurately as a county, in order

of personnel in the municipal (county) government rose by 95 per cent (7 per cent per year) between 1979 and 1989. There is no evidence of any effort to reverse the growth in the size of the state apparatus since then, either nationally or in Xinji. There are at least six reasons for the expansion. First, since 1978 a huge contingent — doubtless into seven figures — of officials who had been evicted from their positions during the Cultural Revolution decade has been officially rehabilitated and returned to former units to work alongside those who had taken their places. Reflecting the post-Cultural Revolution political stalemate, neither group could be evicted from its posts.

Second, the policy of encouraging older officials to retire was largely a failure, for at least three reasons. First, it contradicted the policy of rehabilitation. Those denounced during the Cultural Revolution did not want to go through the difficult process of rehabilitation in order to find themselves immediately retired. And if rehabilitated officials would be retired anyway, there would be no incentive for their units to take rehabilitation work seriously. Second, officials could not feel sure they would have their medical, financial, and housing needs met if they retired, since in China these are still provided by work units, not social services agencies. Moreover, apprehension about access to housing and especially medical services and housing were increasing at this time due to the growing tendency to privatize them. Third, the private, passive life of retirement was not an attractive prospect to officials who had spent active lives in the pursuit and acquisition of power in the public realm.

A third general reason for the expansion of the state administrative apparatus is that no effort has yet been made to restructure the Chinese bureaucracy. The coexistence of dual systems of leadership — vertically organized ministries and mass organizations, their bureaux and sub-units at each level, the CCP organs paralleling and embedded in all of them, and then the horizontal organs

---

to minimize confusion and remind readers that Xinji is, both in its size and its position in China's administrative hierarchy, much more similar to an ordinary Chinese *xian* (which is translated as county) than to an urban area (which is connoted by the word *shi* (municipality or city). The data cited here and, unless noted otherwise, elsewhere throughout this chapter, were supplied by officials of the Xinji municipality government, and refer to the end of 1989. Policy and administrative practices refer to mid-1990.

such as local governments, planning commissions, and party committees — which had contributed to bureaucratic bloating and much administrative confusion in the first three decades of the People's Republic has not been altered. Nor was any effort made to rationalize the provision of government services. Since in the state sector social services were still dispensed largely by production units, not specialized agencies, there were continuing problems of duplication of work and personnel, as myriad factories and government agencies ran their own hospitals, clinics, and housing agencies. In Xinji, collective production units own and operate six times as much housing (measured in floor space) as did the municipal government's Real Estate Management Bureau.

Fourth, it continued to be in the interests of administrative agencies to retain as large a staff as possible. Despite all the attacks on Chinese political culture and administrative practice, it has remained the case that, the larger the unit, the more prestigious it is and the more powerful its leaders. Large units are also better positioned for elevation in the bureaucratic hierarchy, which is a pathway to increased income, prestige, and power for its leaders and members, larger budgets, and better access to scarce goods and services which are allocated through the state.

A fifth factor has to do with educational changes. The number of graduates of tertiary institutions has exploded, starting from 1982, when 457,000 received their degrees — more than twice as many as the previous high of 194,000 (in 1977). Between 1982 and 1988, an average of 410,000 per year graduated.[6] The government was faced with the task of finding employment for all these people, and many (probably most) of those placed were assigned administrative posts.

Sixth, and perhaps most important, the economic and political reforms have themselves promoted administrative growth. The rapid expansion and diversification of the Chinese economy since 1978 have called for a larger and more ramified administrative structure. Compared with 1978, there are now many more train tickets to sell, units from which to collect taxes, roads to build, markets to regulate, housing units to construct and administer, technologies to develop and oversee, types and numbers of consumer goods to supply, threats to the environment to be regulated,

6 *ZTN 1989* (see n. 3), 697.

land use conversions to be monitored, and so forth. In particular, urbanization has proceeded apace, creating the need for expanded city administrative services in areas such as real estate management, town planning, and provision and maintenance of infrastructure such as roadways, power lines, water and sewer lines, trash collection, and cultural services. Political reforms have had the same effect: the elaboration of more complex forms of property and the increasing importance of property rights, along with the general expansion of law and the judicial system, have promoted the development of new legal agencies and administrative tasks. Between 1986 and 1989, the number of agencies of the Xinji government expanded by precisely 50 per cent, from thirty-four to fifty-one. Of these, three were involved in industry, six in commerce, four in political or administrative matters, and three in urban affairs. And in China more widely, the transfer of local security personnel from the military to local governments has also added to the size of administrative payrolls.[7] So has the assignment of demobilized soldiers to government positions as part of the streamlining of the armed forces.

The expansion of government has of course gone hand in hand with increased administrative expenditure. Between 1950 and 1978, government administrative expenditures rose at an average rate of 5.1 per cent per year; as a proportion of total government expenditure, they fell from 75 per cent to 7 per cent. (Taking 1957, the end of the First Five-Year Plan, as a bench-mark, the figures to 1978 are an annual increase of 4.1 per cent and a drop from 14 to 7 per cent respectively.) But from 1978 to 1985, administrative expenditure began a new and much higher average rate of increase of 18 per cent per year, reaching 19 per cent of government expenditure in 1985 (compared with 7 per cent in 1978).[8] In Xinji, county government administrative expenditures rose at an average rate of 6.8 per cent per year in 1950–78 (3.8 per cent in 1957–78), reaching 13.6 per cent of total expenditures in 1978; in 1978–89 they rose at an average annual rate of 18 per cent, reaching 19 per cent of total expenditures.

In conclusion, the size and cost of government administration

---

[7] Some of the problems entailed in this transfer are discussed in 'Hainan: People's Armed Forces Transfer Completed', Hainan Island Radio Broadcast, 16 June 1986, in *FBIS* (PRC Regional Affairs) HK160815 (18 June 1988) P2–3.

[8] Computed from *Yearbook 1989* (see n. 3), 572.

have grown dramatically since the advent of the Chinese reforms. The post-Mao changes have created various new functional needs and political pressures for a larger and more expensive state. This does not bode well for separating the state and economy. In a developing socialist country like China, where the vast majority of economic activity is still owned, managed, and administered by the state, where the economy is still the major preoccupation of the state, where economic modernization is the explicit policy of the present leadership and the broadly shared goal of all social groups, the rapid growth of the state bureaucracy can only mean that more officials will be well positioned, inclined, and expected to exert power over the economy.

Reform of the State Sector

Managerial Autonomy

It was not until almost six years into the reform period that a major programmatic statement on reform of state sector enterprise was made.[9] A key element was the manager responsibility system. 'It is . . . necessary to establish a unified, authoritative and highly efficient system to direct production and conduct operations and management. This calls for a system of the director or manager assuming full responsibility.'[10] But this new policy withheld from the managers the authority which this 'full responsibility' would have to entail. While 'Party organizations in enterprises should actively support directors in exercising their authority in giving unified direction to production and operations', they were instructed in the same breath to 'guarantee and supervise the implementation of the principles and policies of the Party *and the state*, strengthen the Party's ideological and organization work in enterprises, improve their leadership over the trade unions and Communist Youth League organizations and do effective ideological and political work among the workers and staff members',[11] the latter of which included management staff. Moreover,

---

[9] 'Decision of the Central Committee of the Communist Party of China on Reform of the Economic Structure', *BR* 27 (29 Oct. 1984), pp. i–xvi.

[10] Ibid., p. xi.

[11] Ibid. Emphasis added.

While the director assumes full responsibility, we must improve the system of congresses of workers and staff members and other systems of democratic management, give play to the authority and role of the trade union organizations and workers' and staff members' deputies in examining and discussing major decisions to be taken by the enterprises, *supervising administrative leadership* and safeguarding the legitimate rights and interests of the workers and staff members.[12]

The 'Decision' was, it is plain, no decision at all. It was, rather, a grab-bag of statements which could be mobilized by all those involved in running, administering, and overseeing state sector enterprises to justify their policy positions, pursuit of interests, and exercise of power.

The result has been something of a free-for-all. Where managers were able to assert themselves, some have engaged in practices that are questionable from a socialist point of view. They have hired former 'class enemies', many of whom had spent time in prison for engaging in 'speculation' or other economic offences, because they were precisely the entrepreneurial sorts required by the reform-programme. They have engaged in illegal trade, for example by purchasing equipment or materials at low state prices and reselling them on black markets. They have increased their own salaries. Some with the right access imported large quantities of foreign goods for resale at high profits, and turned fortunes from black market exchanges of Chinese currency.[13]

Yet in other places managers were tightly constrained by state officials. In general, they lacked significant power over planning, investment, profit disposition, technical upgrading, input procurement, output disposition and pricing, and transformation of product line.[14] Indeed, they were even frequently denied the personnel authority to hire, promote, or transfer — not to mention fire — their

---

[12] Ibid. Emphasis added.

[13] An epidemic of this kind broke out on the island of Hainan, where, under cover of duty exemptions for goods to be used locally, 89,000 motor vehicles, 2,900,000 colour TVs, and over 250,000 videotape recorders were imported for resale on the mainland. Enterprises of all sorts got in on the act, including e.g. the *Hainan Ribao (Hainan Daily News)*, which turned a profit of Y1,400,000 from the purchase and resale of 400 Toyota vans. Y4,200,000,000 borrowed from Chinese banks was exchanged for foreign currency on nearby mainland black markets. See John F. Burns, 'A Billion-Dollar Misdeed Bursts a Chinese Bubble', *New York Times* (13 Dec. 1985), 2.

[14] David Granick, *Chinese State Enterprises* (Chicago, 1990).

immediate subordinates. This undercut their ability to function as modern firm directors, as well as their political power in their enterprises (which of course they would need to deepen their authority as managers). In a compromise, many have gained the capacity to hire some middle- and lower-level supervisory personnel.

The resulting personnel situation provides a context for several different kinds of conflict. Where these middle- and lower-level supervisory personnel are indeed committed to increased efficiency and therefore discipline the labour force more closely, worker discontent has followed, and found expression partly in a recent wave of strikes, slow-downs, and production sabotage.[15] Both in the enterprises — where state officials are still strong — and the wider political system, these have played into the hands of critics of thoroughgoing reform. Conflicts between state (particularly party) officials and managers have been widely reported, some so serious as to be characterized as 'civil wars'.[16] The managers are not well placed to win them: 'Young factory managers . . . are often forced to resign because of local hostility to their new ways.'[17]

Though objections to the manager responsibility system are usually couched in ideological terms, such as the need to preserve socialism's commitment to party control, workers' interests, or democratic management (themselves often contradictory goals), they are rooted in the concerns of state officials about their loss of power or even function if authority in enterprises is turned over to managers. These anxieties are only heightened by party officials' experiences of having been shunted aside during the Cultural Revolution. Put more positively, they did not fight to be rehabilitated from the political eclipse of those years only to yield their newly regained position, influence, and power to factory managers. In general, too, there tend to be deep differences in outlook between state officials and factory managers. Many of the former attained their positions during the revolution or the immediate post-revolutionary period, while managers tend more heavily to have

[15] Chen Ji, of the Chinese Trade Union Federation, recently admitted that 49 strikes had occurred in the first six months of 1988. The number is undoubtedly higher.
[16] For some lively examples, see L. do Rosario, 'Managers' Bruising Battles on the Shop Floor', *FEER* (8 Sept. 1988), 131.
[17] 'AFP Views Machine Factory Wage Bonus Plan', *FBIS* (30 June 1986).

been recruited and educated in the 1960s, 1970s, and 1980s. A correlate of this is that managers tend to be younger and better educated than state officials.[18] In Xinji, the problem is indicated by a concerted, carefully organized, multi-year effort to raise the educational levels of state officials. Managers have usually been recruited on the basis of their education, whereas state officials' career pathways came through political, administrative, or military posts. So there is good reason to expect sharp disagreements among them on matters of enterprise management and the role of the enterprise in a socialist country. Neither the 'Decision' discussed above nor the more recently promulgated Enterprise Law could resolve them.[19] In fact, according to a party circular, the Enterprise Law was intended to address 'the lack of separation . . . of government administration and enterprise management . . . [which] is still a major obstacle to making enterprises more productive and profitable'.[20] Yet this piece of legislation continued to equivocate, subjecting managers' authority over pay schemes to approval by workers' congresses, and leaving in the hands of local government departments the power to 'issue unified mandatory plans for the enterprises' and to 'appoint or remove, reward or punish the factory director . . . [and] the leading administrative cadres at the level of vice-director'.[21] The public admissions and complaints about the failure to separate state administration from management (which were frequent in 1988 and the first half of 1989)[22] have died down in the wake of the climacteric of 4 June 1989. No new offensives or policy experiments were afoot on this front in Xinji in mid-1990. The problem remains unresolved.

To the extent that the differences between managers and state officials have to do with the essentially generational differences just discussed, they may fade away with the passing of time, leaving

---

[18] According to one recent survey, nearly 50% of enterprise managers were under the age of 50, but only 35% of enterprise CCP secretaries were. They also averaged better on senior high school educations, a standard to which CCP secretaries did not measure up. These data are cited in Hong Yung Lee, *From Revolutionary Cadres to Party Technocrats: The Changing Cadre System in Socialist China* (Berkeley, Calif., forthcoming).

[19] 'The Law of the People's Republic of China on Industrial Enterprises Owned by the Whole People (Adopted on April 13, 1988 at the First Session of the Seventh National People's Congress)', *CD* (16 May 1988), *Business Weekly*, 2–3.

[20] 'Party Promotes Enterprise Law' (see n. 4).

[21] 'Law' (see n. 19), art. 55.

[22] 'Developing Market Mechanism Crucial', *CD* (26 Sept. 1988).

China with a technocratic corps of leaders at the enterprise level. Indeed, this is already beginning to happen. In a startling twist on previous practice that is still common throughout China, according to which party officials appoint factory managers, in Wenzhou, an epicentre of reform — particularly in the direction of privatization — in the late 1980s, a factory manager *hired the party secretary* of his firm. Moreover, he chose his friend for the job, in order to help him deal with problems the local government posed for the firm.[23] This example shows that such arrangements are as likely to produce audacious new mergers of state and economy as they are to separate them. Indeed, to the extent that a more unified generation of technocrats dominates positions in the state administration and the enterprises, there is a strong possibility that it could form an integrated political–economic leadership or even élite.[24] Since June 1989, Wenzhou has dropped from prominence and fallen into political disfavour, indicating a critique of its free-wheeling approach to state–economy relations.

There is another deep contradiction lurking in the manager responsibility system. As Hong Yung Lee has pointed out, '[I]n . . . management method, the [party] secretary uses the "soft" method of persuasion even if it takes a long time. In contrast, the managers use the "hard method" of administrative orders or economic rewards.'[25] Managers' reliance on administrative fiat stands in direct opposition to the political liberalization which is another prominent aspect of reform. It has undoubtedly been ascendant since June 1989. But the more it is, the more likely it will draw criticism from reform leaders and social groups who are deeply concerned with political change when these issues resurface once the post-June hard line has played itself out. To the extent that this happens, it will expose the cleavages in the diverse and potentially fragile social coalition which backed reform during its first decade.[26]

[23] Edward Gargan, 'Along the Chinese Coastline, Economic Dragon Awakens', *New York Times* (13 Aug. 1988), 5.

[24] Vivienne Shue, 'State Socialism and Modernization in China: Through Thick and Thin', paper presented to the Annual Meeting of the American Political Science Association, Washington, DC, 1–4 Apr. 1988.

[25] Lee, *Revolutionary Cadres* (see n. 18).

[26] It also runs against the grain of a host of participatory management experiments, experiences, and values which, though themselves problematic, have nevertheless formed an important part of factory life for major periods since 1949. Indeed, arbitrary management was a key complaint expressed by workers themselves

Financial Relations between State and Enterprises: The Substitution of Taxes for Profits

Reformers recognized early on that state enterprises would have little incentive to increase productivity or raise profits so long as the state claimed the lion's share of enterprise profits. So one of the first reform moves was the adjustment of profit remission ratios so that the enterprises could keep more of them. This led to several problems. Enterprises proved adroit at negotiating low remission rates with the bureaux that supervised them. In turn this meant that: (1) local state officials spent a great deal of time and effort dickering; (2) profit remission rates were neither standardized nor set according to criteria that were rational economically (such as structural constraints facing the enterprise or sector) or politically (such as leadership priorities about development); and (3) downward pressure was placed on state revenues.[27] It also left the central government agencies constrained by local ones, which — for reasons that remain to be explored fully — had the power to negotiate the low retention rates whose ultimate financial consequences had to be dealt with centrally.

Beginning experimentally in 1983 and then widely promulgated in 1984, the leadership attempted to solve these problems by replacing profit remissions with taxes. It was argued that these would be more standard, predictable, and useful as a lever of macroeconomic regulation.[28] Moreover, since enterprises would now be

---

during the Cultural Revolution. See Stephen Andors, *China's Industrial Revolution* (New York, 1977). That movement and those experiments may be discredited politically, but they also suggest that the leadership could be playing with fire by encouraging the draconian managerial practices which contributed to the radicalism of the past.

[27] From 1978 to 1982, state revenue dropped from 37.2% of national income to 25.5%. 'Over-Decentralization Causes Swell in Capital Spending', *News from the Xinhua News Agency 080911* (9 Aug. 1983), 4. From the start of the profit retention system in late 1978 until 1982, state enterprises retained Y42 billion of their profits, which about equalled the size of the budget deficits run up over the same period. See David Buchman, 'Implementing Chinese Tax Policy', in David M. Lampton, ed., *Policy Implementation in Post-Mao China* (Berkeley, Calif., 1987), 133.

[28] For just one example, 'the state, in defining tax rates, may levy less on such products as should be encouraged and those products selling at a low price or with a small profit. The state can thus use the regulatory rolke of taxation to case the contradictions arising from irrational prices'. 'Reform — Way to Invigorate China's Economy', *News From the Xinhua News Agency 052273* (23 May 1984), 7.

submitting their surpluses to the highly centralized Ministry of Finance and Taxation, local governments would lose financial leverage over or benefit from local enterprises. This in turn would enhance the latters' autonomy from government administration.[29] And since the state was no longer collecting profits, the enterprises could now also be held fully accountable for their after-tax profits and losses, which would, it was theorized, provide an incentive to increase their efficiency. Between 1983 and 1987, Chinese leaders and their press repeatedly sang the praises of the new tax system.

The tax policy seriously damaged the interests of local (e.g. county) governments, which had previously been able to retain a significant share of enterprise profits for themselves in their extra-budgetary funds.[30] In Xinji, these amounted to around one-fourth of total county government budgetary expenditures by 1978. Predictably, local governments fought the new policy. They were successful, forcing the reversal of the policy by early 1987, after just two years of operation. The state leadership had been so heavily committed to the substitution of taxes for profits that when they dropped it, they did so with no public fanfare, evaluation, or criticism of it whatsoever. The centre did not wish to advertise this major victory for local governments.

Political pressure aside, the replacement of profit remissions with taxes probably did not deliver the increased regularity of revenues and enterprise autonomy and efficiency that had been promised for it. An official of the Sichuan's Guanghan County Finance and Tax Bureau said in late 1986: 'Now the system of three distinct types of state, collective and private ownership has been replaced by many more mixed forms. So it's difficult to know which taxes and tax rates apply to a particular enterprise. The regulations can't be clear. It's up to us to decide.'[31] This local government bureau was able to exercise significant leverage over local enterprises. In Xinji, the tax-for-profits system was never even applied to those enter-

---

[29] See e.g. 'Enterprises Benefit from Tax Reform', *News from the Xinhua News Agency* 102422 (25 Oct. 1985), 12–13.

[30] For a description of extra-budgetary funds, see Vivienne Shue, 'Beyond the Budget: Finance Organization and Reform in a Chinese County', *Modern China*, 10/2 (Apr. 1984), 172–80.

[31] Field research notes, 26 Nov. 1986. Guanghan county has been popularized for being in the forefront of economic reform. See note 33 for fuller details on Guanghan.

prises most directly under the control of the county government, which remitted their profits to its extra-budgetary fund. 'In principle, extra-budgetary enterprises implemented the tax-for-profit policy like other factories. But in fact now [late 1986] they pay only the income tax, and they remit all the rest of their profits to the county's extra-budgetary fund, just like before.'[32] The Xinji government simply did not want to part with the revenues it was collecting from these factories, so it fought for the implementation of the tax-for-profit scheme under which these monies would have gone into the coffers of the higher levels of the state through the Ministry of Finance and Taxation.

The system of taxes replacing profits was supplanted by a system called 'profit contracting', under which '[s]tate-owned enterprises which are able to make profits must fulfil an annual quota of profits and increase it each year at a regular rate. The enterprises then share with the state the amount made in excess of the quota.'[33] In Xinji, as of mid-1990,

The word 'tax' still exists, but in fact it's profit contracting. In 1987, because of the increased vitality of the enterprises, the enterprises' departments got a tax target, which in turn sent it down to the enterprises. This was called 'fix the base numbers, guarantee upward transfers [of profits], exceed the revenue target and keep more excess, be responsible for revenue shortages yourself'. The bureaux set these policies for the enterprises. Enterprises' tax targets increase 10% per year, because they are the major taxpayers. Then they can keep 80% of their after-tax profits, and hand in 20% to the Finance and Tax Bureau.[34]

It is difficult to see much difference between this system and the old profit remission system, which had been criticized for allowing too much local government influence over enterprises' finances. At present financial relationships between enterprises and the state are in disarray, with a proliferation of local practices. The state, though critical of the localities for not serving its interests and

[32] Briefing with Xinji Finance and Tax Bureau, 6 Dec. 1986.
[33] 'Contract System may be Changed', *CD* (3 Aug. 1988), 4. In 1986, state-owned enterprises in Guanghan county were remitting 40% of their profits to the state, which in turn was redistributing an average of 40% of these revenues back to the county government (though this last figure could be as low as 10% for very rich counties and as high as 80% for very poor ones). Field research notes, 29 Nov. 1986. The original 40% profit remission figure may well have risen through 1987, when the tax-for-profit system was abolished.
[34] Briefing with Xinji Finance and Tax Bureau, 7 July 1990.

allowing 'government departments [to] interfere too much in enterprises' economic decisions and day-to-day affairs', was in 1987 justifying inaction in the name of continued experimentation.[35] With
the onset of the central government's serious deficits in subsequent
years and the resulting general recentralization of administrative
and financial levers in the wake of the June 1989 events, the issue
has been dropped.

Bankruptcy

Beginning in February 1985, the industrial city of Shenyang began
to moot bankruptcy as an approach to making enterprises
autonomous and responsible for their own affairs. Though no
bankruptcy law yet existed, in September of 1986 the Shenyang
Explosion-Proof Equipment Factory, which was unable to pay
Y503,000 in debt (against assets of only Y302,000), was the first
Chinese firm to be declared bankrupt since 1949. It was sold to the
Shenyang Gas Supply Company at an auction that attracted thirty
bidders. Its seventy-two workers were laid off, though disabled
workers and those near retirement received benefits of three-
quarters of their salaries for an unspecified period.[36]

   This approach to enterprise policy caused a firestorm of controversy in China. Proponents argued that only if enterprises faced
the possibility of bankruptcy would they take responsibility for
themselves seriously and strive to make prudent investments and
management decisions.[37] Opponents on the Standing Committee of
the National People's Congress argued against it on several grounds.
First, it was premature to pass a bankruptcy law until legislation on
workers' rights and unemployment insurance was in place. Second,
it was unfair to hold enterprises responsible for their losses in this
most draconian manner so long as local governments were still exercising power over them. Third, so long as prices remained
unreformed, enterprise profits or losses were often poor indicators

[35] Sun Xiaoliang, 'Problems to Avoid in Contract System', *CD* (29 Sept. 1987), 4;
Zhang Xiaogang, 'Factory Reforms Produce Results', *CD* (27 June 1987), 4.
  [36] 'Bankrupt Firm Sold at Auction', *CD* (27 Sept. 1986); Li Rongxia, 'First
Bankruptcy Shocks China', *BR* 29/36 (8 Sept. 1986), 25–7.
  [37] For one example of many such statements which appeared in 1986, see Sun
Yunling, 'Establish the Enterprise Bankruptcy System, Improve the Enterprise
Behavior Mechanism', *Jingj Cankao (Economic Reference)* (21 June 1988), 6.

of their efficiency and productivity.[38] Away from the pinnacles of power, workers complained that they ought not suffer the economic hardship and 'shame' of unemployment because of the poor management of the plant.[39] Local governments complained that bankruptcies would create a host of problems for them: adding more workers to the already swollen rolls of unemployed jobseekers, putting financial pressure on local social services (as workers would become unable to meet their medical, housing, or children's school expenses), and generally increasing local discontent whose expression could cause political and security problems.

In the face of these difficulties and controversies, the state equivocated. The Eighteenth Session of the Sixth National People's Congress Standing Committee decided in November 1986 to approve a tentative draft of a bankruptcy law for trial implementation in a small number of units.[40] But then bankruptcy has been shelved, with no further closures. Some sabres continued to be rattled through the early part of 1987,[41] though, and bankruptcy retained some supporters, as noted below.

In 1988, it was replaced by a new approach under which unprofitable firms were absorbed into profitable ones. This created new problems. Most significantly, by permitting local governments to allocate the assets of one enterprise to another, it actually increased their power *vis-à-vis* enterprises. This mitigated against the separation of government administration from enterprises, which had been one of the original, overarching goals of the bankruptcy policy. In addition, the new policy saddled the enterprises into which unprofitable firms were absorbed with large contingents of new workers whose labour could not be used efficiently but for whom payrolls still had to be met.[42]

As of mid-1990, the issue is dormant but not dead. In what may be an indication of ongoing controversy over the new approach, in August 1988 the press again began to mention bankruptcy.[43]

[38] Wang Gangyi, 'NPC again Mulls Revised Draft of Bankruptcy Law' *CD* (17 Nov. 1986).

[39] Li Rongxia, 'First Bankruptcy' (see n. 36).

[40] British Broadcasting Corporation, *Summary of World Broadcasts, Part 3: The Far East: 8433*.

[41] 'Four Bankruptcy Warnings Given', *CD* (7 Mar. 1987), 3.

[42] '"Annexing" Firms Can Help Economy', *CD* (7 Mar. 1987), 3.

[43] Yin Jiafei, 'Bankruptcy Law to Doom Thousands of Enterprises', *CD* (22 Aug. 1988).

And at least one bankruptcy of a state sector firm – the Nanchang Motorcycle Manufacturing Company, which had accumulated Y9,500,000 in debt – has taken place.[44] But in the post-June 1989 environment of much more cautious economic policy and political apprehension, bankruptcy has not yet caught on in a major way. By mid-1990 bankruptcy has never been attempted in Xinji, even though the county has had a significant problem of unprofitable enterprises. Most of these simply continued to operate in the red. The only significant attempt to transform a losing enterprise took place in April, 1988 (a period of economic reformist experimentation on the national scene) when, in line with the then-current policy described above, a cotton-oil machinery factory was contracted out to a successful township enterprise. Though this proved a success for all parties concerned – the factory remained open, all its workers kept their jobs (which was a condition of the take-over, indicating the sensitivity of the employment issue), and the ink turned from red to black – the experiment was not extended to other unprofitable firms.

Banking Reform

A major effort to free the economy from government interference, and to have key decisions made on economic rather than political grounds, has centred around banking reform. One of the first and most durable institutional changes associated with the reformist project was the creation or resuscitation of specialized banks for agriculture, industry, and capital construction, and the conversion of the People's Bank, which had formerly been the only bank (except for the Bank of China, which dealt in international transactions), into a central bank. The banks were not only elaborated in this way, but also were to be strengthened and in theory made more autonomous from political control. Whereas in the past enterprises received their capital as allocations through their ministries, now banks became major suppliers of capital in the form of loans. The booming collective sector enterprises rely most heavily on the banks for their credit, but even state and private enterprises have become bank 'customers'. Moreover, the banks have been instructed to

---

[44] 'First State Firm Goes Bankrupt in Jiangxi', *CD* (7 Dec. 1990).

operate according to strict economic principles in evaluating loan applications.

The problem is that at the middle and lower levels such as provinces, prefectures, and counties, where the actual financial decisions are taken, the banks have not been autonomous of local state organs, and thus cannot operate according to purely economic criteria in regulating and distributing credit. In some cases, this has to do with ongoing efforts of the state to plan and shape the economy, reforms to the contrary notwithstanding. For example, in mid-1990, criteria for decisions on loan applications by Xinji banks included whether the enterprise was included in the state plan and whether it was engaged in sectors given high priority by economic planners. Political pressure is often applied by local governments on the banks to support their local enterprises or pet projects, or simply to keep existing enterprises with their large labour forces afloat. In Xinji, the Economic Planning Commission admitted frankly: 'When one of our factories needs a loan and the bank doesn't give it, the mayor has to persuade the bank to give the money.' As a result, in many cases credit is not being allocated according to criteria of efficiency or profitability. Moreover, many banks have been exceeding their quotas in extending new loans. Consequently the money supply has periodically expanded out of control.

The central leadership has responded in three ways. First, it has sought to constrict the dispensation of bank credit by centralizing administrative control over the banks, using this power to enforce strict lending limits. In mid-1990 Xinji bankers said:

We don't have a problem of exceeding loan quotas in any of the banks. This is tightly controlled, and we can't violate it. In the past few years, there was policy regulation that bank loans could increase with rising deposits. But now this policy has been abandoned. The new policy is called scale control. Now, if we have funds on deposit, but we have already reached the ceiling for loan volume, we can't make new loans. And if we have not reached our ceiling but we do not have funds on deposit to cover new loans, we also cannot make new loans.

Even rural credit co-operatives, which formally are collective rather than state institutions, became subject to this 'scale control'.

Second, reforms intended to encourage banks to operate according to goals of profitability have been shelved. In the words of Xinji bankers in mid-1990:

We can make profits, but this is not our goal. Our main purpose is the service and supervision of the socialist economy. We do have a profit target, but this is not the main indicator of our performance. Treating the banks as [state] enterprises is a way of strengthening the management of the banks. Our profit target is soft, not hard. The idea is not for each branch to make a profit, but simply for the banking system to be in the black for the whole country.

In 1987, the agricultural bank began to experiment with profit contracting with the Ministry of Finance. But this failed for two years nation wide, because the differential between loan and deposit interest rates was too small, and sometimes was negative. So in 1989 the experiment was abandoned.

The Xinji bankers are saying two things. First, putting banks on a profit-and-loss basis would deprive planners of a major lever of control over the development of the economy. Second, banks could not turn a profit without deregulation of interest rates. The state was unwilling to do this partly for the same reason. In addition, the attendant rise in interest rates might cause a recession; more specifically, it would endanger the state sector enterprises which are the most dependent on the state banks for loans and also the least flexible in their ability to adjust their operations and prices to reflect changing interest rates.

Third, experiments with private banking, highly publicized as the 'Wenzhou model' after the city in Zhejiang Province where private banking has mushroomed, were shelved. Privatization of banking poses at·least five serious problems. First, private banks, with their flexible interest rates, would provide stiff competition for the tightly regulated state banks. The latter can therefore be expected to bring political pressure to bear within the state to regulate or restrict them. Second, the higher interest rates that the private banks pay and charge could fuel inflation, about which the leadership has recently been so apprehensive that after a false start it backed down on a long-promised price reform in August 1988. (None the less, rising prices were a significant contributor to the discontent that exploded in the spring of 1989.) Third, private banks pose a problem of losing depositors' money or, worse yet, swindling them. And China's government retains its commitment to protecting its people from such losses. Fourth, the Wenzhou model of private banking is not appropriate to many (probably, most) parts of China. As Xinji officials put it:

The Wenzhou model was not really so important. There was a lot written about it in the papers. It is not well suited to the conditions here in Xinji. In Wenzhou [which is located in more prosperous and commercially developed Zhejiang], there is a proliferation of light industries. Wenzhou is on the coast, and it receives great benefits from this. But here in Xinji [on the North China Plain] we are mainly an agricultural area in terms of population. It's harder to get significant capital accumulation from agriculture. So the Wenzhou model wouldn't fit here.

In other words, local officials feel that there is simply not enough surplus extant in the rural economy of Xinji to support or merit opening private financial institutions to supplement the state banks. And Xinji is much closer to the vast majority of Chinese rural areas than is Wenzhou. Fifth, a profit-oriented banking sector would probably only magnify the problem of excessive investment rates in China's overheated economy.[45]

Conclusion and Prospects

In conclusion, state sector economic reforms intended to separate the state from enterprises and enhance the autonomy of the latter have by and large met with failure. The effort to grant managers fuller responsibility for their enterprises has proceeded unevenly and uncertainly at best. In the few places where it has been implemented, it has tended to produce technocratic elitism which does not get the state out of enterprises but only transforms its mode of insertion into them. And increased managerial power poses a serious contradiction with political reform too, by making enterprises more authoritarian. Attempts to use taxation to deprive local governments of the financial power they garnered by appropriating enterprise profits have met with such serious political opposition from within the state and such poor results that they were ignored or, where implemented, reversed. Bankruptcy, another way of making enterprises responsible for their own finances, has up till now gone nowhere too. And the attempt to deregulate or even

---

[45] Overheating of the economy refers to the phenomenon in which construction of new enterprises — spearheaded by local government agencies or collective or even private sector entrepreneurs — has proceeded much faster than the ability of these firms to operate successfully, because of shortages of needed inputs, insufficient markets for their products, bottlenecks in transport, or inability to obtain sufficient financing.

privatize the financial sector in order to reduce political control of
the economy and promote economic rationality has been difficult
to implement, proven inappropriate to the economic conditions
in much of China, contributed to economic overheating and inflation, and incurred political opposition from within the state. Thus
far, then, removing the state from the administration of state enterprises has proven impossible in some places and problematical in
others.

This suggests that the only way to get the state out of the economy
may be to eliminate or at least attack state ownership itself while
also reforming collective ownership. For a time up to mid-1989,
many leaders, policy advisers, and scholars in China were beginning
to think this way. But each offensive in this direction has been
reversed since June 1989. First, there was a raging debate on the
transformation of state ownership into a kind of joint stock ownership.[46] But the conceptual ambiguities, theoretical conundra, and
practical problems of such a development are very great and have
not yet been adequately thought through, much less tackled in
practice, even on a serious trial basis.[47] Many rural collective
sector enterprises have issued shares to their employees. But these
are not tradable, and serve mainly as ways for enterprises to raise
capital from their employees in the context of tightened credit. From
the employees' points of view they also serve as fees for gaining
employment. In mid-1990, stock markets remain moribund, though
there are still those who would like to breathe life into them,
especially in Shanghai and in the Shenzhen Special Export Zone.[48]

Second, for a time before the spring 1989 crisis there was a clear
commitment among many in China's leadership to expanding the
collective and private sectors and restricting further expansion
of the state sector. There are numerous problems in basing China's
economic future on these sectors, though. Even before 1989,
political and administrative obstacles to and harassment of private
businesses, combined with ongoing anxiety about a change in the
state's policy on or attitude towards the private sector, have induced
many private firms to camouflage themselves as collective firms.

[46] Wang Gangyi, 'Opposing Views on Shareholding', *CD* (17 May 1988), 4;
'Businesses Freed From Old Bonds', *CD* (24 Aug. 1988), 4; *FEER* (9 Mar. 1989), 72.
   [47] e.g. it is argued that private ownership of stock in state enterprises 'do[es] not
change the public ownership of the enterprises . . .': 'Businesses Freed' (see n. 46).
   [48] *FEER* (26 July 1990), 54–6.

This has confused the situation and opened many private entrepreneurs to charges of embezzlement when they have tried to claim
their private profits from an ostensibly collective firm.[49] Collective
sector firms have been frequently criticized for being serious
polluters,[50] for their technical backwardness and inefficiency,[51]
their proclivity to excessive or at least unregulated investment,[52]
and their exploitative labour practices (such as child labour or
the reappearance of the 'forbidden stitch' which induces blindness
in embroiderers). Since June 1989, the state sector has been cham-
pioned anew as the core of the Chinese economy, and collective
enterprises have been subject to closure or at least to loudly and
frequently reiterated prohibitions against competing with state
firms.[53] State sector firms have been given priority in allocation of
credit as well.[54]

State sector firms form so central a part of the Chinese economy
that even in the heyday of reform they remained dominant. In
1988 they produced 60 per cent of industrial output value (and
much higher percentages of key sectors such as steel and energy),
employed more than half the urban labour force, took 85 per cent
of urban fixed investment, and accounted for 85 per cent of remissions of industrial profits and taxes.[55] By the end of 1988, they had
only increased their importance, accounting for 68 per cent of
industrial output value, and 69 per cent of industrial employment.[56] For the foreseeable future, even one which includes a
political and policy reversal in the direction of reform, it is unlikely
that this sector could soon become dwarfed by a burgeoning collective, much less private, sector.

If the state sector is here to stay for a significant period of time,
and if previous efforts to remove state control over it have failed,

[49] 'Private Business Suffers Injustice', *CD* (22 Sept. 1988).
[50] Interviews with Xinji Bureau of Urban Planning and Environmental Protection, 14 Dec. 1986 and 28 June 1990.
[51] 'Culling of Needless Firms would Remedy Economy', *CD* (9 Feb. 1990); 'Axing
Superflous Firms Would Strengthen Market', *CD* (12 Jan. 1990).
[52] e.g. see Guo Zhongshi, 'Rural Firms Thrive, but Problems also Grow', *CD* (28
Sept. 1988).
[53] 'State-owned Sector in Official Spotlight', *CD* (8 Nov. 1989); 'Rural Enterprises
to be Readjusted', *CD* (9 Dec. 1989); 'Give Priority to Big State Enterprises', *CD* (20
Dec. 1989).
[54] 'New Bank Loans to Support Major State Factories', *CD* (18 Jan. 1990).
[55] Louise do Rosario, 'China's Broken Engine', *FEER* (8 Sept. 1988), 128.
[56] Calculated from *Yearbook 1989* (see n. 3), 233, 218, 219.

what next? In 1988, there were a few new wisps in the air intended to revitalize the state sector and diminish political control over it. State firms were encouraged to emulate the scrappy business tactics of rural collective firms. This avenue seems unpromising at best. The advice is inappropriate: a large power plant or steel mill cannot be run with the flexibility and hard-nosed management style of a village workshop. A silent admission of this may be found in the fact that the renewed emphasis placed on the state sector since June 1989 has not included such exhortations. (In general, exhortation doesn't go very far any more in China, if it ever did. But the post-June leadership is certainly one which is not reticent about exhortation.) As noted above, share holding, under which enterprises and workers would own minority shares of their enterprises, was making something of a comeback in policy circles in the spring of 1988, and still has its supporters; but many theoretical problems and practical details remain to be worked out and trial runs undertaken. Bankruptcy too may still be on the table, though the time for so bold a move seems to have passed for the moment. If a way can be found to make state banks more truly autonomous of other state agencies, finance may be one area where further progress could be made in reducing political influence in the economy.

That aside, there appears little prospect of a significant new approach either to downgrading the state sector or to removing the power of the state from it. For the foreseeable future, China will probably have to face up to the fact that the real question is not whether to have a state sector or how to get politics out of it, but rather how to restructure the relationship of the state to it in ways which promote the leadership's goals of economic modernization. To that problem we turn next.

Restructuring the Relationship between the State and the Economy. Personnel Policy: Towards Meritocracy?

A necessary condition for such restructuring is the professionalization of state personnel policy. Recruitment of a better educated leadership possessing more experience with modern technology and methods of management would help promote economic modernization. So would the allocation of rewards and promotions according to performance in promoting modernization. Hence the reform leadership undertook a major 'rectification' of the CCP, beginning in 1983, and floated the idea of creating a depoliticized civil service to replace the highly politicized cadre corps that now administers state affairs.

Raising the educational level of the party has been a daunting task. By the mid-1980s, fully 42 per cent of party members still had just a primary education, and another 30 per cent had only finished junior high school.[57] In Xinji, by 1985, only 10 per cent of cadres had any post-secondary education, 24 per cent were high school graduates, and 65 per cent were lower-middle school graduates or less. The party rectification had mainly political objectives, and thus was not concerned directly with removing poorly educated people from the CCP. Moreover, it has proven increasingly difficult to attract intellectuals into the party, because of its low prestige, the fact that party membership is no longer essential for career success or improved material life, the relatively greater attractiveness of and demands made by professional work, and the intellectuals' justified concern that those with lingering doubts about reform may be more heavily concentrated in the party than in other state institutions.[58] Still, intellectuals whom the party does attract will tend to exert greater influence than other new recruits, because of the CCP's commitment to promote them quickly to positions of authority.[59]

Efforts at emphasizing professional and educational qualifications in recruitment, evaluation, and promotion of non-party officials have been half-hearted, halting, and subject to reversals. On the negative side, appointments are made by the immediately superior administrative agency and party committee.[60] In another

[57] *Zuo Hao Zai Zhishifenzizhong Fazhan Dangyuan Gongzuo (Do a Good Job of Developing Party Membership among Intellectuals)* (Beijing; 1985), 58; cited in Lee, *Revolutionary Cadres* (see n. 18).

[58] e.g. Hong Yung Lee points out that many of the more reform-minded party members cannot attend CCP meetings regularly because they are engaged in work-related travel: *Revolutionary Cadres* (see n. 18) ch. 10a, p. 35. The demands which professional work poses for young intellectuals, and the general unattractiveness of the CCP to them, are captured poignantly in the 1982 Chinese film *Ren Dao Zhongnian (At Middle Age)*.

[59] When speaking in late 1986 about the municipality- (formerly county-) level party committee he chaired, one of Xinji municipality Party Secretary Bai Runzhang's most prominent points of pride was its large and still growing contingent of college graduates. Field research, 13 Dec. 1986. For details about Xinji, see n. 5.

[60] The division of responsibility here is complex and unclear. According to Party

contradiction between administrative and political reform, experiments undertaken in the mid-1980s with elections of officials by the members of the units in which they are to serve have tended further to politicize recruitment rather than result in selection of the most educationally or technically qualified persons.[61] And according to 'Questions and Answers on Party Organizational Work', a major reform statement on personnel policy, evaluation and promotion of government as well as party cadres is still handled by party committees, which were to use a list of criteria that began with 'virtue, focusing on political standpoint and character'.[62] Yet there are also countervailing tendencies. In Xinji, a target was set in 1985 that, by the end of 1990, all officials at the county and township levels were to be high school graduates. A complex, multi-stranded and expensive system of training was established for cadres who did not meet the standard, involving extended leaves of absence to participate in protracted courses of study. But, in another 'negation of the negation', in the year when this five-year programme was to be completed, official state policy was once again re-emphasizing political reliability and virtue as the paramount criterion in personnel recruitment.[63]

Promotion and demotion could pose a problem that might be termed a reforming state socialist version of the Peter Principle. In a strongly hierarchical statist system such as that which continues to prevail in China, it is still presumed among state officials at all levels that power accretes upward. Thus reformers concerned with personnel competence would tend to promote the most qualified and demote the least qualified. But this would deprive the enterprises of the most competent people, which contradicts the goal of decentralizing economic power downwards to enterprises (at least in theory if not in practice), where professional competence is so

---

Chairman Zhao Ziyang, local party committees are to 'recommend cadres for key posts in local state organs'. Zhao Ziyang, 'Advance along the Road of Socialism with Chinese Characteristics: Report Delivered at the Thirteenth National Congress of the Communist Party of China on October 25, 1987', *BR* (9–15 Nov. 1987), 30/45, 38.

[61] *Renmin Ribao (People's Daily)* (21 Mar. 1985); cited in Lee, *Revolutionary Cadres* (see n. 18), ch. 13, p. 22.

[62] Melanie Manion, 'The Cadre Management System Post-Mao: The Appointment, Promotion, Transfer and Removal of Party and State Leaders', *China Quarterly*, 102 (June 1985), 227.

[63] *China News Digest* (1 Mar. 1990).

badly needed for the success of the economy and of enterprise-based reform.

One approach to personnel problems which has been frequently mooted and hotly debated in China is the creation of a civil service.[64] Aside from its unpopularity among the large phalanx of poorly educated officials who stand to lose out, there are several other problems involved in establishing such a personnel structure in China. There has been no agreement on a job classification system, a necessary prerequisite for any civil service.[65] In China's highly politicized state, it is a conceptually as well as politically formidable task to distinguish administrative posts, which would be included in a civil service, from political ones, which would not. And even if this distinction could be made, the job of classifying and then grading administrative posts promises to be nothing less than a practical and, more important, a political nightmare. There are good reasons, then, why proposals for a Chinese civil service have generated intense heat but little light. And even if these obstacles could be overcome, a Chinese reform leadership ought to resist the naïve assumption that a civil service really can be apolitical, especially in a one-party state. As of mid-1990, though, they do not require such sagacity, as the issue of civil service reform has dropped from sight in the wake of the 1989 climacteric.

Separation of Party and Government

Personnel issues raise the question of the relationship of the CCP and the government. If the reformers' goal of separating the state from the economy is proving difficult to attain, perhaps the state's involvement in the economy can better serve the goal of modernization if the party can be separated from the government, another frequently advanced reformist goal. According to former Premier and Party General Secretary Zhao Ziyang, in a statement with which even his severest critics would take not the slightest issue, 'the Party exercises political leadership, which means that it formulates political principles, points the political direction, makes

[64] Zhao Ziyang raised it again in his report to the 13th Party Congress in late 1988. Zhao, 'Advance' (see n. 60), 40–1.
[65] Lee, *Revolutionary Cadres* (see n. 18), ch. 13, p. 18.

major policy decisions and recommends cadres for key posts in organs of state power'.[66] The government's role is to administer and provide leadership over practical matters, including economic affairs. Yet, in a statement that might have been more controversial within the leadership, Zhao also said that

local Party committees at the provincial, municipal and county levels should exercise political leadership in local work, . . . ensuring that the decrees *of the central government* are implemented. Their principal responsibilities should be . . . to ensure the implementation in their local areas of directives from *governments* of higher levels and from the State Council; to propose policy decisions on important local issues; . . . to co-ordinate activities of the various local organizations.[67]

Local party officials could hardly be blamed for a certain confusion about the boundaries to which the General Secretary was asking them to restrict themselves, or for using his statement to stick their noses into just about anything they liked. So while Zhao complained in October 1987 about the continuing 'lack of distinction between the functions of the Party and those of the government[,] and the substitution of the Party for the government',[68] neither his speech nor any subsequent developments have produced much progress on this front. The CCP's reassertion of its own pre-eminence since June 1989 suggests that the confusion may in fact have reflected disagreement within the party which Zhao was trying to reconcile or paper over. When questioned in late 1986 about the division of labour between them, Party Secretary Bai Runzhang and Mayor Liu Baolu of Xinji municipality conveyed a clear sense that the important aspect of party–government relations was how closely and easily they worked together in planning and leading economic development, which comprised the bulk of their work. By mid-1990, Party Secretary Wang Zhongyi, who succeeded Bai, clearly ruled the roost among the top leaders of Xinji.[69]

One key element of personnel reform would be the simplification of lines of administrative authority over state officials. The system of 'dual rule' which has evolved in China since 1949 made officials

[66] Zhao, 'Advance' (see n. 60), 38.
[67] Ibid. Emphasis added.
[68] Ibid.
[69] Field research notes, 13 Dec. 1986 and 6 July 1990.

responsible both to their superiors in their particular bureaucratic hierarchy (i.e vertical rule) and also the CCP authorities at their own level (i.e horizontal rule). With two very different authorities to please, it is no wonder that state officials felt confused about what was expected of them, could not discern or pursue a clear career path, and as a result often acted passively. If the reformers seek to develop a more technocratic corps of officials by encouraging their careers, they must abolish the duality of personnel authority over them. There is little indication of this before or since June 1989, or that it could be done until such time as party and government can be separated in a meaningful way. This is a deep catch-22 of administrative reform.

Conclusion

Before June 1989, the reformist leadership in Beijing undertook several initiatives to reorient state administration of the economy. Most failed or at best had very mixed results. Indeed, some parts of the reform programme contradicted others. The state's administrative apparatus did not shrink but in fact grew considerably during a period when the state was supposed to be giving up control over the economy and receding from what it came to criticize as the overweening social control of the Maoist period. Enterprise managers did not gain significant autonomy from local state officials. Administrative reforms to put in place a taxation system that would provide an incentive for enterprise efficiency or at least profitability while depriving local governments of financial leverage over enterprises were reversed, largely because of the opposition of local officials who are themselves key actors in the reformist story. Bankruptcy, which could put enterprises at risk of dissolution, in turn causing difficulties for local governments that have to deal with the consequences, was derailed after great fanfares about its opening run. Banks were not made autonomous or profitable, much less privatized. The state itself was unable to separate its government administration from political control generally, or more specifically to reform and depoliticize its personnel practices.

Since June 1989, there has been nothing in the way of new offensives or experiments in any of these areas, and precious little frank discussion of the problems already encountered before that time.

The new leadership and political climate are clearly responsible for this. Lacking many obvious political allies outside the armed forces, Deng Xiaoping and Li Peng have curried the favour of the state bureaucracy, especially those opposed to or ambivalent, dubious, or worried about reform — and the myriad difficulties encountered by the reforms probably swelled their ranks considerably. On the other side, those continuing to favour reforms of various kinds found themselves both weakened and increasingly disagreeing with each other as a result of the reforms' crisis. They have also been constrained against any positive approach to the situation by the reversals at the top.

Before June 1989, it was possible to discern some structural space for new directions that might help resolve the crises of the first decade of reform. There was latitude for localities to pursue their own pathways in economic development and political change. Two directions for political economics could be made out: one in which local political authorities would act as entrepreneurs, and the other in which they would play a role of creating the infrastructural conditions for economic growth while leaving the entrepreneurship to enterprises.[70] There was room for other new approaches to emerge as well. In the latter half of 1990, such room for manoeuvre as may have existed eighteen months or two years earlier is obstructed. Nothing in the way of a constructive approach to the administrative problems and contradictions posed by China's reforms is in evidence. Except for some anachronistic revivals of old saws and timeworn policies, such as giving primacy to the state sector, for now the crisis of reform is being met with a thunderous silence.

Once the present leadership is swept away, experiments will resume anew. They will doubtless produce their own admixture of success and failure. On the positive side, there are now ten years of experience of reform that can be mobilized in formulating novel policies and practices. On the negative side, the reversals beginning in 1989 may well make reformers more hesitant in the future. And they surely will make the objective economic and political

---

[70] Marc Blecher, 'Developmental State, Entrepreneurial State: The Political Economy of Socialist Reform in Xinji Municipality and Guanghan County', in Gordon White, ed., *The Road to Crisis: The Chinese State in the Era of Economic Reform* (London, forthcoming); M. Blecher, 'State Administration and Economic Reform: Old Dog Snubs Master, But Learns New Tricks', *Pacific Affairs*, 2/2 (1989), 94–106.

problems to be resolved more daunting as the economic crisis worsens with time. The longer the present leadership remains in power and the present course of economic policy and administrative practice continues, the more thunderous will be the storm once the silence ends.

3. Human Rights: The Changing Balance-Sheet

ANN KENT

The forcible suppression of civil rights in June 1989 and succeeding months, together with related international developments, has created an obvious crisis in human rights for China. This crisis is also, however, the legacy of problems caused by heightened popular expectations of improved civil and political rights in the modernization decade preceding June 1989, by the diminution of economic and social rights which occurred in this period, and by the carry-over of social structures and expectations from the Maoist era. It is only by assessing the overall condition of civil, political, social, and economic rights in China since 1949 that the full dimension of China's current human rights problem can be appreciated.

The model of human rights here applied to China is a broad international one, deriving from the International Bill of Rights.[1] Civil rights may be understood as conferring rights of immunity upon the individual, as requiring non-interference from others and as 'not normally dependent upon social conditions'.[2] They include freedom of thought, conscience and religion, expression and association, residence and movement; freedom from slavery, arbitrary arrest or detention; and equality before the law.[3] Political rights may be defined as rights of participation, and include the individual's right to 'take part in the government of his country, directly or through freely chosen representatives'; the right of access to public service; and the right of election and recall of government

---

[1] The International Bill of Rights comprises the Universal Declaration of Human Rights (UDHR) and its 1966 covenants, the International Covenant of Civil and Political Rights (ICCPR) and the International Covenant of Economic, Social, and Cultural Rights (ICESCR). For texts, see A.H. Robertson, *Human Rights in the World* (Manchester, 1972), 185–223.

[2] Eugene Kamenka, 'Human Rights, Peoples' Rights', *Bulletin of the Australian Society of Legal Philosophy*, 9/33 (June 1985), 157.

[3] 'Universal Declaration of Human Rights' and 'International Covenant on Civil and Political Rights' in Robertson, *Human Rights* (see n. 1), 185–90, 202–3. See also L. Henkin, in R. Randle Edwards, Louis Henkin, and Andrew J. Nathan, *Human Rights in Contemporary China* (New York, 1986), 32.

on the basis of 'universal and equal suffrage' by secret ballot.[4]
Social and cultural rights, in the form of claims to benefits from
the state, may be understood as rights of consumption, allowing
access to social security, to education, and to the cultural life of
the community. Social rights include 'the right [of everyone] to a
standard of living adequate for the health and wellbeing of himself
and of his family, including food, clothing, housing and medical
care and necessary social services, and the right to security in the
event of unemployment, sickness, disability, widowhood or lack of
livelihood in circumstances beyond his control'.[5] Economic rights,
which suggest not only the right of consumption but also embrace
the more active right of participation in the work-force, include
the right to work, to free choice of employment, to equal pay for
equal work, and the right to 'reasonable limitations of working
hours and periodic holidays with pay'.[6] They also include the right
to strike which, together with the civil right of freedom of association, comprises a separate category of industrial rights.

In applying this model of human rights to China, it is not suggested that the realization of 'human rights' has been an explicit goal
of the post-1949 Chinese government. On the contrary, despite
the inclusion in each of China's four post-1949 constitutions of a
section on the rights and duties of the Chinese citizen, encapsulating
civil, political, social, and economic rights, China's leaders have
not normally referred to 'human rights' as part of their political
agenda.[7] Nevertheless, Marxist theory has encompassed within
itself the basic content of social and economic rights in the form of
the more equal distribution of resources, and the guarantees of
the right to work and the rights of access to social welfare and social
security, as well as the right to education. In other words, Chinese
leadership, however authoritarian, haş been obliged to legitimize
its rule by reference to some content of 'human rights', even if its
policies have not been defined in those precise terms. Moreover, if

---

[4] Art. 25, 'International Covenant on Civil and Political Rights', in Robertson,
Human Rights, 210–11.

[5] Art. 25(1), 'Universal Declaration of Human Rights', in Robertson, *Human
Rights*, 189.

[6] Ibid., arts. 23 and 24.

[7] For exceptions to this rule, see Ann Kent, *Human Rights in the People's
Republic of China: National and International Dimensions* (Canberra, 1990), 59–61.
See also Roberta Cohen, 'People's Republic of China: The Human Rights Exception',
Human Rights Quarterly, 9/4 (Nov. 1987), 448–549.

one distinguishes between the formal and informal provision of
rights in China, or between 'instrumentation', or formal institutionalization, and 'compliance', or actual implementation, in the
guarantee of China's human rights, the complexity of the overall
human rights situation in China is revealed.[8] Social and economic
rights are seen to have an intricate relationship with civil and
political rights. It becomes clear that from December 1978, the
beginning of the modernization decade, until June 1989, civil and
political rights, although not formally given precedence in China,
began expanding informally, while social and economic rights
contracted. Thus, the normal Marxist emphasis on social and
economic rights, to the neglect and even negation of civil and
political rights, began to be reversed. This process of informal
reversal was, of course, interrupted by the June 1989 events, which
brought the overall condition of human rights in China, whether
civil, political, social, or economic, to an all-time low. Since that
time, China's leaders have been seeking the appropriate mix of rights
which would allow the restoration of a sufficient degree of doctrinal
and performance legitimacy to ensure a return to social stability and
popular support: economic obstacles and the regime's own inability
to relax social controls have, however, militated against their
success.

Human Rights under Mao

Since 1949, as a socialist country, China has traditionally con-
formed with the view of other socialist and Third World countries
which emphasizes the social and economic aspects of human rights
and considers the aspirations of their peoples as realizable mainly
through collective social and economic action. According to this
formal Marxist view, political rights and equality, or 'bourgeois
right', have been seen as symptoms of social and economic in-
equality, with true rights arising from the state ownership of the
means of production and the equal distribution of wealth. While

---

[8] The distinction between 'instrumentation' and 'compliance' is applied to the
respect accorded civil rights in China's legal and judicial system by James Seymour,
'Human Rights and the Law in the Poeple's Republic of China', in Victor C.
Falkenheim and Ilpyong J. Kim, eds., *Chinese Politics from Mao to Deng* (New
York, 1989), 272.

Western states emphasize the universal and abstract nature of the individual's civil and political rights, with social rights as secondary, concrete, non-universal, and contingent, China emphasizes social and economic rights but views all rights as collectively based, concrete, non-universal, and subordinate to state sovereignty and state security. China has also interpreted the collective political right of self-determination of peoples, articulated in Part 1, Article 1, of the International Covenant of Civil and Political Rights (ICCPR), as stipulating the liberation of non-self-governing peoples from colonial domination, which, by extension, means 'the right that foreign states shall not interfere in the life of the community against the will of the government'.[9]

In the Maoist period it can be observed, as a broad and obvious generalization, that this socialist emphasis on social and economic rights in preference to, and almost to the exclusion of, individual civil and political rights, was most fully realized, not only in theory but in practice. Social, economic, and cultural rights guaranteed under China's four constitutions have included the 'right and duty to work', the 'right to rest', the right to 'material assistance from the state and society in old age, illness or disability', the right to a system of retirement for state workers and staff and the 'duty as well as the right to receive education', together with the right to engage in 'scientific research, literary and artistic creation and other cultural pursuits'.[10] Under the post-1949 socio-economic security system, Chinese citizens in the Maoist era achieved an improved standard of living over the pre-1949 years, relatively egalitarian forms of distribution, access (if limited) to health and education services (in the collective sector of the countryside as well as in state enterprises), and access to secure, if overstaffed, jobs. If the result was an equality of poverty, it was none the less a poverty padded with important economic and social safeguards against destitution, starvation, ill health, and ignorance.[11] Crucial in this respect was the provision of the 'right and duty' to work: social and economic rights

---

[9] Antonio Cassese, 'Political Self Determination: Old Concepts and New Developments', cited in Kamenka, 'Human Rights', (see n. 2), 155.

[10] Arts. 42–7, 1982 Constitution, 4 Dec. 1982, *BR* 25/52 (27 Dec. 1982), 17.

[11] On equality of poverty, see David S. G. Goodman, 'Communism in East Asia: The Production Imperative, Legitimacy and Reform', in Goodman, ed., *Communism and Reform in East Asia* (London, 1988), 4. Even in the Maoist era, the relativity of this 'equality' is emphasized by Deborah Davis, 'Chinese Social Welfare: Policies and Outcomes', *China Quarterly*, 119 (Sept. 1989), 579.

were peculiarly conjoined, in that the right of access to social security was historically associated with the right to work. Hence the economic right to work at the same time implied social rights, leading to the notion of the 'iron rice bowl', and many 'social' rights were limited under China's constitutions to the 'working people'. Yet even those outside the state sector, in particular China's peasantry, were during the Maoist era guaranteed a basic rice ration, and, on a collective basis, limited health and education services, from the social welfare system.

On the other hand, civil and political rights were severely limited in practice, if not strictly in constitutional theory. The civil rights guaranteed under all four Chinese constitutions (1954, 1975, 1978, and 1982 — the freedoms of speech, correspondence, press, assembly, association, press and demonstration, of person, religious belief, right of appeal against state functionaries, and the autonomy of national minorities) proved during this period to be nominal ones, cancelled out by other articles of the constitutions, by constitutionally prescribed duties, by other acts of legislation, and by Party fiat. Their very existence in the constitutions, on the other hand, was important, because they still had the potential to be activated or empowered and could fuel rising expectations. However, in the Maoist era, the formal limitations on civil rights were reflected in the practical restrictions on their exercise in the society at large, despite the fact that certain civil rights, such as the right to strike and the 'four freedoms', were guaranteed in the 1975 and 1978 constitutions and were partially invoked. Apart from the nominal and partial freedoms, other civil rights laid down in the Universal Declaration of Human Rights (UDHR) and ICCPR, such as freedom of residence and movement, freedom from forced labour, freedom from torture, and the presumption of innocence, were neither constitutionally guaranteed nor exercised in practice in Maoist China.[12]

Political rights in the pre-modernization phase also reflected in practice the minimalist guarantee under the constitutions of 'the right to vote and stand for election' for all citizens of 18 and over. Since the basic definition of a right is its universal character, moreover, the exclusion from access to this right of 'those persons deprived of this right by law' raised the question of whether such

12 Henkin, in Edwards, Henkin, and Nathan, eds., *Human Rights* (see n. 3), 32.

political arrangements could in fact be called 'rights'. In practice, local elections were regarded as ritualistic procedures in which voters selected from a list of candidates nominated by a committee controlled by party members. The county-level congress delegates elected district-level candidates and so on up to the national level. Representatives were cadres and party members continually re-elected and seldom recalled. Thus, in the Maoist phase of human rights, it may be observed that the formal civil and political rights guaranteed Chinese citizens remained reasonably consistent with their exercise in reality — always excepting the token repetition of the nominal civil rights — in the negative sense that the provisions of the constitution remained close to the reality of a strictly controlled society.[13]

Human Rights during the Modernization Decade

Two years after the death of Mao, with the formal endorsement of Deng Xiaoping's four modernizations programme at the Third Plenum of the Eleventh Central Committee in December 1978, this socialist hierarchy of rights, characterized by the predominance of social and economic rights over civil and political rights, began a gradual reversal. The decade of economic modernization, marked by the change from a centrally planned socialist economy to a 'socialist commodity' economy, brought the decollectivization of agriculture, the rationalization of industrial production, the separation of ownership and management within factories, some market-based pricing policies, and a freer labour market, as well as a new emphasis on the importance of expertise over redness and of competition over egalitarianism. Implicit in these shifts were moves towards the establishment of a rule of law, the decentralization of economic decision-making, the acceptance of a greater degree of political pluralism, unofficial tolerance of the phenomenon of unemployment, and a shift in the notion of social welfare, from a good to be redistributed by the state to a commodity which was seen as the beneficiary of the diffused trickle-down effect of economic growth.

---

[13] These are essentially the findings of Jerome Cohen, 'China's Changing Constitution', *China Quarterly*, 76 (Dec. 1978), 836–41.

The impact of these changes on the condition of China's human rights and the challenges they raised for China's leadership are best demonstrated by the gap which developed in this era between the formal constitutional guarantee of rights and the reality of their informal implementation. The legal framework for the condition of human rights in the modernization decade was the 1982 Constitution, which, although more liberal in some respects, did not reverse the normal socialist hierarchy in its formal reality: rather, unlike the earlier constitutions, it proved incapable either of prevailing over or of accommodating the informal developments in the society at large.

In terms of civil and political rights, the 1982 Constitution was not a liberal document.[14] It allowed for the expansion of some civil and political rights. The 1954 guarantees of equality before the law were restored and the right to vote and stand for office were to be enjoyed without reference to class background. The 1979 congressional organic and election laws were reflected in new provisions which required the direct election of deputies to local people's congresses at county, city, district, and township levels. Popular supervision and political accountability were stressed; the rights of national minorities were restored and enlarged. On the other hand, the right to strike and the 'four freedoms', features of the 1975 and 1978 Constitutions, were dropped from the 1982 Constitution: citizens were still able to be deprived of their political rights by law and the state's power to limit rights by law was continued. The powers of the people's congresses were not altered and a new role for the Standing Committee was introduced, to 'decide on the enforcement of martial law'. Most importantly, the essential ideas underlying the Four Basic Principles — that no exercise of democracy could contradict the socialist road, the people's democratic dictatorship, CCP leadership and Marxism-Leninism-Mao Zedong Thought — were included in the Preamble to the Constitution.

In contrast to the restrictive nature of the 1982 constitution, civil rights in China, relative to the past, showed an enormous expansion at the informal level, in avenues which are generally familiar. Chinese citizens began to infuse life and meaning into the nominally

---

[14] For an excellent analysis of the 1982 Constitution, see Edwards, Henkin, and Nathan, *Human Rights* (see n. 3), 115–20. See also A. Kent, 'Waiting for Rights: China's Human Rights and China's Constitutions 1949–1989', *Human Rights Quarterly* (May 1991).

guaranteed civil rights of freedom of thought, speech, association, assembly, and publication. A bourgeoning of publications in all disciplines, a network of associations and of semi-official consulting and research organizations providing advice to government, brought relatively open policy debate and a new development in China's social and political life. Freedoms not listed in the Constitution, such as freedom of movement and the economic freedom to choose employment, were also increasingly exercised. This gradual development was a function not only of the production imperative but of the uncertainties resulting from the loss of old structures of socioeconomic security.[15] The new commitment to the rule of law and the promulgation of numerous laws added to the expectations of, and calls for, the increased realization of the nominal civil and political rights in the constitutions. In some areas, particularly the civil rights of immunity such as the right to life, freedom from torture, and freedom from arbitrary arrest, the new legal system failed to uphold and enforce the prevailing informal condition of civil rights.[16] Thus, between 1983 and 1988 Amnesty International documented 1,500 executions of criminals and also unofficial estimates of 30,000 executions; in Amnesty's opinion, the appeal procedure and the trial itself continued to be largely formalities, death sentences were excessive and often inappropriate, and arbitrary arrest and torture continued to be widespread.[17] Nevertheless after the imprisonment of the main leaders of the 1978–81 democracy movement, dissidence was treated more as a contradiction among the people than, as in the past, a contradiction between the people and the enemy; political dissenters lost their party membership and other privileges, but were otherwise officially tolerated, albeit unwillingly.

Compared with the expansion of civil rights, the relatively ambitious political reform launched in this modernization decade proved more problematic, precisely because of the need to carry out lasting structural reform to achieve it. Thus, the more lively appearance of NPC sessions and especially of the NPC Standing Committee has been interpreted as 'a manifestation of inner Party struggle' rather than an indication of the strengthening of popular

---

[15] For the production imperative, see Goodman, 'Communism' (see n. 11), 1–8.

[16] See particularly Seymour, 'Human Rights and the Law' (see n. 8), 286–7.

[17] Amnesty International, *People's Republic of China: The Death Penalty in China* (Jan. 1989), 1–7.

participation.[18] The separation of party and state, which required a complex restructuring process, was resisted by entrenched party interests, especially in local CCP committees; the streamlining of the bureaucracy, reflected in the newly pared-down State Council, proved a long-term problem because of the inbuilt momentum for bureaucratic proliferation.[19] And the decentralization of political control led to the ambiguous result that 'the simple relations between state and society based on unconditional obedience to the central authorities [were] superseded in most cases by an unregulated bargaining process'. Finally, although attempts were made to regularize procedures among the top leadership in running state affairs, the events of May–June 1989 revealed how limited the results were.

Notwithstanding the inadequacies in civil and political reform, the popular exercise of civil and political rights in this decade far outstripped both earlier precedent and the provisions of the 1982 Constitution, which represented an attempt to enforce orthodox thought and social stability.[20] Not only was this informal liberalization of civil and political life evident on the domestic scene: it was also reflected in the formal international arena, where Chinese activity in the United Nations in respect of human rights, its membership of the Human Rights Commission, ratification of seven international conventions relating to human rights, and its own statements on human rights, brought China closer than ever before to an acceptance of the need for individual civil and political rights.[21]

Like the constitutional provisions of civil and political rights, the social and economic rights guaranteed China's citizens under

18 John Burns, 'China's Governance: Political Reform in a Turbulent Environment', *China Quarterly*, 119 (Sept. 1989), 510–11. See also Michael D. Swaine, 'China Faces the 1990s: A system in Crisis', *Problems of Communism*, 39 (May–June 1990), 20–7.

19 Burns, 'China's Governance' (see n. 18), 511–16.

20 You Ji, 'Politics of China's Post-Mao Reforms: From the CCP's 13th Party Congress to the Dawn of Beijing Students' Demonstrations', MA thesis, Australian National University, Canberra, Aug. 1989, p. 208.

21 See Kent, *Human Rights* (see n. 7), pp. 57–63; Hungdah Chiu, 'Chinese Attitudes toward International Law of Human Rights in the Post-Mao Era', in Falkenheim and Kim, eds., *Chinese Politics* (see n. 8), pp. 237–70; and *Massacre in Beijing: The Events of 3–4 June and Their Aftermath*, Report by the International League for Human Rights and the Ad Hoc Study Group on Human Rights in China (New York, 1989), 46–7.

the 1982 Constitution also diverged from their exercise in reality. While some provisions were restrictive, others guaranteed rights that no longer existed in reality or contained programmatic rights that were not currently realizable. This distance from reality was due chiefly to the rapid structural changes in the economy which, for reasons of economic optimism, absence of funds, and lack of decisive planning, did not lead to changes in social security legislation and regulations or to the transformation of the social welfare and social-security infrastructure. Thus, the right to work, although still formally guaranteed in the 1982 Constitution, was progressively undermined by the market mechanism: although the rice bowl was not smashed, its surface became marked with hair-line cracks in the shape of redundancy, unemployment, large wage differentials, and inflation. Moreover, the introduction of contract labour into state enterprises implied official sanction for the informal right to choose one's employment (and for the converse right to be unemployed), as well as for the civil right of movement (to find a job), neither of which, as has already been noted, were rights guaranteed under China's constitutions. Yet the economic right to strike, a right guaranteed workers in most advanced economies, was eliminated from the 1982 Constitution. Despite this anachronistic restriction, the right to strike was exercised as never before during the 1980s.[22]

The most glaring inconsistency between the 1982 Constitution and informal reality was the programmatic character of Article 45, which substantially overstated the possible scope of welfare and social security services. It stated that 'citizens of the People's Republic of China have the right to material assistance from the state and society when they are old, ill or disabled'. Moreover, it undertook to 'develop the social insurance, social relief and medical and health services that are required to enable citizens to enjoy this right'. The significance of this article is that, first, by replacing the term 'working people' used in the three preceding constitutions with

---

[22] e.g. a series of bus strikes occurred in Beijing during 1986 which resulted in wage rises. In the first half of 1988, 49 strikes were reported officially, and in 1989 there were wide-spread reports of job action in support of pro-democracy demonstrations. See 'China', *Country Reports on Human Rights Practices for 1989*, Reports submitted to the Committee on Foreign Relation, US Senate, and Committee on Foreign Affairs, US House of Representatives (Feb. 1990), 822. See also Benedict Stavis, 'Contradictions in Communist Reform: China before 4 June 1989', *Political Science Quarterly*, 105/1 (1990), 45.

the term 'citizens', it signalled the end of the close nexus between social rights and the workplace that had been an integral feature of socialist rights, and implied acceptance of the existence of unemployment. Secondly, the formal universalization of the provision of social rights served to disguise a number of negative developments in the area of social security and social welfare which during the 1980s led to a severe diminution of social and economic rights and which widened the gap between the constitutional guarantees and the reality of those provisions. These were: (1) the commodification of social welfare;[23] (2) the increase of the rural–urban gap in the provision of social services;[24] (3) the devolution of the state's responsibility for social welfare and social security onto enterprises, the individual, and private insurance schemes; and (4) the lack of a comprehensive unemployment insurance system. Finally, the formal universalization of rights was not accompanied by the development of new structures to institutionalize them, despite the fact that the state's undertaking to 'expand' social services indicated the acceptance of some legal obligation to implement progressively the new guarantees. This failure was recognized in April 1988 by the Minister of Civil Affairs, Cui Naifu, when he pointed out that 'China's social security system is more and more out of alignment with the development of the socialist commodity economy'. Particular aspects of his criticism included the lack of universality of the social security system (inaccessible to peasants and workers in small collectives), its organization according to work units rather than on a national basis and the failure to spread equal responsibility for contributions between the state, enterprises, and the individual.[25]

The resultant inadequacies and inequities of China's social welfare and social security system in this decade have been convincingly documented by others.[26] But whereas the 1982 Constitution may be seen as having overstated the provision of social welfare and retirement benefits to all 'citizens' of China, its most crucial failure was its neglect of any universal provision for unemployment relief,

[23] This concept was first used by Davis, 'Chinese Social Welfare' (see n. 11), 596.
[24] Ibid.; and Jeffrey R. Taylor, 'Rural Employment Trends and the Legacy of Surplus Labour, 1978–86', *China Quarterly*, 116 (Dec. 1988), 753–8.
[25] Cui Naifu, 'Seeking a Social Security System with Chinese Characteristics', *ZGNJ* (1 Apr. 1988), 631–2.
[26] See Ch. 5 by A. Chan. See also Davis, 'Chinese Social Welfare' (see n. 11).

as required under Article 25 of the UDHR.[27] Statistics showing unemployment to be the most potentially explosive issue in China abounded, with the *Economic Daily*, for instance, estimating in May 1989 that China would have 240 to 260 million surplus workers by the year 2000, most of them in the rural areas.[28] The reason for the failure of the state to remedy, as opposed to its readiness to recognize, this problem was not only its inability to afford such a crippling burden: the continued guarantee in the 1982 Constitution of the 'right to work' to all citizens, despite its inappropriateness to the new socialist commodity economy, made it difficult to accept officially the existence of unemployment due to a shortage of jobs. Although much political energy was spent trying to find a solution to the problem of unemployment, the Constitution still only formally recognized the social rights of those who had lost the physical ability to work.[29]

Faced with this problem of real and incipient unemployment, the government had before mid-1989 adopted a variety of solutions. Since October 1986, an unemployment insurance system had covered only workers and staff in state-owned enterprises and contract workers in government organizations. Those who had worked over five years qualified for 60–75 per cent of their monthly standard salary for twelve months and 50 per cent for another year, those who had worked less time qualified for 60–75 per cent for a year only. Efforts were made to train redundant state workers and relocate them. Redundant workers in non-state enterprises, however, had little or no unemployment insurance coverage or superannuation.[30]

As to those outside the state system, a number of solutions had been devised. The *laissez-faire* solution of finding or creating one's own employment, either through the forty-four labour markets set up throughout China after 1985 or through private initiative, was

[27] Art. 25(1) of the UDHR states: 'Everyone has the right to a standard of living adequate for the health and wellbeing of himself and of his family, including food, clothing, housing and medical care and necessary social services, and the right to security in the event of unemployment, sickness, disability, widowhood, old age or other lack of livelihood in circumstances beyond his control'. See Robertson, *Human Rights* (see n. 1), 210–11.

[28] *CD* (8 May 1989). Also Taylor, 'Rural Employment' (see n. 24), 737.

[29] For the six categories of 'shi laodong nengli di zhigong' who have the right to social security, see He Jinming, ed., *Jingji Gongzuo Shouce* (Shanxi, 1983), 565.

[30] *BR* (19–25 Dec. 1988), 20.

obviously seen as the first priority. For surplus rural labour, migration to the cities was discouraged: the rural unemployed were in preference channelled into small town construction work and enterprises, industry, and service industry work in villages and towns, although millions still found their way into the big cities.[31] Failing employment, the neo-traditional solution was invoked. In 1986, the Minister for Civil Affairs, Cui Naifu, pointed out that 'because the concept of the family remains strong among the Chinese people, there is no need to shift insurance functions from the family to society. Responsibility for supporting old people should be shouldered by the family'.[32] This statement was reinforced by the new obligation outlined in the 1982 Constitution that 'parents have the duty to rear and educate their minor children, and children who have come of age have the duty to support and assist their parents'.[33] This solution simply compounded poverty.

The long-term and most important solution, however, was seen as structural change which would reflect the transfer from the command economy to a 'reformed' command economy with market characteristics. Thus the Seventh Five-Year Plan called for research and experimentation in, and gradual implementation of, a social security system for individual urban and rural workers, although any national insurance system could not exceed existing financial capacities. It also called for the devolution of total state responsibility for social security to a system combining the resources of the state, enterprises, and the individual.[34] Within the economic research institutions, proposals were made to 'change the ineffective insurance system, syphon off part of consumption and establish social security funds'. More importantly, it was suggested that employment be separated from welfare and job security, thus severing the traditional nexus between employment and the social security system. The proposed replacement of employment security with unemployment compensation was seen as 'a breakthrough point in reform of the whole employment system'.[35] But, as of

[31] Zhao Dongwan, Minister of Labour and Personnel, 8 Sept. 1987, *ZGNJ* (1988), 614.

[32] *Liaowang* in *CD* (13 May 1986).

[33] Art. 49, 1982 Constitution, p. 18.

[34] 'Proposal of the CCP Central Committee on the Implementation of the Seventh Five Year Plan', *ZGNJ* (1986), 91.

[35] Huang Xiaojing and Yang Xiao, 'From Iron Ricebowls to Labor Markets: Reforming the Social Security System', in Bruce Reynolds, ed., *Reform in China:*

mid-1989, this breakthrough had not occurred.

Thus, in the decade prior to 1989, China was caught between two systems, rejecting the nexus between social security and guaranteed employment established under the command economy, but not yet able to erect the safety net provided in most *laissez-faire* economies to protect citizens from the 'fall-out' factor in the market economy. Added to these structural problems in 1989 were the familiar short-term economic and social problems. As of 1987, the 10–11 per cent GNP increase in real terms over the previous three years had far outweighed a 7.3 per cent inflation rate. In 1988, however, the high inflation rate, somewhere in the range between the official estimate of 18.5 per cent and an unofficial estimate of 30 per cent, had the effect of transforming the 22.2 per cent increase in nominal per capita income over the year to an actual rate of increase in real income of 1.2 per cent. More significantly, it led inevitably to a redistribution of income, so that a sampling survey in thirteen cities revealed that the income of 34.9 per cent of all families had actually decreased purely because of price rises.[36]

In this way, the fall in real living standards served to expose the defects of a dual system in which the old machinery of socio-economic security had yet to be replaced by coherent mechanisms reflecting the new socio-economic circumstances. It also served to highlight the yawning gap which existed between the social and economic rights guaranteed under the 1982 Constitution and those rights which could be exercised in reality.

Thus it may be concluded that the formal rights guaranteed China's citizens under the 1982 Constitution were substantially out of gear with the civil, political, social, and economic rights actually accorded them in the modernization decade: in terms of civil and political rights, formal provisions lagged behind realities, while in the case of social and economic rights, the formal provisions both outstripped reality and lagged behind it. Not only did the

---

Challenges and Choices, Summary and Analysis of the CESRRI Survey prepared by the Staff of the Chinese Economic System Reform Research Institute (New York, 1987), 149, 154, 159.

36 State Statistical Bureau, 'China's Economy in 1988', *SWB* FE/0401/C1/5–6 (6 Mar. 1989). Cf. earlier improved standard of living reported in State Statistical Bureau, 'Changes in the Life-Style of Urban Residents', *BR* (14–20 Nov. 1988), 26–7; *ZGNJ* (1988), 623; and in 'Seventh Five-Year Plan', *ZGNJ* (1986), 80. For more complete treatment, see Stavis, 'Contradictions' (see n. 22), 40–52.

1982 Constitution fail to synchronize with reality, but the normal Marxist priority of social and economic rights, which it formally still partially upheld, was in fact overturned by events. China, by mid-1989, was a country not only in need of a new constitution formally expanding, and giving legislative support to, the civil and political rights already being exercised in society. It also required a restructuring of the institutional base of the social system to accord with the new socio-economic constitutional guarantees, as well as a specific constitutional guarantee of unemployment relief which reflected the new socio-economic circumstances.

Human Rights, May–June 1989

China's ongoing search for solutions to these challenges was brought to a temporary halt by the events of May to June 1989. The popular demonstrations throughout China from April to May can be seen as the ultimate point of collision between the old structures of Maoist rights and the new rights of the modernization decade: the democracy movement was the outcome of a revolution of rising expectations in the arena of civil and political rights and of a combination of rising expectations and relative deprivation in the area of social and economic rights. The official response to this spontaneous eruption of popular feeling, in the form of the declaration of martial law in Beijing on 20 May and the repression of the peaceful demonstrations throughout China in early June, abruptly reversed the gradual evolution of civil and political rights. With the imposition of martial law, not only were the civil freedoms of speech, press, association, and assembly denied the people of Beijing, but those basic civil rights of immunity embodied in successive Chinese constitutions (and in the Universal Declaration of Rights) were in theory negated. These included the right to life, the freedom from arbitrary arrest and detention, from torture and mistreatment, and equality before the law. With the physical suppression of the democracy movement in June, the theoretical denial of rights was starkly realized.[37] The abuse of civil rights

---

[37] See Asia Watch Committee, *Punishment Season: Human Rights in China after Martial Law* (New York, 7 Feb. 1990); and Economic and Social Council, United Nations, 'Question of the Violation of Human Rights and Fundamental Freedoms in Any Part of the World, with Particular Reference to Colonial and other Dependent

which the suppression entailed was matched by continued deprivation in the area of social and economic rights. China was brought
to a nadir in its overall condition of human rights.

Human Rights after June 1989

As a result of the massive resort to armed force against civilians in
Beijing on 3–4 June and the following week, the problem of the
1980s in meeting the challenge of human rights became, for China's
leadership, a much more serious issue of the management of a crisis
in human rights, an issue which promises to fester well into the
1990s. Against a background of perceived leadership corruption, a
vacuum in national ideology, and the failure of Deng's reforms to
guarantee the economic well-being of the majority of Chinese
citizens, that act of violence and the subsequent state of martial law
in Beijing precipitated a crisis of legitimacy for the current power-
holders which precluded the long-term restoration of past political
practices. Having imposed a simple and drastic military solution
to the problem of the maintenance of political power, China's
leaders were, and are still, caught in a web of dilemmas. In terms
of legitimating principles they hesitate between the compulsions of
the individualistic philosophy underlying the market element within
the economy and their need to seek refuge in old collective
orthodoxies. And in political and economic terms they are caught
between the citizens' egalitarian and welfare expectations derived
from the Maoist era and the pluralism and individualism borne of
the officially endorsed pursuit over the decade of individual political
and economic self-interest.

The political, economic, and social policies that have been
adopted since 4 June bear witness to the eclectic and often contradictory nature of their choice, synthesizing as they do important
elements of Maoist policy with lesser strands of the reform platform.
This uneasy and dynamic synthesis has been maintained by the

Countries and Territories: Situation in China, Note by the Secretary-General',
46th session, Agenda Item 12, E/CN/4/1990/52 (30 Jan. 1990). For more general
report, see 'China', *Country Reports on Human Rights Practices for 1989*. For impact
of June repression on rule of law, Jerome Cohen, 'Tiananmen and the Rule of Law',
in George Hicks, ed., *The Broken Mirror: China after Tiananmen* (London, 1990),
323–44.

resort to instruments of coercion and to emotionally charged propaganda, manipulating nationalism, even chauvinism, historical
fears of foreign influence, of national destabilization and disintegra-
tion, and the more recent concerns about a return to the chaos
of the Cultural Revolution.[38]

In human rights terms, the post-June period divides roughly
into two main, if overlapping, phases. The first phase reflecting
the general retreat back to more orthodox Marxist-Leninist policies,
brought a re-emphasis on social and economic rights, with little
mention of political issues and a stringent clampdown on civil
rights. The second phase, a phenomenon of the 1990s, is characterized by a continued close grip on the exercise of civil rights, but
with official expressions of support for the renewed reform of
the political system, in parallel with ongoing economic reform.

In the first phase, extending roughly from June to December
1989, choice of policy was partly determined by the ideology and
general constituency of the new Jiang Zemin–Li Peng leadership,
which could be said to draw its support in general from a coalition
of central planning institutions, from heavy industry and its related
bureaucracies, financial interest groups, the propaganda apparatus,
parts of the military, and an unknown proportion of the peasantry.[39] Choice of policy was also determined by the need to win
over erstwhile or potential supporters like disaffected workers
and ordinary citizens demonstrating against inflation and the loss
of social rights, whose presence in the student demonstrations
served to turn an élite movement into a mass one. Finally, the
leadership sought to woo the 'swinging voter', including undecided
elements of the urban population, those parts of the military whose
loyalties had not been determined, and a mass of peasants who,
although politically inert during the April–May demonstrations,
appeared to have substantial economic grievances.[40]

The new policies were thus designed to outflank the intellectuals
and students. They combined ideological and political propaganda

---

[38] Clemens Ostergaard, 'Citizen Groups and a Nascent Civil Society in China:
Towards an Understanding of the 1989 Student Demonstrations', *China Information*, 4/2 (Autumn 1989), 39–41.

[39] Ibid., 40. See analysis in You Ji, 'Politics' (see n. 20), 35.

[40] See Jorgen Delman, 'Current Peasant Discontent in China: Background and
Political Implications', *China Information*, 4/2 (Autumn 1989), 42–64; and Jonathan
Unger and Jean Xiong, 'Life in the Chinese Hinterlands under the Economic Reforms',
Bulletin of Concerned Asian Scholars, 22/3 (July 1990).

with recentralizing economic policies which stressed planning, the strengthening of state-owned enterprises, and constraints on small, collective, and private enterprises. Pledges to control inflation and corruption and to give priority to agriculture were aimed, among other things, at strengthening the basis of the regime's support. The expansion of a national labour insurance system was sought to meet the needs of all employees working under different systems of ownership; and the Ministry of Public Health announced new plans for a rural primary health care programme to help meet the 'national target of providing every Chinese with health care by the year 2000'.[41] The practice of stimulating production through consumption was discarded in favour of a policy justifying rule on the basis of public ownership and the provision of material and cultural needs. There was a renewed emphasis on distribution according to work and on the prevention of an excessive wealth gap and 'unjust' distribution, although 'egalitarianism in distribution' was attacked and the notion of 'some people becoming prosperous' maintained.[42] On the other hand, curbs on further civilian political activity were devised in the form of firm controls over education and media institutions, a constricting new law on demonstrations, and the deepening and extension of the purge, which ensured universal (if temporary) compliance from the urban population.

By December 1989, however, a number of developments, in parallel with the jockeying for power at the élite level, had created pressures for a readjustment to this renewed and almost exclusive emphasis on social and economic rights. First, the efforts to base claims to mass legitimacy on achievement in areas of social and economic welfare were stymied by the parlous state of the Chinese economy and the need to maintain an anti-inflationary austerity programme: ambitious social programmes became difficult to implement and unemployment increased.[43] Secondly, international repudiation of the June massacre and the ensuing economic sanctions severely limited China's room for economic reform. The speed

[41] *CD* (5 and 11 Aug. 1989).

[42] Jiang Zemin, 'Speech at the Meeting in Celebration of the 40th Anniversary of the Founding of the People's Republic of China', 29 Sept. 1989, *BR* (9–15 Oct. 1989), 18.

[43] e.g. 'Beating around the Gooseberry Bush', excerpts from *Xuexi yu Yanjiu Yuekan (March 1990)*, *Inside China Mainland* (June 1990), 10; and Chen Te-sheng, 'Mainland China's Economic Reform Policies in the Wake of the Fifth Plenum of the CCP's Thirteenth Central Committee', *Issues and Studies*, 26/3 (Mar. 1990), 25–42.

and scope of political reform in Eastern Europe, moreover, although initially discounted by the Chinese leadership, had an inevitable impact on Chinese domestic opinion and on the regime's sense of its room for political manœuvre. The combination of these internal economic limitations and external political pressures was decisive in producing a discernible if modified trend back to a liberalization in China's attitude to political reform.

Thus, on 12 December 1989, Premier Li Peng called for the reform of China's political structure to be carried out simultaneously with reforms of the economy: at the same time he stressed that political restructuring should aid the country's stability and prosperity and not cause social disturbances. In his 'Report on the Work of the Government' submitted to the Third Session of the Seventh National People's Congress in Beijing, Li said that political restructuring involved continued efforts to perfect the system of peoples' congresses, to pursue multi-party co-operation, and establish and improve the procedures and systems for democratic decision-making and supervision. On 11 June 1990, Jiang Zemin also stated that 'political structural reform should keep pace and co-ordinate with economic structural reform and the two should promote each other'. The content of this political reform, however, appears to resemble closely the old idea of mass line and to depend on the enhanced contact between CCP members, the leadership élite, and the people, with communication proceeding downwards rather than in the opposite direction. Moreover, its close resemblance to the corporatist system of political organization is reflected in the provisions of new laws on mass rallies and demonstrations, and on the organization of urban and rural residents' committees as well as of the regulation on the registration of social organizations issued at the end of October 1989, and the 21 December 1989 circular calling for CCP leadership over mass organizations as 'bridges and ties for the Party to link with the people as well as important pillars of state power'. Elements of corporatism are also evident in the much acclaimed document, 'Guidelines of the Central Committee of the Communist Party of China for Upholding and Improving the System of Multi-Party Co-operation and Political Consultation under the Leadership of the Communist Party of China'.[44]

[44] For Li Peng call, *CD* (14 Dec. 1989); Government Work Report, *SWB* FE/0720/C2/1–19 (23 Mac. 1990); Jiang Zemin, 'Jiang Zemin Replies to American

In the final analysis, the content of these renewed calls for political reform will depend on whether the current controls on the exercise of citizens' civil rights are loosened. That is, the question remains whether the current purpose of political reform, focused as it is on 'improving socialist democracy and the socialist legal system' is, in fact, as Jiang Zemin now claims, 'to ensure effectively that the people enjoy status and rights as citizens of the country'. Since the lifting of martial law in Beijing on 11 January 1990, 881 political prisoners have been released from custody. Such actions, however, appear to have been more closely related to achieving the removal of international economic sanctions than to any liberalization of domestic policy. Currently, pressure is still being maintained on the media, with the censorship of publications and the press continuing into 1990. The publication of the *Code of Collegiate Student Behaviour* and of the *Regulations on the Management of College Students* has served to reinforce control over educational institutions. There have also been calls for the expansion of the judiciary, in view of the doubling of China's crime rate in 1989; and another wave of execution of criminals has begun.[45]

In social policies, continued attention is being paid to the problem of unemployment, with the *Economic Daily* reporting that the urban 'job waiting' rate might exceed 4 per cent in 1990, rising further in 1991. In 1990 urban job hunters were expected to exceed ten million, of whom 3.78 million were laid off in 1989. The country was reported to have more than 300 million rural labourers, with only 180 million needed for farming, and over 120 million surplus farmers having to look for their own jobs. There have been calls from the Ministry of Personnel and the Minister for Labour for a national labour insurance system, and especially an unemployment pension system, along with reports that in 1989 three million rural enterprises had been closed and 20,000 projects postponed or cancelled. Suggestions as to the means of resolving the unemployment crisis have included the renewed expansion of village and township enterprises, lower wages and increased employment for

Students', *B R* (25 June–1 July 1990), 8–12; regulation on social organizations, *C D* (1 Nov. 1989); circular, *C D* (2 Feb. 1990); democratic parties, *C D* (9 Mar. 1990). For recent political reforms, Swaine, 'China' (see n. 18), 27–9.

45 For Jiang, *B R* (25 June 1990), 10; political prisoners, *B R* (18–29 June 1990), 6–7; Code of Collegiate Student Behaviour, *C D* (25 Nov. 1990); Regulations, *C D* (10 Feb. 1990); crime rate (ibid.).

workers, and a dual and 'flexible' employment system differentiating between different kinds of enterprises, with large enterprises operating on the basis of production efficiency and small enterprises adopting labour-intensive methods. Draft labour laws are planned for 1990 and, in view of the lower inflation rate (currently reported around 6 per cent) and the easing of credit, reinvestment in rural industries has begun, with an anticipated expansion rate of 15 per cent in 1990; at the same time, measures have been undertaken to stop the mass exodus of surplus rural labour, with 1.3 million rural workers being sent back from cities in 1989 and plans for the return of another 900,000 in 1990. One of the main means of facilitating the absorption of surplus labour into the economy has been the setting up of a labour service network, with 3,000 sub-agencies throughout the country: their functions, however, have included not only the location of jobs for unemployed urban workers but the return of unemployed rural workers to the countryside.[46]

In parallel with continued work on the expansion of a primary health care system in China, the government is setting up a timetable for providing basic education for the whole population and for eliminating illiteracy among young people and adults. Despite the economic austerity policy, the government has granted a 4.38 billion yuan increase for 1990 in education, an area which is now being accorded top priority. It is also increasing state wages and subsidies and attempting to resolve the housing problem. Finally, it is putting renewed emphasis on its programme of poverty relief, claiming to have fed and clothed 70 per cent of its poor farmers since the commencement of the five-year plan to relieve rural poverty (defined as 200 yuan or less annual income) by 1990. For 1990, the government has pledged a further four billion yuan (US $0.85 billion) in grants, low interest loans, and materials to poor regions.[47]

---

[46] For urban unemployment rate, *CD* (28 Feb. and 19 Apr. 1990); rural labourers, *Workers' Daily* in *CD* (23 Jan. 1990); calls for unemployment pension system, *CD* (29 Nov. 1989, 31 Jan. 1990); rural enterprises, *CD* (6 Dec. 1989); solutions to unemployment, *CD* (6 Dec. 1989, 23 Jan. 1990); labour laws, *CD* (28 Nov. 1990); rural workers' return, *CD* (20 Mar. 1990); labour service network, *CD* (20 Mar. 1990).

[47] On primary health care, *CD* (6 Feb. 1990); illiteracy, *CD* (9 Dec. 1989); education, *Xinhua* (21 Mar. 1990) *SWB* FE/0719/C2/1 (22 Mar. 1990); on other measures, Swaine, 'China' (see n. 18) 32, and *CD* (21 Feb. 1990); and on poverty relief, *CD* (21 Feb. 6 Mar., 16 Mar. 1990).

It is likely that this trend of giving cautious priority to social and economic rights and at the same time allowing a measure of informal political change will continue in the 1990s. It is now clear that a simple reversion to the Marxist hierarchy of rights favouring social and economic rights exclusively, which was the initial policy reflex of the post-June government, can no longer be relied upon as a solution to China's problems or those of her leaders. First it appears that, despite the recent easing of inflation and credit, the current state of China's economy will not allow a sufficient expansion of social and economic rights to cover the needs of workers and the pool of unemployed which has enlarged as a result of the austerity measures. Rural poverty, once geographically contained and disguised as underemployment, is spilling over into the cities, despite the government efforts to stem the flow, in the form·of millions of surplus labourers seeking work. This significant alteration to the social configuration in urban areas, this merger between urban and rural 'have-nots' has had, and will have, important implications for China's political system. Secondly, as suggested, the articulate and educated sector of China's population, the most easily mobilized for political action, has already experienced considerable civil and political freedoms, freedoms which, if currently forbidden, are still being underwritten by the combined command-market structure of China's economic system. That same sector of urban dwellers, comprising both manual and mental labourers, has since the 4 June repression become thoroughly disillusioned with its political leadership; and its members are aware that elsewhere in Asia, and in the socialist bloc, people have been taking to the streets with the cry of human rights and political change.

The expansion of social and economic rights in China in the 1990s is thus likely to become a more gradual one, paralleling a limited increase in political rights. Until a radical change in China's leadership occurs, however, the exercise of those political rights will continue to be modified in the sense that expressions of political pluralism will be incorporated into, and to a large extent neutralized by, existing political institutions.[48] Moreover, any expansion of political rights will not be accompanied by an amelioration of civil

---

[48] For an excellent discussion of this problem, see David Strand, 'Protest in Beijing: Civil Society and Public Sphere in China', *Problems of Communism*, 39 (May–June 1990), 1–19.

rights. And here lies the essential dilemma for China's leadership in the 1990s as it grapples with its human rights crisis. On the one hand, it will be unable to shoulder the crippling burden of expanding social and economic rights to a degree sufficient to meet popular needs and expectations. On the other, any attempt to give real content to the pledges of political reform will continue to be thwarted by its simultaneous concern to shackle, through the medium of legislation and the legal system, the freedoms of thought, speech, press, association, and assembly of China's citizens. This inherently unstable condition of rights threatens to further undermine the Chinese political system in the years to come.

4. The Chinese Communist Party and the Beijing Massacre
The Crisis in Authority

LAWRENCE R. SULLIVAN

The military crackdown on pro-democracy demonstrators in Beijing and other cities on 4 June 1989 represented a major crisis for the Chinese Communist Party. In one night of indiscriminate killing by People's Liberation Army troops, the CCP squandered much of its political legitimacy — which had already been severely weakened by the Cultural Revolution (1966–76) and, more recently, by the enormous corruption of party leaders at all levels of the apparatus to which the pro-democracy movement was a reaction. In addition to the popular outrage against party leaders, particularly Li Peng, the unleashing of military forces against peaceful protests indicated that the CCP was incapable of resolving fundamental conflicts through political means.

The Beijing massacre resulted from a profound *institutional* failure of the CCP, that is, an inability by China's leaders to establish political structures accommodating social–economic changes over the last decade of reform. Deng Xiaoping's policies liberalized the economic system and opened China up to substantial outside influence, especially from the West, thereby creating an increasingly pluralized society with competing interests. Yet, politically, Deng and other conservative leaders refused to alter a CCP organization that had been formed forty years earlier during the party's struggle for power. The social explosion in Chinese cities reflected this fundamental 'contradiction' between rapid social change and a rigid political structure and outworn ideology. Since 4 June 1989, conservative leaders have attempted to reinforce this highly centralized structure, while dealing with the enormous political fall-out from the crackdown, particularly a more assertive army and a deteriorating social order. China under current CCP rule is a society increasingly ruled under the jackboot, led by a leadership committed to maintaining 'stability' with security forces, while seriously concerned with the loyalty of its own army.

The CCP and Beijing Spring

The mass movement in Beijing and at least a hundred other cities would not have occurred without serious divisions within the CCP. Under the leadership of General Secretary Hu Yaobang (whose death on 15 April 1989, sparked the demonstrations) and his successor, Zhao Ziyang, the party underwent important internal changes which strengthened the political influence of the 'pro-reform' or 'freedom' faction within the apparatus.[1] Significant increases in educated personnel from universities and high schools, along with a more youthful party membership, created a critical mass of party members supportive of Hu's and Zhao's model of a reformed party.[2] Yet, despite the establishment of pro-reform think-tanks under Zhao's tutelage, and innumerable conferences, books, and newspaper articles on 'structural reform', real institutional changes had not been realized. Deng Xiaoping himself had advocated radical reform measures in an August 1980 speech, but by the late 1980s the old leader refused to give his imprimatur to Zhao's rather moderate plans for political liberalization. Confronting an organization still controlled at the 'commanding heights' by conservatives, recently recruited intellectuals, well-educated workers, and even wealthy entrepreneurs and rich farmers, thus joined the spring 1989 protests against the CCP's and 'Stalinist system'.[3]

The failure of Zhao Ziyang to push through fundamental reforms

---

[1] Ming Ruan, 'Hu Yaobang and I', lecture, Fairbank Center for East Asian Research, Harvard University, 9 July 1990. Mr Ruan, a former high-level official at the CCP Central Party School, argues that since the 1940s the CCP has been divided into three basic factions: A 'pro-Soviet' group composed of individuals like Wang Ming and ex-security chief, Kang Sheng, whom Mao opposed in the 1940s; a 'militarist' faction which relied heavily on guns, now represented by Wang Zhen; and a 'freedom and democratic' faction which, though weak in the 1940s, has been strengthened over the past decade.

[2] Party members with senior high school education or above increased from 17.8% in 1984 to 28.5% by late 1987. Stanley Rosen, 'The Chinese Communist Party and Chinese Society: Popular Attitudes Toward Party Membership and the Party's Image', *Australian Journal of Chinese Affairs*, 24 (July 1990), 57–8. Rosen also notes that, as college-educated party members were recruited, applications from workers were often ignored (p. 60).

[3] Big-character poster, Beijing Normal University, 'Defects of the Stalinist Political System', 25 Apr. 1989, in Suzanne Ogden et al., eds., *China's Search for Democracy: Documents of the Student and Massed Movements, 1989* (Armonk, NY, 1990).

in the CCP comparable to Gorbachev's *perestroika* was evident from 1987 onwards. Zhao's report at the Thirteenth Party Congress that year (which was reportedly edited by Deng Xiaoping) contained few new initiatives on political reform, except for a vague promise to carry out the separation of party and government which Deng had advocated in 1980.[4] Zhao had also called for 'giving the people more freedom in their lives', for instance by proposing the abolition of the pervasive 'personal dossiers'. But Zhao and his supporters were generally unable to carry out reforms beyond organizations and enterprises under his direct control.[5] It is true that during Zhao's tenure as general secretary, the authority of party secretaries in educational institutions and factories diminished considerably. In one celebrated case in a Shaanxi factory, the newly elected factory manager successfully fired the party secretary for violating factory rules.[6]

Ideologically, party members were also exposed to radical ideas at seminars and lectures run by party schools. Beijing party members, for instance, were lectured on the American system of separation of powers — an anathema to Deng Xiaoping but which some rank-and-file party members evidently found very persuasive — and the democratic model of pressure groups strongly favoured by Zhao Ziyang.[7] However, by the end of the decade China had made little real political progress: conservative leader Wang Zhen declared any discussion of Deng's 'retirement' an 'act

[4] Zhao Ziyang, 'Report to the Thirteenth CCP National Congress', *BR* 30/45 (9–15 Nov. 1987), 37–43. Zhao's additional proposal at the congress, to dismantle the CCP's pervasive apparatus of 'small groups' and 'branches' established in virtually every state and mass organization, was apparently not acted on. As for Zhao's report, Deng reportedly cut out all references to any significant separation of powers, arguing that Zhao was trying to introduce the American system in China.

[5] State-run companies closely tied to Zhao had begun to dispense with dossiers, while Zhao also favoured increased democracy in labour unions as indicated by his appointment of the relatively liberal, ex-propaganda chief Zhu Houze as vice-chairman of the All-China Federation of Trade Unions. According to Liu Binyan, trade unions had increasingly demanded more participation in government over the last few years: *China's Crisis, China's Hope* (Cambridge, Mass., 1990), 28, and Wu Guoguang, 'The Issues of Participation in the Political Reform: Pressures and Limitations', paper presented to the Conference on 'China: Crisis of 1989 — Its Origins and Implications', SUNY Buffalo, 16–18 Feb. 1990.

[6] *Quanguo Haozinwen* (*The Best News Stories in China*, 1988). Many elections of factory managers apparently occurred in Chinese factories in 1988.

[7] Anonymous interview, research associate, Political System Reform Committee (*Zhengzhi tizhi gaige weiyuanhui*), Summer 1990.

of treason', while in March 1989 Li Peng ruled out further political reform in his address to an exceptionally compliant National People's Congress.[8] While Zhao had introduced the ideas of political reform and democracy to a more well-educated party membership, Deng Xiaoping, Li Peng, and other conservatives obstinately prevented their realization.

The Revolt of the Rank and File

The Beijing mass movement was not an anti-CCP uprising, at least before 3 June 1989. Until conservative leaders unleashed their military assault against unarmed citizens, the protests focused more on pressuring central leaders into acting on the reforms which had been discussed for a decade, rather than overthrowing the CCP. To be sure, demonstrators called for Li Peng to 'step down' and Deng Xiaoping to really 'retire'. (One banner, in fact, wrote out an entire retirement application form for Deng complete with name, date of birth, and occupation!) But opposition to CCP rule *per se* was not a major theme in the protests, at least not until the hunger strike (beginning on 16 May when 'Down with the Communist Party' was heard more frequently in opposition to the obstinate hard-line leadership.[9] Most protest speeches and banners, including those by CCP members, were, instead, directed at the leadership's failure to implement changes which even the party-controlled press had advocated for years.

First among the needed changes was the continuing corruption of party authorities. Economic liberalization and the opening up to the outside world had created enormous opportunities for corrupt party officials to line their pockets through networks of personal connections. In the absence of a law protecting a free press (which had, in fact, been discussed for several years and yet never finalized) and an independent legal system, powerful party patriarchs were beyond control. With the CCP reserving the right to punish its own officials through secret disciplinary

---

[8] Ming Ruan, 'Hu Yaobang' (see n. 1). After relatively open sessions in the mid-1980s, the NPC became substantially less critical of party policy by 1988-9.

[9] At this point, Beijing citizens began to compare CCP leaders unfavourably with countries like South Africa where protesting hunger strikers had elicited government response.

procedures that were easily subject to back-door influence, rank-and-file party members and the general population saw party bigwigs and their families (the so-called 'prince's faction') living outside the law.[10] Just as the economy began to stagnate in the late 1980s, the free-wheeling business activities of the sons of Chen Yun, Deng Xiaoping, and Zhao Ziyang, and the spending of public funds by government officials on expensive imported cars, increasingly aggravated ordinary people and rank-and-file party members who were suffering under unprecedented inflation in an ostensibly socialist state. Like 'errant priests' in the Catholic Church, party leaders were violating their own doctrine, especially the old Maoist dictum of selflessly 'serving the people' which more and more party members realized was virtually ignored by the top leadership. Despite the enormous problem of high-level corruption, however, the tightly controlled political system provided no outlet for popular grievances, as leaders who publicly railed against corruption often privately benefited from it.

Other issues raised during the demonstrations had been part of the reform agenda since the December 1978 Third Plenum, but still remained unresolved. Although Deng Xiaoping's personal authority did not equal Mao Zedong's, party members still complained that the CCP was a 'Stalinist system' in which one man's word dictated policy.[11] Party policies and even speeches by Deng Xiaoping had criticized the 'overconcentration of authority' and 'patriarchal despotism' in the CCP for years. But the reality remained that, despite paeans to 'collective leadership', Deng's word was final on crucial issues, a fact publicly revealed by Zhao Ziyang during his meeting with President Gorbachev in May 1989, and which subsequent CCP statements never denied.[12] Deng's 'cult of personality'

---

[10] Rosen, 'CCP' (see n. 2), 84, emphasizes that relatively few party cadres, especially high-level leaders, were expelled from the CCP for corruption. The Central Discipline Inspection Commission is empowered to investigate corruption in the CCP, yet its subordination to powerful party secretaries at the provincial level and below undermines its investigative authority, as does the commission's deep involvement in partisan political struggles.

[11] 'Defects' (see n. 3).

[12] Zhao Ziyang further confused the situation, however, by supporting arguments by his think-tank intellectuals in favour of 'new authoritarianism', the notion that a strong leader be given extraordinary authority to effect changes leading ultimately to democracy. Such arguments alienated many party liberals, such as ex-*People's Daily* editor Hu Jiwei, who believed it would merely reinforce China's despotic political traditions.

never reached the fanatic levels of the Mao cult in the 1960s. But for some party members the glorification of leaders prevented the shift of authority in the CCP from persons to institutions – another goal of the reforms which Deng had failed to effect.

Unlike modern countries in the West and Japan, China was saddled with a 'feudal' bureaucracy in which individuals, irrespective of their ability or age, superseded institutions. Thus Deng continued to wield nearly absolute authority, even though he no longer sat on the CCP's ruling bodies. As one frustrated party member explained: '[S]ince Deng was neither a member of the Central Committee nor a member of the Politburo, why should the Central Committee listen to his every word?' And while Deng remained a member of the Central Military Commission, that body was not subordinate to the party, as formally stipulated in the CCP's constitution, but to Deng personally.[13] Western history learnt by Chinese had stressed the importance of institutional developments, from the formation of an independent judiciary and legal codes, to the creation of corporate political structures in which individuals adhered to procedure and accepted subordination to the office. American leaders from George Washington to Ronald Reagan had clearly demonstrated the superiority of institutional authority over personal charisma in the West, which, many Chinese have argued, accounts for the West's capacity for sustained development and political stability. In China, everything depends on one man at the centre and 'little tyrants' throughout the hierarchy, which not only ensured a highly arbitrary political system, but, as clearly demonstrated in the Cultural Revolution, an unstable one as well. Until China made the transition to an impersonal, institutional authority, party intellectuals like Yan Jiaqi believed the country would continue to experience paroxysms of political chaos and violence.

A final concern of many newly recruited party members was the profound anti-intellectualism which still influenced party decision-making and intra-party life. Despite the increased recruitment of university graduates into the CCP and a substantially more liberal environment fostered by Hu Yaobang and then Zhao

---

[13] Alterations of the CCP constitution at the 1987 13th Party Congress eliminating the previous rule requiring the chairman of the CMC to sit on the Politburo so as to accommodate Deng's retirement from the latter body, was another indication that personal authority superseded institutional procedures.

Ziyang, especially in CCP propaganda organs, party conservatives were still able to mobilize periodic campaigns against liberal values. The 'anti-spiritual pollution' and 'anti-bourgeois liberalization' campaigns of the 1980s, though less intense than either the Cultural Revolution or the 1957 Anti-Rightist movement, demonstrated the power of illiberal ideology, especially among old conservatives such as Wang Zhen, Deng Liqun, and Hu Qiaomu. Hu Yaobang's reputation for having protected intellectuals from the likes of Wang, Deng, and Hu endeared him to party liberals, which is why his death during a period of conservative resurgence created such anxiety. Although China's film and TV industry engaged in highly provocative productions, namely the culturally iconoclastic television series *River Elegy* and the movie *Red Sorghum*, both these productions came under intense conservative criticism.[14]

The 26 April 1989 editorial of *People's Daily*, with Cultural Revolution rhetoric not seen for years, clearly indicated that Deng Xiaoping's purported commitment to 'emancipating the mind' was a sham. Indeed, the fact that the editorial was actually written by Xu Weicheng, an old protégé of the Gang of Four and current vice-mayor of the conservative Beijing party committee, indicated the extent to which 'leftist' ideology had been revived.[15] After ten years of reform, the ideological rigidity and cultural conservatism reminiscent of Maoism and even Stalinism were still powerful forces in the CCP.

CCP members' participation in the democratic movement took many forms. Although all party members were subject to enormous pressure to avoid the demonstrations, many took to the streets even before Zhao Ziyang's fate had been sealed by party hard-liners. Students and teachers at CCP 'party schools' were the most active participants, in Beijing and even relatively 'backward'

---

[14] Wang Zhen criticized both productions, claiming that *River Elegy* deprecated China's 'glorious' cultural traditions, while *Red Sorghum* accentuated China's backwardness and portrayed peasants resisting the Japanese invasion without CCP leadership.

[15] Cultural Revolution rhetoric not seen for years appeared in the editorial's title — 'We must Firmly Oppose Turmoil' — and throughout the text in such key terms as 'beating, smashing, looting, and burning' and 'a small group'. Xu Weicheng had also been a member of the notorious 'radical faction' during the Cultural Revolution and launched frenzied attacks in *Beijing Daily* against intellectuals during the 1986–7 'anti-bourgeois liberalization' campaign. See He Xin, 'An Analysis of the Current Student Protests and Forecasts concerning the Situation', *Australian Journal of Chinese Affairs*, 23 (Jan. 1990), 66 n. 51.

areas like Ningzia.[16] As institutions established to upgrade party members' education, these schools, including the Central Party School, had played a critical role in Hu Yaobang's and Zhao Ziyang's efforts to liberalize the CCP.[17] It is, indeed, ironic that party institutions established to train the membership and interpret the doctrine (such as Su Shaozhi's Institute of Marxism-Leninism-Mao Zedong Thought) proved to be centres of liberal thinking. As for newly recruited and veteran party members at universities, many decided publicly to withdraw from the party to protest at the 'narrow-mindedness and stupidity of its peasant-like characteristics'.[18] Convinced that the CCP could no longer 'represent the interests of the people', this group from People's University declared what party conservatives considered the ultimate heresy: the formation of an opposition party modelled on Poland's Solidarity.

Such radical actions were, to be sure, generally restricted to university campuses. Yet as pressure on Zhao Ziyang to resign increased in mid-May, party members around the country issued unprecedented protests, including 300 CCP members in Shanghai.[19] The centre's decision to declare martial law and contemplate military action against the demonstrations reportedly generated even greater internal opposition as the Central Committee was, according to one reliable source, inundated with telegrams and phone calls from outlying party organizations urging the leaders to exercise restraint. Ironically, such open defiance of the top leadership within the CCP — and, more ominously, in police organs and even the military — may have convinced Deng and his coterie of party elders to launch the assault with highly loyal units like the 27th Army, thereby frightening deviant members

---

[16] *Ningxia Ribao* (19 May 1989), 1, in FBIS China (9 June 1989), 58.

[17] The Central Party School organized several forums on political reform under the tutelage of Liao Gailong, and attended by provincial party officials, many of whom opposed proposals for separating party and government. Interviews conducted by this author at the Beijing city party committee party school in 1986 indicated substantial revisions of the curriculum to prepare students for political and economic reform.

[18] Big-character poster by some party member teachers at People's University, 'A Proposal for Quitting the Communist Party and Preparing to Establish a "Society to Promote the Chinese Democratic Movement" ', late April 1989, in Ogden *et al.*, eds., *China's Search* (see n. 3).

[19] Roy Forword, 'Letter from Shanghai', *Australian Journal of Chinese Affairs*, 24 (July 1990), 287.

back into line. The total loss of authority by party conservatives both within the CCP and Chinese urban society, left the leadership with to use force as the only alternative.

The CCP and the Beijing Massacre

The political and institutional weakness of the CCP was clearly evident throughout the crisis, especially in the days leading up to the military crackdown. Lacking the institutional capacity to resolve fundamental internal divisions exacerbated by the demonstrations, decisions were made by a small coterie of leaders without regard for formal decision-making procedures. Not once during the entire crisis did the Central Committee or even the full Politburo meet, as hard-line leaders feared internal opposition to their policies. Basic decisions were, instead, restricted to the five-man Standing Committee in which Deng Xiaoping swung the political balance against Zhao by insisting on having a vote.[20] Contrary to formal stipulations, Zhao's resignation was 'accepted' by the Standing Committee, rather than by a full Central Committee plenum where he undoubtedly could have won considerable political support.[21]

Critical decisions on troop movements were also made within the CMC 'without the signature of Zhao Ziyang' who remained first vice-chairman.[22] This reportedly led the commander of the 38th Army stationed in Baoding to challenge the validity of 'individual' decisions by Deng Xiaoping and Yang Shangkun (also members of the CMC) to move troops to Beijing. Unfortunately, with Deng's enormous personal authority and Yang Shangkun's network of relatives in key military positions, such 'legalistic'

[20] Deng's insistence on participating in the crucial 18 May Standing Committee meeting apparently swung the votes of Hu Qili and perhaps Qiao Shi against Zhao, thereby ensuring his defeat and the decision to declare martial law. Yi Mu and Mark V. Thompson, *Crisis at Tiananmen: Reform and Reality in Modern China* (San Francisco, 1989), 62, and anonymous interview, 1990.

[21] In this sense, the CCP is still more institutionally underdeveloped than was the CPSU in 1957 when Nikita Khrushchev prevented his purge at the hands of the ruling presidium by insisting on a full plenary session in which he won key support.

[22] Faculty members, party members, and graduate students of Universities in Beijing, 'Smash the Counterrevolutionary Coup Carried Out by Li Peng and Yang Shangkun' (21 May 1989), in Ogden *et al.*, eds., *China's Search* (see n. 3).

protests failed to sway critical forces. The 38th Army commander, Xu Qinxian, was court-martialled (along with several hundred officers and more than a thousand troops who also reportedly resisted orders), while the 27th Army commanded by Yang Shangkun's nephew moved into Beijing and crushed the demonstrations.

On 5 June 1989 a document issued in the name of the Central Committee claimed that pro-democracy demonstrators had planned to 'kill all 47 million Communist Party members'.[23] Thus began the campaign to convince CCP members that the decision to crush the 'counterrevolutionary rebellion' had been taken in their interest. In an obvious attempt to paint Zhao Ziyang as the real 'conspirator', a secret document — read to party members on 10 June to ensure against its duplication — claimed that Zhao Ziyang had planned to use 4,000 troops under his direct command to stage a coup. The very 'survival' of the party had been at stake, hard-line leaders such as Li Ximing (first secretary of the Beijing party committee) claimed, and thus severe measures were necessary. The democracy movement had been stopped in Beijing and other cities, but the political crisis was far from over.

The CCP after 4 June: The Politics of Barracks' Communism

Since the military crackdown, hard-line leaders in China have been obsessed with security and control. Despite claims that only a 'very, very small number of people' in the CCP and Chinese society had been directly involved in the 'riot', the major concern of top leaders has been to prevent further social explosions and even a possible military coup. The overthrow of the Romanian regime has had a particularly chilling effect on Chinese leaders, especially since the loyalty of some PLA units has been in question ever since the declaration of martial law on 19 May 1989. Equally serious is the regime's fear of renewed social disorder, particularly as its economic retrenchment policy (inaugurated in 1988) has created increasingly severe problems of unemployment among the growing 'floating population' of itinerant workers in China's cities.[24] In a country which relied on local 'units' to maintain social

---

[23] 'Party and State Letter to the People on the Tiananmen Crackdown', (5 June 1989), *China Report*, 25/4 (1989), 450–2.

[24] CIA Report, *The Chinese Economy in 1989 and 1990* (28 June 1990), 7.

order, the post-crackdown regime has increasingly turned to beefed-up police and security forces to prevent social challenges to its power.

Following the military crackdown, the most immediate reaction of hard-line leaders was to purge the CCP of pro-democracy and Zhao Ziyang supporters. While Zhao and high-level allies, such as his secretary Bao Tong, were placed under house arrest, intellectuals who had provided key ideological support to the pro-democracy movement, like Wen Yuankai, were purged. Provincial party secretaries, governors, and other personnel who had not 'resolutely opposed the turmoil' were also dismissed or demoted, while promotions were given to officials who had taken a particularly hard line, such as Shaanxi governor Hou Zongbing.[25] Large-scale purges were also ordered in Beijing, where a sizeable percentage of party members had actively participated in the movement, and in the party organs of provinces and cities where massive demonstrations had broken out, such as Shenyang city and Guizhou province.[26] After writing obligatory 'reports' on their activities during the '50 days of turmoil' and two days of 'riot', Beijing party members were to 'register'—a common procedure for dismissing 'disloyal' members.

Yet, demonstrating the hard-line leadership's isolation from CCP rank and file, party secretaries in the capital and elsewhere protected their personnel to the point that Beijing First Secretary Li Ximing complained of a 'perfunctory rectification' that evidently yielded little result.[27] After a year or so the 'investigations' petered out, while even high-level party figures previously purged, such as Li Rui (a secretary to Mao Zedong and a Zhao sympathizer), were reinstated though, as will be discussed later, organizational

---

[25] Hefei, Anhui, Provincial Radio Service (26 July 1989), in SWB (29 July 1989), B11. Hard-line Beijing officials Chen Xitong and Li Ximing were not promoted, however, while Li Ruihuan and Jiang Zemin were (to Politburo member and general secretary, respectively), perhaps because they resorted to relatively peaceful means to stop the protests. Hou Zongbing was promoted to party secretary in Henan. Altogether, 13 provincial party secretaries and governors were shifted. *Tangtai* (Hong Kong), 32 (7 July 1990), 15–16.

[26] In Guizhou 1,000 were punished, though their cases were connected to vague accusations of 'corruption' rather than specific charges of participating in the democracy movement. The same was true in Shengyang. *Renmin Ribao* (10 July 1989) and Shenyang, Liaoning Provincial Service (11 July 1989).

[27] *Xinhua* (25 Aug. 1989) and *Beijing Ribao* (14 June 1990), 1. Other areas, such as Zhenjiang province, played down the entire process and purged few, if any, party members for their involvement.

changes were effected to pre-empt further 'rebellions' within CCP ranks.

The CCP and Internal Security

The leadership's half-hearted effort to 'ferret out counterrevolutionaries' in the CCP reflected its greater concern with major security problems created by the June massacre. First and foremost was the question of loyalty within the PLA. Although Deng Xiaoping evidently retains great stature among army commanders, the 'Yang family', CMC members Yang Shangkun and his brother Yang Baibing, are apparently deeply resented. As the army bore the brunt of popular resentment after the crackdown, China's civilian leaders became increasingly concerned that army units which had refused to deploy force against the citizenry (not just in Beijing but apparently in other cities as well) might seek to overturn the current leadership and 'reverse' verdicts on 4 June 1989 to refurbish the PLA's tattered image. Deng thus decided that during future crises the CMC would exercise direct control over military units nationwide, while political commissars were given increased authority over operational matters.[28] Even though Deng had retired from the CMC by turning over his position to new CCP General Secretary Jiang Zemin, a 'special leading group on military affairs' was reportedly formed with Deng and Yang Shangkun as members.[29] Finally, for only the third time in PRC history, a major transfer of military region commanders was ordered, along with a big shake-up in the Beijing military region command structure and the People's Armed Police, all to prevent opposition from coalescing.[30]

These organizational changes were matched by a sustained propaganda campaign aimed at ensuring PLA loyalty, especially after the Romanian revolution. With some hard-line and even

[28] *South China Morning Post* (Hong Kong, 2 Jan. 1990), 10. The Air Force had apparently stood down during the entire crisis.

[29] *South China Morning Post* (22 Nov. 1989), 8.

[30] *Ming Pao* (Hong Kong, 6 May 1980), 18. The only other occasions when this occurred was in 1973, soon after Lin Biao's attempted coup, and 1985, when Deng reduced the number of military regions from 11 to 7. Changes in Beijing included promotions of Generals Wang Chengbin and Zhang Gong to region commander and political commissar, respectively.

old leftist army personnel evidently questioning party supremacy, the press and the CCP's internal propaganda machine sent an unequivocally clear message to the PLA: it must 'uphold the party's *absolute* leadership'.[31] While top CCP leaders frequently visited military units, party publications aimed at refurbishing the army's image and praising soldiers by reiterating *ad nauseam* their 'heroic' role in putting down the 'riot' and protecting China from suddenly hostile forces from the West. A major 'regularization' of army structure and training procedures was also effected to strengthen loyalty and rein in semi-independent units.[32]

Army propaganda made it clear, however, that, while some PLA units opposed the use of force against the students (including several old generals like the unrepentant Zhang Aiping), others were convinced that the CCP's lax policy on political and ideological education had produced the 'turmoil'. Over the past year, the most blatantly 'leftist' statements, including a call to renew 'class struggle' and warnings of a 'war threat', have come from PLA organs, especially *Liberation Army Daily*.[33] Although the centre's decision to increase the military's budget might be expected to mollify restive commanders, there is great fear of continuing opposition from both the left and right sides of the political spectrum in the military. Guaranteeing that the 'barrel of the gun is firmly grasped in reliable hands' has become for CCP leaders vital to the 'long-term stability of the nation'.[34]

The other major security threat comes from an increasingly volatile society. As cities reported 'grim' security conditions resulting from petty crime to outright sabotage and seizure of weapons, party leaders took extraordinary measures to ensure 'stability'.[35] A new 'PRC Law on the Protection of Military Installations' was passed, while several provincial organs held special meetings to

---

[31] *Renmin Ribao* (16 Apr. 1990), 5. Emphasis added.

[32] *Renmin Ribao* (14 May 1990), 3, *Jiefang Junbao* (30 Mar. 1990), 3, and *Beijing Ribao* (1 Mar. 1990), 1, which reported Li Ximing lavishing troops with medals and honours. Even some democracy supporters, such as news reporter Dai Qing, expressed concern about the army becoming 'independent'.

[33] *Jiefang Junbao* (13 and 16 Feb. and 27 Mar. 1990). The paper also called for a renewed purge of the CCP in March. *AFP* (Hong Kong, 13 Mar. 1990), *FBIS China* (13 Mar. 1990), 12.

[34] *Jiefang Junbao* (12 May 1990), 1, 4.

[35] Anhui Provincial Service (20 Feb. 1990), and Shanghai City Service (31 Mar. 1990), in *FBIS China* (6 Mar. 1990), 40, and (31 Mar. 1990), 43.

deal with problems of 'managing weapons and explosives'.[36] In addition to rocketing crime rates in the cities, several minority areas experienced small-scale uprisings, with the most serious occurring in Xinjiang among Kirghiz people irate over the CCP's discriminatory religious policy.[37] Compared to the Soviet Union's policy of loosening central controls over non-Russian areas, CCP nationalities' policy was toughened as major changes in party personnel occurred in nearly all minority provinces and autonomous regions.[38] With public and state security organs now constituting approximately one-third of all government employees, China has assumed the characteristics of a 'garrison state' in which the party's overwhelming concern is to maintain control and 'stability'.[39]

'Rebuilding' the Party

The response of CCP leaders to internal dissension in party ranks was to reiterate well-worn communist party principles. While Mikhail Gorbachev introduced radical innovations into the CPSU and the Soviet political system, China's leaders reaffirmed the organizational practices and orthodox ideology which had been the target of the democracy movement: Democratic-centralism, internal party discipline and obedience, and Marxist-Leninist-Mao Zedong Thought. Contrary to the relatively liberal ideological line of the past few years which had encouraged the rank and file to speak their minds with a critical, relativistic perspective, unquestioning obedience and absolute loyalty have become the

[36] *Jiefang Junbao* (24 Feb. 1990), 1, Hubei Provincial Service (7 July 1990), Lanzhou, Gansu Provincial Service (6 July 1990), and Shandong Provincial Service (29 June 1990), in *FBIS* China (6 Mar. 1990, p. 33; 11 July, p. 57; 19 July, p. 50; and 3 July, p. 38, respectively).

[37] *Xinjiang Ribao* (26 May 1990), 1–2, in *FBIS* China (19 July 1990), 51. According to Amnesty International, executions in China have substantially increased in the past year, and include people accused of 'counter-revolutionary' religious activities during the pro-democracy movement. *New York Times* (13 Sep. 1990).

[38] Party secretaries or governors in Ningxia, Qinghai, Tibet, and Guangzi were all changed.

[39] 11,262 people, or 62% of total employees for various departments under the Beijing government, are in Public or state security, or labour reform work. *Tangtai* (Hong Kong), 21 (21 Apr. 1990), 8–9.

model attributes party members should emulate.[40] 'The most important factor to consider when choosing [party] leaders', Beijing Mayor Chen Xitong demanded, 'is whether or not they will swear full allegiance to the Communist Party.'[41] Confronted with possibly fatal challenges to party rule from hostile domestic and international forces, all CCP members, it was emphasized, must carry out Central Committee decisions 'to the letter'. 'Whoever fails or resists . . . implementing a party Central Committee decision', Qiao Shi warned 'will be regarded as having undermined party unity and violated party discipline.'[42]

Several measures were employed to enforce this rigid discipline. In the immediate aftermath of the crackdown, party officials called to Beijing to ratify hard-line decisions purging Zhao Ziyang and reversing political reforms met under tight security and reportedly were forced to vote almost at gunpoint.[43] The Central Discipline Inspection Commission and Central Advisory Commission (both heavily influenced by Chen Yun) investigated and often dismissed many party members suspected of supporting the democracy movement on purported charges of 'corruption', as occurred with the provincial governor of Hainan.[44] Veteran cadres ostensibly retired were also reactivated to reinstil younger cadres with the devotional 'Yan'an spirit' and the selfless leadership style cultivated in the supposedly 'golden years' of the 1950s and early 1960s.[45] With renewed emphasis on the 'simple' political fealty shown by Lei Fang and the 'Good Eighth Company of Nanjing Road', post-crackdown leaders wanted to create a pliant membership who would never again challenge their authority in the streets.

Recent changes in recruitment policies and ideological education also reflected this highly politicized goal. Concerned that the recent infusion of irreverent intellectuals into the party had created the social basis of pro-democratic policies, the party has targeted more 'naturally' loyal peasants and workers for membership, while

---

[40] Criticism was thus directed at Hu Jiwei for purportedly 'concluding that if one was "obedient" to the leadership, one would commit mistakes'. *Renmin Ribao*, overseas edn. (5 Apr. 1990), 6, in *FBIS* China (23 Apr. 1990), 5.

[41] Quoted in *Cheng Ming* (Hong Kong, Nov. 1989), 1.

[42] *Xinhua* (30 Jan. 1990).

[43] Anonymous interview, Summer 1990.

[44] *Renmin Ribao* (29 June 1990), 1.

[45] Ibid. 3, and Shandong Provincial Service, 30 June 1990.

barring private entrepreneurs altogether.[46] After years of heavy emphasis on bringing in new members with technical expertise, recruitment guide-lines, reminiscent of Mao Zedong's call for 'red and experts', now call for balancing 'ability' with 'political integrity'. Intra-party education has also shifted almost exclusively to indoctrination of Marxism-Leninism, especially as the collapse of communist regimes in Eastern Europe and Gorbachev's *perestroika* reforms have raised serious doubts about the viability of socialism.[47] Political education at the grass roots has been particularly emphasized as top leaders realized that it was the CCP's local organs which failed to prevent members from taking part in the democracy movement and then resisted efforts at purges directed from the top.[48]

Despite concerns over the loyalty of the CCP, however, the party's control of mass organizations and institutions, particularly universities and newspapers, has been increased. Reacting to the formation of independent trade unions and wildcat strikes (which increased dramatically in China, even before the pro-democracy movement), the party's leadership has been consolidated to 'make these organizations keep a correct political orientation'.[49] Previously autonomous factory managers must also now compete with rejuvenated factory party committees, as the former, though still technically in command, are advised to seek 'the party organization's advice'.[50] At universities, the relationship between academic officers and party committees is more clear cut: 'school presidents [must] assume responsibility under the leadership of party committees' which are in the leading position.[51] As for the press, party conservatives make it abundantly clear that newspapers will remain an arm of the party without the autonomy promised under the previously proposed 'editor-in-chief responsibility system'. 'The power of leadership over propaganda work and public opinion must be in the hands of Marxists', Shanghai's *Liberation Daily* proclaimed, with the 'party as the core of leadership over all

---

[46] Rosen, 'CCP' (see n. 2), 87. Over 1 million new members joined in 1989, though no precise figures are provided on occupational composition.
[47] *Xinhua* (15 Mar. 1990).
[48] 'Communique of Sixth Plenary Session', *Xinhua* (12 Mar. 1990).
[49] CCP Circular, *Renmin Ribao* (31 Jan. 1990).
[50] *Xinhua* (29 June 1990).
[51] *Hebei Ribao* (22 June 1990), 1, in *FBIS China* (20 July 1990), 54.

journalistic work'.[52] Although new Politburo member Li Ruihuan called for newspapers to lighten up (evidently to the great consternation of Li Peng), the days of free-wheeling journalism, epitomized in the 1980s by Shanghai's *World Economic Herald*, are clearly over.

Conclusion

In the midst of the 4 June military crackdown, outraged citizens declared that the 'Communist Party is finished'. Relying on raw military and police power, however, the CCP has survived as conservative leaders attempt to wrest control of the institution from the pro-reform groups cultivated by Zhao Ziyang. While the press obediently follows central dictates, the failure to 'ferret out' pro-democracy sympathizers and Zhao supporters has left the CCP just as divided as before 4 June. The purge of Zhao and his think-tank intellectuals has substantially reduced reform-minded leaders at the top. Yet the promotion of Li Ruihuan to the Politburo and retention of Shanghai Mayor Zhu Rongji (a close ally of Zhao) could possibly revive political reform in the event of a shakeup in the central leadership. In the cities and key institutions such as universities and advanced industrial installations, moreover, many CCP members remain highly receptive to reform as they wait for the death of the old leaders to create an opportunity for a new leadership to emerge.

But just as Mikhail Gorbachev has circumvented the CPSU apparatus in building new political institutions and social bases supportive of reform in the Soviet Union, so too may reform-minded leaders in China be forced to adopt a similar strategy. The CCP's enormous loss of authority since 4 June 1989 makes the prospect of the communist party leading the country towards liberalization and democratization in the future extraordinarily difficult. Spring 1989 may, in fact, have represented the party leadership's last opportunity to guide the reform process without unleashing various political forces which will topple, or at least

---

[52] *Jiefang Ribao* (12 Oct. 1989), 1, 3. This prescription was reinforced by the transfer of security personnel, including from the military, into newspapers, and the appointment of conservative ideologues, such as Gao Di, to important journalism posts.

seriously weaken, the CCP. Deng Xiaoping's fatal decision to crush the movement, rather than harnessing it for political ends which he has periodically supported, leaves the country with a ruling body that lacks the enormous reserve of authority and popular will necessary to effect the difficult transition from orthodox to reform communism. The current reliance on repression can only increasingly alienate the population and spur even more emigration of the students and intellectuals on whom the country's prospective development relies. Yet if reform and liberalization are attempted in the midst of the hatred and desire for revenge created by 4 June, China may experience a period of social violence comparable to the civil war of the 1930s. Whether China follows the violent path of Romania or the relatively peaceful transition accomplished in Czechoslovakia may, then, depend once again on Deng Xiaoping who, concerned over his historical legacy after the Beijing massacre, may revive reform through leadership charges that send the 'butchers of Beijing' packing.

5. The Social Origins and Consequences of the Tiananmen Crisis

ANITA CHAN

When mass protests erupted in Beijing in April 1989, the world was caught by surprise. Glowing reports of China's decade-old open-door economic reforms in the Chinese press, echoed by the Western and even some of the Eastern bloc press, had caused many to slight the subterranean social tensions that had been building steadily in China during the preceding few years. Even dire warnings made by none other than Deng Xiaoping himself were duly overlooked. In June 1988, about two weeks after the Chinese government had withdrawn subsidies for four main food items in the cities, Deng made a surprising statement to a group of foreign guests. He said that, as the government tried to tackle the thorny issues of price and wage reforms, the Chinese economic reforms had arrived at a 'critical stage . . . Our work must rest on facing big risks and preparing countermeasures so that the "sky won't fall down".[1] Deng did not elaborate further on what he meant by 'risks' or 'countermeasures'. But it is not every day that China's top leaders so forthrightly and publicly reveal their inner worries. There was a shade of wavering confidence, yet doggedness. On the very day Deng expressed these fears, student unrest broke out on the campus of Beijing University. The upheaval was quickly quelled, only to resurface a year later. The Beijing Spring of 1989 proved that the 'risks' and 'countermeasures' that so worried Deng were no exaggerations. In mid-1988 the mass dissatisfaction that Deng feared could be sensed when I spent a month in Kunming, the capital of Yunnan province, interviewing Chinese from all walks of life. The types of grievances that they expressed would soon be played out in the mass occupation of Tiananmen Square and the protest movements that simultaneously engulfed all of China's cities during 1989.

[1] *BR* (13 June 1988), 5.

Currents of Dissatisfaction

As of mid-1988, one might have expected the Chinese people to be relatively satisfied with their government. Living standards, for one thing, were considerably higher for the vast majority of the Chinese people than they had been a decade earlier. Yet that was not an impression strongly shared by all city-dwellers. An opinion poll carried out in forty Chinese cities that year revealed that only 60 per cent thought their lives had improved since 1978.[2] Had the poll asked whether people's lives had improved since 1985, not 1978, the percentage of affirmative responses very likely would have dropped dramatically. My interviews in Kunming indicated that the reforms had begun turning sour in people's minds by the mid-1980s. It was then that the new economic policies had begun to take root and that the new patterns of social stratification began to have a more visible shape.

When Deng Xiaoping first returned to power in 1978, much of the populace had held high hopes for the promised reforms. The most dramatic success was a quick increase in agricultural output. Until the mid-1980s, improved opportunities seemed to be opening for all. The pie was to become bigger and everyone was promised an equal opportunity to acquire a fair share. By 1988, as was obvious from my interviews in Kunming, such hopes were giving way to frustration.

Unrealistic expectations were partly to blame; and the CCP's own propaganda and slogans were responsible for creating and fuelling them. Glowing figures on national production only pointed up one's own meagre income. Lavish praise heaped on the '10,000 dollar households' and the 'big capable entrepreneurs', holding them up as national models to be emulated, only bred frustration and jealousy. Beating the drums for people to 'look forward' infused impatience that the promised land was still not in sight.

These unrealistic expectations were coupled to complaints about equity. Within the previous few years, it had become obvious to most of the populace that a bigger pie did not always mean a bigger share, less still a fairer share. But the identities of the real winners and losers were not always apparent to people. Very often their envy was directed towards the wrong groups.

2 *BR* (18 July 1988), 26.

The Scapegoats of Frustration

Almost invariably, when I asked who was doing well under the reforms in China, urban people answered, with an unmistakable tone of resentment, the 'private households', the workers in profitable collective enterprises, and the peasants. But these were all misplaced targets of frustration.

The 'private households' include the self-employed repairmen, the street hawkers selling breakfast pancakes or smuggled imported clothing, the taxi-drivers who own their own cabs, and the family-operated noodle shop owners. The average income of these small-time entrepreneurs in 1988 came to 3,000 to 4,000 dollars a year, one to two times more than the average national urban income of 1,400 dollars.[3] What the complainants did not take into account, though, is that these 'private households' were not entitled to any of the benefits enjoyed by state employees, such as access to almost free housing, workplace, subsidies, labour insurance, medical care, or pensions, and that their incomes were erratic and the survival of their business precarious, not to mention the long working hours.

The second group that bore the brunt of popular frustration were the workers in collective enterprises, which had mushroomed in the previous half-decade. The popular image was that, due to more flexible management practices than in the state-owned factories, these enterprises had begun turning over huge profits and were distributing handsome bonuses to their employees. This was true of a highly publicized small minority of firms, but the reality of the situation, according to government statistics, was that the average annual income of the 35 million collective employees in 1988 was only 1,436 dollars, 417 dollars less than the earnings of the 99 million state-employed workers.[4] Moreover, collective employees normally have had to work harder during work hours, have not enjoyed as many fringe benefits, and have had less job security than those in the state-run sector.

The third group who were making a lot of money, people complained, were the peasants. Yet this, too, was a grossly distorted picture. The peasants who were doing well were those whom the urban people came into contact with—those resident in the suburban counties. Through vegetable sales, for example, they could

---

[3] *Guangming Daily* (31 Mar.1988), 3.
[4] *ZTN 1989* (Beijing, 1989), 114, 142, 146, 101.

afford consumer goods and build private homes far more spacious than the cramped accommodations of city-dwellers. But these peasants were a small minority. The reality is that, like many other developing countries, China suffers from a noticeable urban bias. In 1988, while the average net income of a peasant was 545 dollars, an urbanite received 1,747 dollars, a ratio of 1:3.[5] Slightly more than half of a peasant household's net income has to go towards food, with little disposable income left for other necessities. Moreover, peasants do not receive most of the social benefits that are provided to the urban populace. In earlier decades, they did enjoy some rudimentary medical insurance at the collective's expense. Today, after decollectivization, with the general deterioration of collective social institutions, especially in poor areas, even these have disappeared. Peasants do not receive any pension, and have to provide their own housing, which has always devoured the lion's share of their lifetime savings.

It was therefore surprising that these three groups were singled out by interviewees as the recipients of unduly high incomes, whilst there do exist groups which are making ten, twenty, even a hundred times more than the national average income (more about these groups later). A possible explanation is that all three of the former groups have had very low status in socialist China. For many years, a state-sector job had been the most sought after. A job with a collective enterprise was second best. No matter how Maoist ideology had attempted to raise the status of the peasants, it was ingrained in the popular consciousness that the peasants were still at the bottom of the heap. The 'private household' trades, for their part, had been abolished back in the 1950s and were allowed to revive only in the early 1980s as a measure to reduce urban unemployment. Initially, only the retired elderly and unemployed young people were willing to start a private endeavour. It was regarded as a stop-gap livelihood for those who could not participate in the state-sector mainstream. Only a few years earlier, in 1982, in one survey of senior high school graduates, out of thirty-eight job categories, self-employed worker had ranked last in desirability.[6] The animosity and envy felt by

[5] Ibid. 138, 746. The ratio is calculated from the figures given in the tables.

[6] Lan Chengdong and Zhang Zhongru, 'Aspirations and Inclinations of this Year's Senior High School Graduates', *Chinese Sociology and Anthropology*, 16/1–2 (Fall–Winter 1983–4), 38.

interviewees should be understood in these terms: the feeling that suddenly, within the space of a few years, all of these lowly people without any respectable skills had begun making more money undeservedly.

The Intellectuals — How Much are They Worth?

Those most resentful of those three groups have been the 'intellectuals'. In Chinese, the term encompasses a wide range of professions, from nuclear physicists through factory technicians to primary school teachers. As a group they have been articulate and vocal in recent years in agitating for higher pay. Primary and secondary school teachers are indeed quite poorly paid, so low that there is now a great staff shortage and teachers' training colleges have difficulty recruiting students. But the most vociferous demands for more pay have come from the university teachers and research personnel, the 'high-level intellectuals'. Now that modernization, not revolution, was said to be the route to China's salvation, academics and professionals openly argued that their mental labour was worth considerably more than manual labour and deserving of correspondingly high pay. Throughout the 1980s, they claimed repeatedly in print and in conversations that they were discriminated against, that their salary was so low that they suffered from malnutrition, that because they work and read at home at night they were entitled to better housing, that middle- and high-level intellectuals have tended to die prematurely compared to the national mortality rate, that those who suffered most were middle-aged intellectuals groaning under the financial burdens of elderly parents and children.[7]

This chorus of complaints notwithstanding, academics were actually doing somewhat better financially, not worse, than the average worker. Among the eight occupational groups in the civil service pay scale, academics were ranked second highest, after state-organ officials.[8] National statistics showed, moreover, that the status and influence of the 'intellectuals' had greatly

---

[7] *Jiushi Niandai* (*The Nineties*) (Apr. 1988), 19–21; *Inside China Mainland* (Taipei, Oct. 1987), 1–4.

[8] John P. Burns, 'Civil Service Reform in Contemporary China', *Australian Journal of Chinese Affairs*, 18 (July 1987), 77.

improved during the past decade. Of the ten million personnel with 'special technocratic skills' (excluding primary and secondary school teachers), 30 per cent had joined the CCP, about three million had received awards or recognition of various types, one million had taken up leadership positions in the party,[9] and 50,000 had gone abroad to study for extended periods,[10] a figure that does not include the many academics and cultural and administrative personnel who had been able to travel abroad on shorter visits.

Whilst the government had been put under pressure to provide salaries commensurate with the improved status of intellectuals, however, the central treasury had been facing deficits throughout the 1980s. In this circumstance, the government remained unwilling to dig deeply into the state budget to raise their salaries substantially. Consequently, starting in the mid-1980s the government began to allow academics and professionals to supplement their incomes by taking up second jobs full-time or part-time. By 1988 about 15 per cent of the ten million had done so.[11] To further augment the salaries of academic staff, the government even began encouraging university departments to institute a 'create income' programme, under which departments have been free to run businesses or offer services to enterprises to supplement departmental budgets. The extra income is divided among the university administration, the department, and the faculty and staff. Through this, Qinghua University in Beijing, China's premier science university, was able to distribute a 600 to 1,000 dollar bonus to each faculty and staff member at the end of 1987.[12] Academic departments without marketable skills desperately improvised. When I visited Yunnan University in 1988, the history department collectively was operating a fruit stall on campus to augment salaries. In primary and secondary schools, teachers selling snacks to students after class became a common sight.[13]

Not surprisingly, given these circumstances, the urban white-collar professionals were becoming increasingly vociferous in

[9] *Renmin Ribao* (25 May 1988), 1.
[10] *Inside China Mainland* (July 1988), 27.
[11] *CD* (28 May 1988), 3.
[12] *Renmin Ribao* (13 Apr. 1988), 1.
[13] See *Guangming Daily*, (3 May 1988), 1, for other means by which primary school teachers tried to make extra money.

pressing their catalogue of complaints in the press. But, to the government's advantage, the intellectuals distanced themselves from other sectors of society. Indeed, if one sifts carefully through the writings of Chinese intellectuals of all persuasions of the past several years, one is hard pressed to find any mention of working-class grievances. On the contrary, the economists and political scientists associated with Zhao Ziyang's think-tanks strongly advocated precisely those economic reforms which caused anxiety among the workers; and most professionals and university students took those economists and political thinkers as their intellectual mentors. Whereas dissident Polish intellectuals had, by the mid-1970s, begun to make common cause with workers who wanted independent trade unions, Chinese intellectuals never adopted a similar stance. Instead, their chorus of complaints that workers and peasants were making more money than themselves had been loud and aggressive.

The Workers — Losing the Iron Rice Bowl

Though they did not have any spokesmen in the mid to late 1980s to articulate their grievances, workers had their own fair share of frustrations, as they saw their previously superior status under Mao challenged and manual labour relegated to a position inferior to mental labour.[14] Materially, to be sure, they were doing better during the 1980s than they ever had before. For a number of years after the introduction of the reforms, their wages were buoyed by bonuses handed out by factory managements eager to seem benevolent. But during the second half of the 1980s these wage increases began to be eaten into by inflation, and signs of worker discontent were beginning to infect industry. Without releasing statistics, official reports admitted that, after 1987, the incidence of strikes in factories throughout the country rose dramatically. The reasons were clear: not only was inflation biting into wages, the reforms meant to the workers tighter control over work schedules, rising work quotas, monetary penalties for shoddy

---

[14] See *Gongren Yuebao* (*Workers' Monthly*), 1 (1986), 18–19. According to an opinion poll carried out by a trade union, to most workers the most urgent problems are wages, prices, housing, jobs for their children, and public order.

work, partial lay-offs, and even full-time unemployment.[15] In particular, the new system of contracting out enterprises to individuals, which was spreading across the country, tended to bring labour reductions in its wake.[16] While a law permitting bankruptcies continued to be debated heatedly within the national leadership, the jobs of many workers in state enterprises and collective enterprises had already been put on the line.

Skilled workers could take advantage of the emerging free labour market to job-hop, and in some trades their incomes had increased substantially in the process. But to the ordinary unskilled and semi-skilled workers, threatened by job insecurity, a free labour market seemed very much a mixed blessing. Nation-wide there were estimated to be thirty million surplus workers,[17] about a quarter of the urban work-force. Economic streamlining would, according to the government's own figures, render ten to twenty million of these workers redundant over the following several years. Once laid off they would have to compete for jobs with thirty million new arrivals to the labour market, a figure that did not include the uncountable number of rural migrants who had begun crowding into the urban areas.[18] The future prospects seemed dim, in short, for a sizeable number of workers.

In these circumstances, it is not surprising that when the intellectuals incessantly complained in print that their working conditions were arduous and that their salaries and housing conditions ought to be considerably better than the industrial work-force's, they aroused the workers' resentment.

The Peasants — Entering Troubled Times

As noted earlier, though the lot of the peasants improved after 1978, their living standards were still far below that of the urban populace.

---

15 See e.g. *Renmin Ribao* (21 Apr. 1988), 2.

16 'After the Risk Mechanism Makes its Way into Enterprises . . .' *Jingji Ribao* (*Economic Daily*) (27 July 1987), 1. This interesting article upholds as a good example the manner in which rationalization and labour savings were implemented in one factory after it was contracted out to a new manager (the previous deputy Party secretary). The manager cut personnel by a quarter to turn a profit. To do this he transferred his relatives and the relatives of the deputy managers from the staff offices to the shopfloor, and then fired workers to reduce the labour force from 260 to 201.

17 *BR* (29 June 1988), 7.

18 *China News Analysis*, 1299 (15 Dec. 1985), 6.

To a large extent this was and is due to a pricing system that is biased against agricultural products *vis-à-vis* manufactured goods. The current 'contract' system for grain still binds many peasants to deliver grain to the government at an artificially depressed price.[19] At one and the same time, the soaring price of agricultural inputs was cancelling out much of the peasants' remaining gains. Economic activities outside agriculture provide the major means by which peasants are able to prosper,[20] and in the isolated and backward areas where farmers have to live almost entirely off grain production, living conditions had barely improved or had actually dropped. In one impoverished county in Shanxi in 1985, peasants who concentrated on grain only made 100 dollars per capita a year, one-third of the already very low average rural income for the county,[21] and one-quarter of the national peasant average of 397 dollars.[22]

Freeing the peasantry to pursue their sideline endeavours and the return of a free market did succeed in raising most peasants' income in the years immediately after decollectivization. But these increases could not be sustained, year after year, without capital investment. The government's policy, however, has been to concentrate on industrial modernization and to let the peasants pull themselves up by their own bootstraps. From 1980 to 1986, the share of capital investment in agriculture had declined from 9.3 per cent to 3.3 per cent of the national budget, in absolute terms from 530 million to 380 million dollars. In a similar fashion, within the villages private funds are being diverted away from agriculture and into more lucrative endeavours. By the late 1980s the effects had become apparent, with rural irrigation systems deteriorating, land being depleted, agricultural machinery old and in disrepair, and a serious shortage of expert agricultural personnel.[23] Grain production had begun sliding after reaching a record high in 1984. By 1987 shortages of pork had reappeared in the cities, and ration

---

[19] Jean C. Oi, 'Peasant Grain Marketing and State Procurement: China's Grain Contracting System', *China Quarterly*, 106 (June 1986), 272–90. Also see Jonathan Unger and Jean Xiong, 'Life in the Chinese Hinterlands Under the Rural Economic Reforms', *Bulletin of Concerned Asian Scholars*, 22/4 (Summer 1990).

[20] For a case-study of this see J. Bruce Jacobs, 'Political and Economic Organizational Changes and Continuities in Six Rural Chinese Localities', *Australian Journal of Chinese Affairs*, 14 (July 1985), 127.

[21] *China News Analysis*, 1323 (1 Dec. 1986), 3.

[22] *ZTN 1987*, 697.

[23] *Liao Wang*, 15 (11 Apr. 1988), 20–2.

tickets for meat and other essentials had to be reintroduced. Worse even than the price squeeze that faced peasants, necessary agricultural inputs were becoming all but unavailable; and what was particularly galling to peasants was the fact that corrupt officials had begun deliberately creating chemical-fertilizer shortages during the planting seasons in order to jack up prices. In response, during 1987, several million peasants took the law into their own hands in 100,000 separate incidents, looting fertilizer plants and waylaying trucks bearing fertilizers.[24] Across much of China, the army had to be called upon to guard supplies, and unknown numbers of peasants were killed. Yet the government did little to clamp down on the corruption. In the spring of 1989, Chinese newspapers were publishing the same charges, and the same stories of desperate peasants. The press in 1989 even reported that officials out for a quick buck had been knowingly selling dead seed-grain to peasants, who subsequently were reduced to hunger when their crops did not germinate.

There was yet another frustration among peasants. Whilst the intellectuals and workers had gained some ground under the reforms in freeing themselves from the yoke of the bureaucrats who sat directly above them, the peasants had been less fortunate. A popular image is that with the dissolution of the collective system, the state has got off the peasants' backs. The reality is that the peasants are still very much under the thumbs of local cadres. The cadres no longer organize the peasants' daily work routine, but as one Western scholar puts it, 'cadres have not so much lost power as refocused it. The personalized authority of cadres and clientelistic politics characteristic of the pre-reform period have not been eliminated: they have merely taken on a different form.'[25] They continue to have substantial control over the peasants' lives, especially in their discretionary power over the distribution of agricultural inputs and other materials. Rather than a relatively free system of small-scale entrepreneurship emerging in the countryside, the economic reforms have opened the door to new forms of patronage relationships that benefit the local officialdom.[26]

[24] *CD* (22 Apr. 1988), 4, and *Shehui* (*Society*), 2 (Mar. 1987), 14–15; *Jiushi Niandai* (Sept. 1988), 82.
[25] Jean C. Oi, 'Commercializing China's Rural Cadres', *Problems of Communism* (Sept.–Oct. 1986), 2.
[26] Jean C. Oi, 'Peasant Households Between Plan and Market: Cadre Control over Agricultural Inputs', *Modern China*, 12/2 (Apr. 1986), 230–51.

The New Monied Élite—the True Winners

While none of the broad social groups saw themselves by the late 1980s as having made dramatic gains by way of the economic reforms, a new stratum that could be called a 'monied élite' had arisen under the government's slogan that some should 'get rich first'. They comprised the '10,000 dollar households', the owners of 'private enterprises', the lessee-managers of state and collective enterprises, and lastly, officials and their offspring who were and are raking in large sums by privately serving as middlemen in commodity sales. They are, for China, the counterparts of the multi-millionaires of capitalist economies.

The '10,000 dollar households' are, for the most part, peasants or village officials who started off accumulating capital as 'specialized households': those which had acquired permission to free themselves from the burden of unprofitable grain-production contracts so as to be able to concentrate on lucrative industrial, agricultural, or service industries, at the same time enjoying preferential treatment from the government.

'Private enterprises' are officially defined as those employing eight or more workers. Their owners sometimes began humbly as 'private households', but their numbers also include the families of officials who have taken advantage of their influence to acquire the required licences and capital. By 1988 there were some 225,000 private enterprises, employing some 3.6 million workers in all.[27] Their size and scope had expanded rapidly, some having acquired capital assets of a million or more dollars.[28] For some years these enterprises had been basking in the glow of *'laissez-faire* socialism', taking advantage of lax enterprise laws to evade taxes. Only in June 1988 did the State Council take steps to publish enterprise laws to bring these firms more effectively under control.[29]

The endeavours of these two new groups of monied élites are essentially 'capitalistic' in character. The third and fourth groups, on the other hand, are the products of the hybrid planned-free-market economy, in line with a new 'socialist' concept that has played upon a distinction between ownership rights and use rights.

[27] *B R* (18 July 1988), 6. This figure is actually on the low side since an unknown number of private enterprises are registered as 'collective enterprises'.
[28] *B R* (21 Mar. 1988), 14–17.
[29] *B R* (18 July 1988), 6–7.

Thus the third group within the new monied élite are the so-called 'lessees' of public enterprises who, at some personal financial risk, guarantee to generate increased profits for the firms they take over. More often than not, the 'lessee-managers' had been CCP secretaries or directors of the very same enterprises before they were leased. So lucrative has this 'leasing-management' practice become that a heated debate on whether it constitutes 'capitalism' began cropping up in the public press.[30] The lessees sarcastically were referred to as 'capitalists without capital', meaning that they operate as capitalists without even having to furnish their own initial capital.

The fourth type of endeavour that generates high personal profits tends to be monopolized by the political élite and their offspring. Taking advantage of China's planned-free-market mixed economy, they have spun their political connections into wealth by securing huge consignments of commodities at a low state-plan price for immediate resale at the free market price, as much as two or three times higher. According to official Chinese statistics, an absolute majority of all the registered private firms in China are comprised of these so-called 'trading companies' that do not themselves transport or wholesale goods, but simply parasitically feed off the dual-price system.[31] And practically all of these 'attaché-case companies' are controlled by the offspring of the political élite at all levels, from the Politburo down to the powers-that-be in counties and towns. The largest such firm in China, until its doors were closed in the wake of the Tiananmen massacre, was controlled by Deng Xiaoping's quadriplegic son Deng Pufang. Other children of the political élite — including those of Zhao Ziyang, Wan Li, He Long, and a good part of the top army brass —

---

[30] The controversy has centred on a famous 'lessee-manageress' by the name of Guan Guangmei who had been a former cadre of the grocery enterprise she began leasing. Within a couple of years, she won the contracts for most of the other food stores that were bid out in her city and gained control of half of the volume of the city's grocery retail business. See a daily serialized debate over the 'capitalistic' or 'socialistic' characteristic of this form of leased enterprise in *Jingji Ribao* (*Economic Daily*), June to July 1988.

[31] Literal corruption is sometimes involved, and is much talked about in China and in Hong Kong. The nature of such economic crimes can be gleaned from *BR* (1 Aug. 1988), 6–7; (8 Aug. 1988), 4; *Guangming Ribao* (12 Apr. 1988), 1. On the new patterns of corruption in general, see Keith Forster, 'The 1982 Campaign against Economic Crime in China', *Australian Journal of Chinese Affairs* 14 (July 1985), 1–19.

had been able to set themselves up as the official agents for China's military hardware sales abroad, which were soaring during the 1980s. Others secured, free of charge, the extraordinarily lucrative import–export licences for goods in short supply. It is a rare leader who has not allowed relatives to enrich themselves in these ways. In many respects, ironically, their kith and kin have become 'socialist compradors', the equivalents of the pre-liberation compradors who were labelled as hated 'enemies of the people' when the communist government first took power.

This form of corruption, a bastard child of the economic reforms, had been growing at an exponential rate ever since 1984, when the reforms to urban industry began to be implemented. The economic reform programme had never met concerted resistance from the local officialdom at least partly, we may assume, because the new hybrid planned-free-market economy provided them with these extra openings for corruption.

In the days of Mao corrupt officials had also abounded, but corrupt practices then were more discreet and of a different order. They had existed mainly in the form of perks and privileges, screened off from the gaze of ordinary people, and, most significantly, in non-economic abuses of one's position and power, in the persecutions of subordinates who got in one's way. Under Deng, the official policy of 'letting a few people get rich first' has legitimized private wealth and conspicuous spending and has sparked off the scramble among officials to enrich those near and dear to them.

Quite naturally, popular resentment began running high against these leaders and their families. Sarcastic sayings abounded like 'to be rich you have to have been an official' and 'the road to riches is to quit being a county head and become a factory manager'. Towards the self-made *nouveaux riches*, however, resentment has been more subdued and often mixed with respect.[32] There was as yet no open objection to the emergence of genuine 'capitalism' and 'capitalists' *per se*, so long as the fortunes were not made through official connections and sleight of hand. What irked the

---

[32] The *nouveaux riches* from humble origins have succeeded in protecting their interests and gaining good images in part by philanthropically donating to social services and education, building factories for the handicapped, etc., activities that were widely publicized by the government as commendable means to redistribute wealth.

Chinese whom I spoke with in 1988 was the lack of equal opportunity for all to partake in the scramble to become rich.

The Widening Income Gap

In only a matter of half a decade, from the early to mid-1980s, the income gap in China had widened very considerably, and is well illustrated in the accompanying graphs from the 1987 Statistical Yearbook (Figs. 5.1 and 5.2).[33] But such statistics did not put the economic reformers on the defensive. The 'get rich first' slogan and the ideological catchphrase of 1987–9, 'China is still in the primary stage of socialism', were nailed in place as a counter to any criticism. In fact, Su Shaozhi, the former director of the Marxism-Leninism-Mao Zedong Thought Institute of the Chinese Academy of Social Sciences, a supporter of reform who fled into exile after the Beijing massacre, argued:

Under the violent stimulation of the mechanism of market competition, the emergence of *great* disparity in income is *inevitable*. The disparity is natural. As long as the majority of society's members are benefiting from the reforms (although the speed at which prosperity is attained varies), we should not be afraid of this kind of disparity.[34]

Also inevitable, Su purported, are problems such as inflation, unemployment, and rampant consumerism, but excessive differences between rich and poor could be avoided by taxation and welfare programmes.

Yet it was evident that adequate taxation mechanisms had not been promptly or effectively put into place to tax the newly rich. Tax laws relating to personal income and private enterprises were not promulgated until 1987 and 1988 respectively, and with tax evasion of all kinds notoriously widespread, it was obvious that any regularized collection of taxes would need very considerable time to take root.

As for the assertion that welfare programmes could be utilized as a levelling mechanism, the irony was that, quite to the contrary, China's economic reforms were rapidly dismantling the socialist

---

[33] *Zhongguo Tongji Nianjian 1987* (see n. 22), 714–15.
[34] Su Shaozhi and Wang Yishou, 'The Two Major Historical Missions of the Reforms', *Renmin Ribao* (5 Mar. 1988), 5; emphasis added.

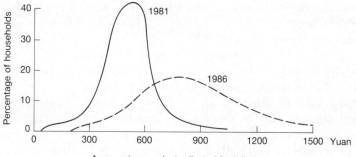

Fig 5.1 *Per capita urban income*

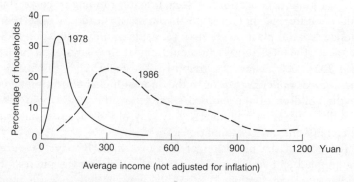

Fig 5.2 *Per capita rural income*

welfare system, without any commensurate increase in alternative welfare provisions. We have already seen how the streamlining of enterprises was expected to throw millions out of work within the course of a few years; yet the state has not yet introduced a comprehensive programme of unemployment benefits, and even if it were to attempt eventually to do so, it would be hard pressed to shoulder such an expense.

Similarly, in terms of health care the ordinary people were confronted with a crisis. During the 1980s, state and local funding for hospitals and medical services had dwindled. Medical institutions were asked to fend for themselves by raising the charges paid by patients.[35] The 90 per cent of China's populace outside

---

[35] *CD* (25 May 1988), 3; *Guangming Daily* (12 May 1988), 1.

the state-employed sector, who have never enjoyed free medical services, were now threatened with astronomical bills some three times their monthly salary if hospitalized for a month.[36] Even the privileges of the 10 per cent enjoying free medical coverage were rapidly eroding.[37] The proposed scenario was that a new system of medical insurance paid for by the work unit and the individual would alleviate the crisis facing the ill. Notwithstanding this, a very sizeable part of the urban population is today, and will remain, uninsured.

In the sphere of education, too, the reform policies were shifting the financial burdens onto the collectives and private shoulders. The first casualties have been impoverished rural districts, which began witnessing primary-school closures and a declining student body. In higher education, as seen already, funding to cover staff salaries fully had not been forthcoming. Instead, to raise more money, special places were now set aside in universities for 'independent students', those who could pay their own annual tuition of 1,800–2,000 dollars.[38] Obviously, the main effect of this new recruitment policy was to open the door of higher education wider to the children of the monied élite, who otherwise would have had difficulty entering university by way of the cutthroat national university-entrance examinations.

Reforms in the provision of housing similarly have favoured the monied élite and have impinged adversely on the interests of ordinary urban families. Ostensibly inaugurated to raise funds to ease the urban housing shortage and to stamp out corrupt practices in the distribution of housing, a plan was announced in 1987–8 to raise rents per square metre by sevenfold or eightfold, which in turn would partially be offset by a housing subsidy equal to 22 per cent of one's basic salary.[39] But the net effect would be to force an average-income family occupying an average flat to absorb a rent increase of some 25 dollars, a 500 per cent increase. The overall result would be to squeeze poor families into smaller

[36] According to an informant who stayed in hospital for 57 days, the hospital charges (excluding medicine) totalled 800 yuan.

[37] *Guangming Daily* (12 May 1988), 1.

[38] *Renmin Ribao* (8 Aug. 1988), 12–15; *China News Analysis*, 1314 (15 July 1986), 3.

[39] *Renmin Ribao* (9 Oct. 1987), 2; *Yunnan Ribao* (19 May 1988), 4; *BR* (2 May 1988), 8–9; *Jiushi Niandai* (Sept. 1988), 18.

living units, opening up the larger flats for wealthy families at high rentals. The new policies also encouraged wealthy families to purchase new flats at several tens of thousands of dollars apiece. Understandably, as one report observes, these impending policies were 'grating on people's most sensitive nerves'.[40]

Fuelled by inflation, all of these new social policies were eroding the material well-being of low- and even middle-income families. This was apparent even by the mid-1980s. In 1986, 161 million people were targeted for state-funded social relief, a 7.3 per cent increase over the previous year. Of these, fifteen million were urban poor, a surprising jump of 65 per cent from the previous year. Though eligible for relief, only a small percentage received any: 2 per cent of the urban poor and 39 per cent of the rural poor.[41]

Consequently, a large group of very underprivileged urban poor was in the making. Their numbers were rapidly being supplemented from the countryside, where there is a labour surplus of some 30–40 per cent.[42] Starting in the early 1980s, when the barriers to internal migration began to be progressively lowered, peasants swarmed into the cities and market towns by the millions, taking up the most menial and heavy jobs, sometimes legally, sometimes illegally.[43] As one example, in Guangdong province in 1982, 340,000 peasants were working without legal authorization in urban state enterprises.[44] In Beijing, migrants by the mid-1980s made up 12 per cent of the population; and a third of these migrants

[40] *Renmin Ribao* (9 Oct. 1988), 2.

[41] These figures are taken from a book of Chinese government statistics. Thanks are due to John McCallum for sharing with me some 10 pages of these valuable tables which he brought back from Beijing in 1988. Unfortunately, they were given to him without a reference source.

[42] Richard Conroy, 'Laissez-faire Socialism? Prosperous Peasants and China's Current Rural Development Strategy', *Australian Journal of Chinese Affairs*, 12 (July 1984), 12.

[43] *CD* (21 May 1988), 4. In Anhui province, 80,000 peasants had entered Heifei city, *Renmin Ribao* (17 Jan. 1985).

[44] Wojtek Zanfanolli, 'A Brief Outline of China's Second Economy', *Asian Survey*, 25/7 (July 1985), 727. As of 1986 another 200,000 Guangdong peasants from poverty-stricken districts had moved into the delta areas to rent land, entering into share-cropping relationships with local households who can make a better living outside agriculture. These migrants live in makeshift tents or pigsties without any security of tenancy. Hein Mallee, 'Rural-Urban Migration Control in the People's Republic of China: Effects of the Recent Reforms', *China Information* (Leiden), 1/4 (Spring 1988), 16–17.

were sleeping at construction sites.[45]

The pressures of this influx were felt even more painfully in 1988–9, as the central government under Li Peng sharply tightened up on bank loans in an effort to staunch inflation that was galloping out of control. The pinch was felt most painfully in the county-town enterprises that have mushroomed this past decade, thriving on cheap peasant labour. Cut off from bank credit, they very quickly experienced cash-flow problems and went under by the thousands during 1988–9, deliberately sacrificed by the government as the means to brake a runaway economy. The millions of former peasants who were thrown out of work saw no point in returning to the land, where increases in labour input could no longer squeeze out higher yields. Roaming the country in search of a living, they joined the armies of unemployed laid off by the urban construction industry, the other sector most hard hit by economic retrenchments. This 'blindly floating population', as they have come to be called, soon reached tens of millions. In February 1989, during the few days of Chinese New Year alone, a crowd of 2.5 million desperate job-seekers swarmed into the relatively rich province of Guangdong, near Hong Kong. These hordes of migrants strained China's already overloaded transport system and contributed to a rapidly climbing crime rate. Complaints about a breakdown of law and order — complaints directed towards the central government — began to grow louder in the cities in 1988–9.

In August 1988, shortly after returning from Yunnan province, I wrote an essay about these findings.[46] The frustration and political dissatisfaction that had come through so clearly in the interviews in Yunnan had led me to believe that growing political unrest and perhaps upheaval lay in China's future, and the 1988 essay concluded with words of despair:

China's social and moral fabric is under challenge from the enormous changes that are being put in place by a government that has proved itself far more concerned with economic development than equity. Those who see themselves as the losers are worried and growing impatient. Ordinary people increasingly perceive the officialdom as morally bankrupt, and

---

[45] Hein Mallee, 'Migration Control' (see n. 44), 18.
[46] Anita Chan, 'The Challenge to the Social Fabric', *Pacific Review*, 2/2 (Apr. 1989), 131.

believe that the large portion of the new monied elite that has ties to bureaucracy is attaining its wealth through illegitimate means. A troubled decade for China lies ahead.

The flashpoint — the mass upheaval from below — came all too soon. In less than a year's time, in the spring of 1989, the people of Beijing and of most other cities in China would be crowding the streets in a vast campaign of protest.

Protest and Repression

The CCP leadership was well aware of, and jittery about, the dissatisfaction and social unrest that were mounting among the major sectors of society. The government in 1988 was already making preparation for a crackdown, if and when that became necessary.

Special police squads had been sent to Poland a couple of years before Tiananmen to learn the techniques of crowd control that had been used by the Polish government to suppress Solidarity in 1981. Borrowing a lesson also from the US South and South Africa, electric cattle prods became standard equipment in dealing with disturbances. In July 1988, as government newspapers began to worry in print that the people's 'threshold of endurance' might soon be reached, Premier Li Peng openly instructed security personnel to prepare to deal yet more harshly with social unrest. Thereafter, the several large and small-scale incidents that the West came to know about were quelled with a brutality that had not been employed for a decade.

First came the heavy-handed and degrading treatment meted out to African students in the midst of racial disturbances, with an official front of indifference to international press coverage. Then in March 1989 came the atrocities and mass arrests in Tibet, unleashing a savagery against non-Chinese that foreshadowed the Beijing massacre against fellow Han.[47] Less known, but almost as ruthless, was the indiscriminate clubbing in Beijing's outer suburbs in early 1989 of a thousand peasants who were demonstrating over industrial poisons that endangered their crops; an unknown number died.[48] And in April 1989, according to an

[47] *The Asian Wall Street Journal* (29 Dec. 1988).
[48] *New York Times* (7 July 1988).

Amnesty International report, in Hebei province 4,000 policemen armed with electric batons descended upon a Catholic village of 1,700 people; more than 300 were injured, a hundred very seriously so, including the elderly and small children. Local hospitals were forbidden to treat them.[49] The description of the assault's savagery surpassed even those of the bulldozing of Crossroads and other black townships in South Africa. The villagers' only offence had been to insist on erecting a tent as a makeshift church. All these incidents, and possibly many others that never made it into the international press, were preludes to the machine-gunning of 4 June 1989. These precursors had been launched in a 'spirit' of brutal suppression from on high.

The Conflict of Spring 1989

The stage was set for major upheavals. Resentment against the rise of the new political monied élite was reaching explosive proportions. All that was needed was a catalyst. This was provided in April 1989 by the death of Hu Yaobang, the former CCP general secretary who had been ousted in January 1987. Hu's downfall, it was believed by many Chinese, had been largely due to two reasons: his attempts to initiate an anti-corruption campaign targeting the children of high-level officials, and charges by his enemies that he purportedly had fanned the flames of the student protests that year. Hu was actually far from being the liberalizer that he was made out to be, and the students knew it, but the myth of a righteous and liberal official served well the students' purposes when they began their protest actions. Hu, in death, could be mourned for his fall; the mass commemoration ceremonies for Hu on 22 April tacitly turned the spotlight on the CCP's unwillingness to tackle its own corruption or to tolerate peaceful dissent.

Within weeks, to the students' own surprise, they were joined by packed truckloads of industrial workers, flying banners that read 'Here come your elder brothers' and 'The workers are no longer silent'. Beijing's populace had been awaiting an opportunity to register its own protest: that common desire to protest gave

[49] *Amnesty International 'Urgent Action' News Release*, UA 117/89 (3 May 1989).

the different sectors of society a common cause. They all rallied under the students' banners opposing corruption and autarchy.

When the Beijing students tabled opposition to corruption as one of the original seven-point demands that they presented to the government, they included the stipulation that all officials should make public their own and their offsprings' assets and bank accounts. From beginning to end, there were never any calls from the students' organizations for the establishment of alternative or oppositional political parties, as had already been officially achieved in Poland and Hungary. The students' demands centred instead on calls for the CCP to live up to its own principles. On the face of it, the demands could be said to be non-threatening to the existing structure of the state. I would emphasize, however, that the banners raised against corruption signified a powerful hidden political agenda. It was not only an effort to humiliate and discredit the supreme powers-that-be at a very personal level. It was, more than that, an attempt to frustrate the solidification of a new kind of social class, the new political monied élite that the party leadership had been creating within the hybrid planned-free-market economic structure.

The second demand that brought the workers and the rest of the urban populace out into the streets in support of the students was that call for 'democracy'. By 'democracy' the students did not mean what the term normally implies in the West. It was not a call for elections based on universal suffrage. Very few intellectuals — not even the most famous of China's dissident political liberals, Liu Binyan and Fang Lizhi — wanted to see China's leaders selected by the 70 per cent of the population who are peasants. 'Democracy' instead holds several other potent meanings for the Chinese. To the students and intellectuals, it means the institutionalization of a more pluralist decision-making system, in which professional associations and independent commissions and forums comprised of intellectuals and specialists should help determine government policies. It means also the right to be safely at odds with the political leadership: an institutionalized right to speak up, a right to demonstrate, an independent press, the recognition of student associations independent from government control, and an independent judicial system safeguarded from the party leaders' commands.

'Democracy' also held a third connotation, one that excited

students and workers alike. For the past third of a century, urban residents had been at the mercy of the leadership at their work-units. To obtain a flat, to get travel permits, to get assigned to a good job when you graduated at university, or to switch employers later in life, even to get married or have a child, one had to curry favour with the various officials at one's all-powerful work-unit. Even in the 1980s, your life was at the mercy of a set of capricious bureaucrats. It was demeaning; it was suffocating. That potent word 'democracy' had begun to bear a meaning similar to 'freedom': freedom from all the petty restrictions and humiliations that were daily imposed. In April and May 1989, when the residents of Beijing and of other cities throughout China overcame their fears and poured into the streets in a vast sea that swept aside the forces of authority, they experienced an exhilaration of release, what they called 'liberation'. Some years ago, when I conducted interviews for a book on the Cultural Revolution, again and again people remembered having felt that same heady sense of 'liberation' in 1966–7 when they had first joined colleagues in casting free from subservience to their work-unit leadership.

Divisions under One Banner

The nation-wide protest movement on the face of it imprinted an image of great solidarity. Almost the entire populace of Beijing city had come out to support the students. All over the country protest actions rallied around the slogan of 'Support the Beijing students'. The rhythm of the provincial movements followed closely behind Beijing's, falling and rising with the same beat.[50]

Does this then connote that the social cleavages among the various groups had been bridged by a momentous emotionalism? To some extent this was indeed the case. The common enemy provided a force for cohesion. Yet even though large numbers of workers in Beijing and elsewhere poured into the streets in 1989 in support of the student protests, the students and intellectuals sought during the protest movement to keep them at arm's length.[51] The

[50] Jonathan Unger, ed., *The Pro-Democracy Process in China: Reports from the Provinces* (New York, 1991).

[51] See e.g. Anita Chan and Jonathan Unger, 'Voices from the Protest Movement, Chongqing, Sichuan', *Australian Journal of Chinese Affairs*, 24 (July 1990), 259–80;

spring of 1989, in short, witnessed a tenuous united front in which workers provided support for the demonstrators but received little in return. The students and intellectuals were intent on pursuing their own agenda in the protest movement, still almost oblivious to worker concerns. Their clamour for speedier economic reform, if anything, actually went against the interests of the workers. Organizationally, the students and workers had only a very loose working relationship on Tiananmen Square.[52] The workers and others, in fact, set up a separate broadcasting station to compete with the students in efforts to draw an audience. In the subsequent hunt for protest activists after the Beijing massacre, the worker activists were not linked up to the underground railway that the student leaders had pre-arranged with their Hong Kong pro-democracy movement supporters. One consequence was that the working-class activists have been the main casualties of the suppression — arrested, imprisoned, tortured, or executed. Not surprisingly, interviews that I conducted in Hong Kong and New York with post-massacre political refugees of working-class background revealed that they had felt deep resentments against the students and intellectuals both during and after the pro-democracy protests.[53]

The exiled students and intellectuals' vast outpouring of speeches, essays, and political treatises during 1989–90 barely recognized the role played by the workers and the ordinary people in the movement, nor paid tribute to the many who are still in jail or died for the cause. At the same time that six student and intellectual exile groups were negotiating an amalgamation, some fifty or so exiled worker activists set up their own separate 'China's Overseas Workers Autonomous Association'.[54] If the relationship between student-intellectuals and workers in exile reflects in any way the relationship of these social groups inside China proper, it would appear that the events of 1989 have, if anything, exacerbated the

also in Jonathan Unger, ed., *The Pro-Democracy Protests in China: Reports from the Provinces* (Armonk, NY, 1991); also see Anita Chan, 'Protest in a Hunan County Town: The Profile of a Democracy Movement Activist in China's Backwaters', in Unger, ed., *Pro-Democracy Protests*.

[52] This information was provided by a member of the Workers Autonomous Union who was in charge of broadcasting on Tiananmen Square.
[53] Also see *Zhengming* (Oct. 1988), 79–82; *Zhengjing Zhoukan* (*Hong Kong Herald*), 24 (19 May 1990), 12 and 23; *Shijie Ribao* (New York, 4 June 1990).
[54] *Zhengjin Zhoukan*, 24 (19 May 1990), 12.

distrust between them. The students and intellectuals do not seem to realize that for their cause to succeed they need to forge a united front with the workers and the rest of the Chinese people.

The ruling CCP octogenarians appear to recognize, better than the intellectuals, the importance of solidarity across class boundaries in any protest movement, and measures have been taken by the government to forestall such co-operation in future. As an initial step, in the months immediately after the Beijing massacre, Deng and the party's hard-liners revived the slogan 'dictatorship of the proletariat', the term that had been used to justify suppression of dissent under Mao in the name of the working class. 'Dictatorship of the proletariat' was, in particular, the rallying cry of the Cleansing of Class Ranks campaign of the late 1960s, arguably the most vicious campaign in the previous forty years of CCP rule, in which many tens of thousands of people died. During that campaign, vigilante workers' corps were mobilized to take control of universities and schools, and were called upon to ferret out and 'struggle against' a vast number of targeted victims.

The revival of this old tactic of divide and rule sought to woo back workers and to pit them and the peasants against the intellectuals. Though the CCP had lost the support of most workers, the former party faithful of past decades were still at the worksites, and many of them undoubtedly yearned for the status and power that they had enjoyed in those earlier campaigns of repression. As we have observed, moreover, they and their workmates had reasons to harbour resentments against intellectuals. Newspaper editorials during the autumn of 1989 began playing upon such sentiments among the workers, lashing out against the insensitivity of 'bourgeois liberal' intellectuals toward the working class.[55]

In addition, efforts were made to placate the work-force at the large state-owned factories in the major cities. During the campaign of economic retrenchment of 1989–90, the workers at these large strategically located factories were to be protected more than others. By government decision, lay-offs largely hurt workers in the collective and private sectors, particularly in the small cities and rural areas.

Having been blamed by protesters for turning a blind eye to

---

[55] *Cheng Bao* (27 Aug. 1989).

blatant corruption and to mounting economic and social chaos, the CCP also began making vigorous efforts to regain its long-lost image among the working classes as the party of morality and law and order. Alongside the political purge that followed the June massacre, it mounted a highly publicized crackdown against soft-core pornography, prostitution, gambling, and the much-despised alleged petty corruption of private vendors. But like all of the other anti-corruption campaigns of the 1980s, the party still had not mustered the will to sacrifice any big fish (high-level leaders or their children) to allay popular anger.

In all of these efforts to appeal to urban workers, the party leadership has seemed anxious to ward off a repetition of the nightmare that had haunted them in the spring of 1989: the potential of a grand coalition of intellectuals, students, vendors, and workers *à la* Solidarity. To a CCP leadership that for decades has based its legitimacy on its claims to represent the interests of the 'proletariat', the most frightening part of that nightmare was the mass participation by workers in Beijing and other cities. This goes far in explaining the post-massacre efforts to turn working-class opinion against the other groups, and equally explains the very harsh examples made of those workers who were bold enough openly to join independent workers' unions. As one exiled worker who had been a Cultural Revolution rebel and a 1980 democracy-wall protester related to me, 'the people the Communists are most scared of are not really the intellectuals, but those critics from among the workers who have intellectual ability'.

The CCP leadership's efforts simultaneously to appeal to and frighten workers are little more than desperate stop-gap measures to stave off in the short term another wave of worker unrest. But the longer term prospect of placating the populace rests ultimately with the success of economic reforms, which would need to be accompanied by a reasonably equitable redistribution of the nation's wealth.

Yet more than a year after the Beijing massacre, the economic programmes that have been implemented are not intended to resolve the basic problems inherent in the reform policies of the 1980s. Measures like slowing down the economy by tightening bank loans, plugging up tax loopholes for the private sector, and closing down inefficient rural industrial enterprises[56] provided

[56] *CD* (10 July 1990).

only marginal and temporary remedies – and had the effect of plunging the economy into a recession, raising unemployment, and further depressing wages. The long-term problems intrinsic to the reform package were not, in short, dealt with in any fundamental way. One of the most resented of these, of course, involved the self-enrichment of the political élite and its transformation through corruption into a hybrid monied–power élite.

Much of China expects another explosion within the next three or five years, once most of the octogenarians who today control China have died. The prospects for success of the next upsurge of protests will hinge on whether the several major social classes can forge a united front. Much depends on whether the students and their mentors take stock of their own failures and begin to reach out to working-class interests. At the same time, it is possible that the workers themselves will emerge as an independent force and join the students and intellectuals on an equal footing, just as they did during the Cultural Revolution of 1966–8. That was the last time social groups cut through class lines and coalesced in a grand alliance called the Rebel Faction.[57] Whether a similar coalition can be forged is one of the question marks hanging over China's future.

[57] For an elucidating interpretation of the socio-political nature of the Rebel Faction in the Cultural Revolution, the Yang Xiguan (alias Yang Xiaokai) 'Ping "Zhongguo Wenge Shinianshi" ' ('Appraising the Book "Ten Years of the Chinese Cultural Revolution" ') *Zhengming* (Aug. 1990), 69–75; Yang Xiaokai, 'Liusi Shengwu: Wei Wenge Zaofanpai fan'an' (The June 4 Reawakening: An Appeal to Reverse the Verdict on the Cultural Revolution Rebel Faction), *Zhongguo Zhi Chun* (Aug. 1990), 42–5.

6. China's Army, China's Future

HARLAN W. JENCKS

The calamitous events of 1989 saw senior leader Deng Xiaoping repeat many of the mistakes made by Mao Zedong in his declining years. Deng severely damaged the political arrangements with which he had hoped to assure a peaceful transition after his own death, and left the People's Liberation Army as the primary institution that will determine China's future.

Deng is not solely to blame. His hand was forced by the size of the increasingly disruptive demonstrations that were spawned by his reforms, and encouraged by his more progressive supporters. He and his fellow reformer, President Yang Shangkun,[1] were forced to accede to, and join with, a coterie of elderly hard-liners who had opposed Deng's reforms all along. Today, Deng is 'first among equals' in a 'gang of elders' including himself, Yang Shangkun, Li Xiannian, Yao Yilin, Chen Yun, Wang Zhen, Wan Li, and Peng Zhen. They have ultimate political authority, even over the Politburo of the CCP. The authority of this uneasy coalition is entirely extra-legal, based on personal prestige, influence, and patronage networks.

Deng's basic mistake, the one that Mao made before him, was that, although he wished the party to control the PLA, he used the military to buttress his own power and enforce his own policy preferences, overriding the party's internal decision-making and control mechanisms. This is ironic because, since his return to power in 1977, Deng has laboured, with limited success, to re-establish the organization and prestige of the CCP. He also attempted to mark out separate roles for the party, the PLA, and the government. These reforms implied that the military would no longer be used to settle political disagreements within the party. In the 1989 crisis however, the party failed to function as an institution, largely because Deng (the party's *de facto* maximum leader) opposed Zhao Ziyang (its legal leader). In some ways, Deng has done more institutional damage than Mao did. This time, the PLA, as well

---

[1] Yang Shangkun generally supported Deng's reforms throughout the 1980s. He was given overall responsibility for reforming military manpower and organization in 1983. Yuan Houqun, 'Brief Stories of the Chinese PLA Reorganization and Force Reduction Process', *Kunlun* (Mar.–Apr. 1987), 6–7.

as the government and party, is badly discredited. Urban Chinese are disillusioned and politicized to an extent not seen since the 1960s.

Virtually all students of civil–military relations agree that the strength of civilian political institutions is the crucial determinant of the character of civil–military relations.[2] Weak or unstable political systems spawn military praetorianism. A common syndrome in politically developing states is that when civilian political institutions (democratic or otherwise) become discredited, they are vulnerable to military penetration. Even a professional officer corps may intervene, regarding itself as the 'guardian' of national virtue.[3] By resorting to brute force in June 1989, Deng brought enormous discredit upon PRC political institutions, and increased his dependence on the army. That may have put the PLA officer corps in a position to question Deng and the 'gang of elders'.

Although the PLA has shown little sign of disloyalty or disobedience, Deng Xiaoping and Yang Shangkun have shown great concern about military loyalty since the Tiananmen incident. Their concern was reinforced by events in Romania in December 1989. The violent collapse of the Ceauşescu regime, especially the spectacle of security police fighting soldiers in the streets (with Chinese weapons), caused the old men in Zhongnanhai to become extremely concerned about the reliability of their own police and military forces.[4]

Especially since Romania, Deng and the 'gang of elders' have sought to reassert their authority with traditional 'Maoist' methods. They have tried to strengthen surveillance over society, government, and the army. They have instigated mass campaigns to indoctrinate the population and to strengthen the PLA's internal political control system. Ironically, like Mao in the early 1960s, Deng and Yang hold up the PLA as a political model for the rest of society, even as they strive to shore up PLA loyalty. The relation-

[2] Amos Perlmutter, *The Military and Politics in Modern Times* (New Haven, Conn., 1977), 9. The following discussion draws heavily on Samuel P. Huntington, *Political Order in Changing Societies* (New Haven, Conn., 1977), ch. 4.

[3] On 'guardianship', see Huntington, *Political Order* (see n. 2), 225–223. Perlmutter, *Military and Politics* (see n. 2), describes 'arbitrator' praetorianism in similar terms on pp. 104–7 and 141–4.

[4] *AFP* (Hong Kong, 27 Dec. 1989) reported a secret Politburo meeting on the Romanian situation. Also see Willy Wo-lap Lam, *South China Morning Post* (27 Dec. 1989). Both reports are reprinted in *FBIS-* China 89-247, p. 10.

ship of the PLA to the party is being recast in strongly Maoist terms. Lei Feng, the perennial PLA model hero, is once again held up for emulation.[5] 'Redness' is again regarded as more important for cadres than 'expertise'.[6]

Internal Security Forces

The 'gang of elders' have accorded unprecedented attention to China's internal security forces. The People's Armed Police (PAP) was specifically organized to maintain domestic security. PLA units have been converting into PAP for a decade. In almost every city except Beijing, it was PAP who restored order in June 1989. In the capital, however, the PAP was vastly outnumbered by demonstrators by the time authorities decided to act. At the time, there were about 500,000 PAP nationally, with perhaps fifteen regiments in Beijing municipality. Some PAP units did participate in the suppression on 3–4 June, but that was mainly a PLA operation. Between June 1989 and January 1990, several more division-sized units from various group armies in the Beijing area reportedly transferred to the PAP as well.[7]

The police also began to get more publicity. Pictures appeared showing them engaged not only in riot control training, but also in counter-terror exercises like hostage rescue. Élite PAP units were organized into 'shock attack units'. Such publicity was intended to improve the morale and image of the PAP while warning dissidents that the police were ready to deal with them in a no-nonsense fashion.[8] In early 1990, party authorities called for 'an anti-riot force system be set up at provincial, prefectural and key county levels', and for formation of special riot-control forces in all large cities.[9]

[5] *Xinhua* (24 Feb. 1990), in *FBIS* China 90–042, pp. 23–4; and *Xinhua Domestic Service* (6 Mar. 1990), in *FBIS* China 90–046, pp. 35–6.

[6] Wang Chenghan, 'Uphold the Party's Absolute Leadership over the Army with Great Firmness', *JFJB (Liberation Army News)* (18 Dec. 1989), 2, trans. in *FBIS* China 90–033-S, pp. 37–9; and Luo Yi, 'The Gun should be Put Firmly in the Hands of People Loyal to the Party', *JFJB* (13 Feb. 1990), 3, trans. in *FBIS* China 90–042, pp. 24–5.

[7] Nicholas Kristof, *New York Times* (15 Apr. 1990), A3.

[8] *JFJHB (Liberation Army Pictorial)*, 9 (Sept. 1989), 8–9; and *JFJHB* 10 (Oct. 1989), 26–7.

[9] *Tang Tai (Developments)* (Hong Kong), 14 (3 Mar. 1990), 7–8, trans. in *FBIS* China 90–046, p. 16.

In autumn 1989, as European communist regimes crumbled, military authorities in PRC coastal provinces expressed concern for the security of militia weapons storage installations, and instituted inspections and other measures.[10] The Standing Committee of the National People's Congress took up a 'Draft Law on Protection of Military Installations', which it passed in February 1990.[11] Several provincial governments decided to reinforce the PAP by establishing rapid-response militia and reserve detachments. These detachments were to set up a 'contingency system throughout the province with an emphasis on the coastal areas and cities'.[12] In December 1989, although Chinese public response to events in Romania was non-existent beyond a few college campuses, the central leadership reportedly placed PAP forces, plus eight group armies in the Beijing and Shenyang military regions, on maximum alert.[13]

On 5 February 1990 the governments of China's four main cities (Beijing, Tianjin, Shanghai, Canton) were delegated authority to declare martial law in the event of public disorder, and to use force without prior clearance from Beijing. In late February, the CCP Central Commission of Political Science and Law issued a circular calling for public security procuratorate and court systems to step up their suppression of dissent. The circular also called for better political intelligence work. Specifically, command centres of provinces, prefectures, and key cities were to be reorganized and reinforced. Anti-riot police forces and tactical units of the PAP were to be organized to struggle against 'sabotage, subversion, and infiltration'. The circular further called for strengthened ideological and political work in the PAP and in the public security forces.[14]

[10] Hangzhou Zhejiang Provincial Service (19 Dec. 1989), in *FBIS* China 89-247, p. 33; and Nanchang Jiangxi Provincial Service (6 Nov. 1989), trans. in *FBIS* China 89-219, p. 61.

[11] Xinhua (New China News Service) Domestic Service (22 Dec. 1989), trans. in *FBIS* China 89-247, p. 16; and *Renmin Ribao (People's Daily)* (24 Feb. 1990), 3, trans. in *FBIS* China 90-041, pp. 35-6.

[12] Hangzhou Zhejiang Provincial Service (27 Feb. 1990), trans. in *FBIS* China 90-043, p. 41; and *JFJB* (20 Jan. 1990), 2, trans. in *FBIS* China 90-033-S, pp. 39-40.

[13] Tai Ming Cheung, 'Haunted Dreams', *FEER* (18 Jan. 1990), 16-17.

[14] *Tang Tai*, 14 (see n. 9), 7-8.

Strengthening the 'Party's Absolute Control'

In late 1989, there were rumoured to be as many as 3,500 PLA and PAP commanders and commissars under investigation for alleged misbehaviour during the spring crisis. Few of them were formally charged, and most were expected to get off with reprimands for such activities as signing petitions, expressing sympathy with demonstrators, or opposing the use of violence. A few serious cases were dealt with quite sternly. The most important of these was Lieutenant General Xu Qinxian, former commander of 38th Group Army, who feigned illness to avoid commanding his troops in the armed suppression of the capital. Reportedly, Xu was court-martialled and imprisoned. In an address to army cadres in November 1989, General Political Department Chief Yang Baibing reportedly said that twenty officers at division level and above, and thirty-six officers at regimental and battalion level, were under investigation for serious crimes.[15]

Deng Xiaoping and the 'elders' were particularly dissatisfied with People's Armed Police performance during the 1989 crisis. Being mainly local people, some Beijing PAP units and commanders evidenced divided loyalties. Even before the traumatic example of Romania in December, the 'gang of elders' had been concerned that some PAP soldiers had openly supported the demonstrators in May and June.[16]

On 14 February 1990, *People's Daily* announced a major reshuffle of the People's Armed Police leadership. The commander, Lieutenant General Li Lianxiu, and the political commissar, Major General Zhang Xiufu, and their deputies were replaced by regular army officers. The new commander is Zhou Yushu, who commanded the 24th Group Army when it pacified Beijing's university district during the June crisis. The 24th Group Army reportedly did its job with better discipline and less violence than most other units.[17] The reshuffle resulted in the PAP having four deputy

---

[15] Tai Ming Cheung, 'Rank Insubordination', *FEER* (1 Feb. 1990), 22.

[16] Id., 'Security Reshuffle', *FEER* (1 Mar. 1990), 20; and *Tang Tai*, 10 (3 Feb. 1990), 8, trans. in *FBIS* China 90–033-S, pp. 31–2. I am grateful to Ellis L. Melvin for sharing his meticulous order-of-battle analysis of the 4 June incident (private correspondence, 5 Apr. 1990).

[17] *FEER* (22 Feb. 1990), 14; and Nicholas Kristof, *New York Times* (15 Apr. 1990), A3.

commanders instead of three, and two commissars instead of one, which tends to corroborate the reports of PAP expansion.

During the reshuffle, foreign reporters made much of the PAP being officially placed under the Central Military Commission (CMC). Actually, the CMC has always ultimately controlled the PAP.[18] Moreover, PAP units have long responded to military commanders at regional, provincial, and local levels. There is no evidence that CCP leaders intend to separate the PAP from the military, to create a countervailing force like the Soviet MVD and KGB troops.

When the Fifth Plenum of the Thirteenth Central Committee met from 6 to 9 November 1989, Deng Xiaoping resigned as chairman of the party CMC, and announced that he would resign as chairman of the State CMC during the National People's Congress session in March 1990. The plenum appointed Jiang Zemin as chairman; Yang Shangkun as first vice-chairman; Liu Huaqing, vice-Chairman; and Yang Baibing, secretary-general. Yang Baibing was also elevated to the secretariat of the Central Committee.[19] Following the plenum, from 10 to 12 November, there was an 'enlarged meeting' of the party CMC. As its name indicated, this meeting was attended by most of the high command, probably including all commanders and commissars down to at least group army level.[20]

In his 'farewell' speech, Deng called on the PLA to persist in 'revolutionization, modernization and regularization'. The reversed order of these three goals is significant. Before Tiananmen, 'regularization' was always listed first. Deng told senior officers that 'ours is an army of the Party, the socialist state, and the people, it should always remain loyal'.

Though Deng is officially retired, 'all participants agreed' that 'the theory and principles he raised for army building will be followed'.[21] The military hierarchy is not likely to accept Jiang

---

[18] Evidence of CMC control before 4 June is that Minister of Public Security Wang Fang, who theoretically supervises the PAP and is nominally PAP First Political Commissar, was not discredited along with 'his' troops. Wang remained in office, accompanying Premier Li Peng to Moscow in May 1990.

[19] 'Deng Retires, Jiang Appointed Military Chief', *BR* (20–6 Nov. 1989), 5–6.

[20] 'Deng Urges PLA to Stay Loyal', *BR* (27 Nov.–3 Dec. 1989), 9. The group picture of the CMC 'enlarged meeting' included at least 350 people. *JFJHB* 12 (Dec. 1989), 6–7.

[21] *JFJHB* 12 (Dec. 1989), 7.

Zemin as the 'core of the leadership'. He has virtually no authority or prestige within the military, so Deng will have to support him indefinitely. There was an almost plaintive tone in Deng's assertion that Jiang was the 'qualified chairman of the military commission because he is the qualified general secretary of the party'. Jiang Zemin called for the strengthening of the CCP's (read: Deng's and his own) 'absolute leadership over the army'. Party organs at all levels had to strengthen and improve ideological work 'in a bid to keep the army and the central committee united'.[22] Jiang's call for 'party building' was more than rhetorical. The party apparatus within the PLA really did deteriorate seriously during the 1980s; many CCP committees were little more than shells by 1989.

The CMC meeting allegedly directed that 70 per cent of PLA training time be devoted to politics.[23] An All-Army Political Work Conference convened on 11 December, and promulgated a document 'Concerning Certain Problems in Strengthening and Improving Political and Ideological Work in the Army Under the New Situation'. It cited the dangers of 'bourgeois liberalism' and 'peaceful evolution' which domestic and foreign 'anti-socialist elements' were trying to infiltrate into the PLA.[24]

A common practice in PRC politics is to have a major policy change announced by someone known to have opposed it.[25] So it was that Chief of the General Staff Chi Haotian, a leading proponent of military professionalization and modernization, enunciated the neo-Maoist view on party–army relations in a long *Qiushi* (the party's major theoretical journal) article in January 1990. General Chi emphasized that the PLA must 'ensure the party's absolute leadership over the army . . . this must be regarded as the most important task in the building of our army'.[26]

---

[22] Ibid. 9.

[23] Tai Ming Cheung, 'Rank Insubordination' (see n. 15), 22.

[24] *Renmin Ribao*, overseas edn. (18 Dec. 1989), 1; and *Tang Tai*, 6 (30 Dec. 1989).

[25] Examples include Liu Shaoqi's announcement of the Great Leap Forward in May 1958; Jiang Qing's denunciation of radical Red Guard violence on 5 Sept. 1967; and Hua Goufeng's presentation of the 'Resolution on Questions of Party History' to the 6th Plenum in June 1981.

[26] Chi Haotian, 'Strive to Raise the Leadership Level of the Party Committees, and Ensure the Party's Absolute Leadership Over the Army', *Qiushi (Seeking Truth)*, 2 (16 Jan. 1990), 2, trans. in *FBIS* China 90-046, p. 36. The article is based on a speech to political committee secretaries of the general staff.

Chi wrote, 'Under the new historical conditions of reform, opening up and modernization, the basic principle of the party's absolute leadership over the Army is seriously challenged by the major and minor climate both at home and abroad', including bourgeois liberalization. Bourgeois liberalization includes the notion of 'non-politicization of the army' and 'separation between the party and the army'. Such doctrines, according to Chi, were blindly copied from the bourgeois military theories of the West by a 'tiny number of people' influenced by Western thought. They were to blame for spreading the idea of weakening the party's absolute leadership. Chi reiterated the Marxist view that every army serves a particular class, and quoted a famous aphorism from his 1929 Gutian speech that 'political power grows out of the barrel of a gun. Our principle is that the party commands the gun, and the gun should never be allowed to command the party.'[27]

The PRC Constitution of 1982 created the State Central Military Commission. At the time, Premier Zhao Ziyang commented that it was necessary because 'the army is an important component of the state'.[28] This was a controversial position, advocated by reformers like Zhao, Hu Yaobang, and (presumably) Deng Xiaoping. It was opposed by many of the old revolutionaries who were forced to retire in the mid-1980s, but who have since re-emerged from the 'second line' leadership.[29]

Chi's *Qiushi* article addressed the matter of the 1982 Constitution, holding that, while the armed forces serve the people and the state, the Constitution also stipulates that the party leads the state and the people in all things. Therefore, the army is still ultimately the servant of the party. Those who argue that party and army should be separated, and the army depoliticized, are trying to 'sow discord between the army and the party'.[30] That assertion ignored the efforts Deng and the other reformers, including Chi Haotian himself, made through the 1980s to disengage party committees from the day-to-day affairs of state, army, and economic enterprises.

According to Chi, because the PLA is the greatest barrier to

[27] Ibid.

[28] *NHK-TV* (Tokyo), 4 June 1982 interview with Premier Zhao Ziyang.

[29] Ian Wilson and You Ji, 'Leadership by "Lines": China's Unresolved Succession', *Problems of Communism*, 39/1 (Jan.–Feb. 1990), 28–44.

[30] Chi Haotian, 'Strive to Raise' (see n. 26) 37.

those who would seize state power and destabilize China, the PLA faces a 'very complicated environment' and 'certain numbers of military men have been confused'. The remedy is reconstruction of the party committee system at all levels. It must ensure that the troops are kept fully in line with the central authorities, 'ideologically and politically and in their actions'.[31] Although party organizations are a 'unified nucleus of leadership and unity of the troops', they must carry out 'a scientific division of work. They are not allowed to assert their independence, or scramble for military power'. Thus, Chi reasserted the traditional division between political command and military command, personified in every PLA unit by the political commissar and the military commander.

As often happens in CCP literature, Chi skirted the real issue. Military loyalty to the CCP was never in question, but the decade of reforms and 'depoliticization' implied that the army would no longer be used as an instrument in intra-party factional conflict. Richard Latham observes that Chi could hardly admit that the real issue in 1989 was not 'seizure of state power', but of *party* power. When martial law was declared on 19 May the PLA, as a military force, was drawn into the internal CCP policy dispute, despite the objections of some senior active and retired soldiers. Chi's sermon on 'party control' obfuscated that real issue. Monte Bullard supports Latham's point from the PLA unit-level perspective: 'Separating party and army functions does not necessarily mean depoliticization of the army[,] nor does it mean any lessening of the degree of party control over the army.' On the contrary, 'it could mean a better relationship between commander and commissar because the commissar returns to doing what he was designed to do[,] which supports the commander. He ceases intermeddling in purely military decisions'.[32]

It is not clear whether the re-emphasis on political control and commissars will mean a return to the traditional political control functions of the General Political Department. Jonathan Pollack recently noted the emergence of the Discipline Inspection Commission of the party CMC. First identified in the press in 1988, this body may have assumed the political control functions

---

[31] Ibid. 38.
[32] Private correspondence with Richard Latham and Monte Bullard, July 1990.

previously associated with the GPD. Its increased visibility since June 1989 seems to confirm its role; and its secretary is Guo Linxiang, concurrently a deputy-director of the GPD.[33]

Chi Haotian devoted the longest part of his *Qiushi* article to the troublesome relationship between collective leadership, personified by the party organization and political commissar, on one hand, and the individual responsibility of commanders, on the other. In terms reminiscent of the early 1960s, he called upon military and political cadres to learn from each other and to train 'military cadres who are both red and expert'.[34]

In February, a *Liberation Army Daily* editorial called for 'stability, concentration and unification . . . to guarantee the important requirement that the Army will always be politically qualified'. This was necessary to 'smash the peaceful evolution conspiracy of hostile forces within and without the country . . . and for revolutionizing, modernizing and regularizing the army'.[35] The editorial thus confirmed the new order of priorities. 'Revolutionization' and especially 'political qualification' clearly are code words for supporting the party faction in power.

At the NPC session in March 1990, the new defence budget of RMB 28.97 billion was announced, up from the 1989 budget of RMB 25.1 billion. This was 11.4 per cent of the total national budget. Perhaps more important, it constituted a 15.2 per cent increase, compared to an overall increase of only 4.8 per cent in government spending.[36] This was the first real increase in military spending in almost ten years.[37] Over the past decade, there had been slight increases in renminbi amounts, but inflation caused an effective annual reduction of about 7 per cent. Since 1980,

---

[33] Jonathan D. Pollack, 'Structure and Process in the Chinese Military System' (30 Nov. 1989), unpubl. paper, p. 19.

[34] Chi Haotian, 'Strive to Raise' (see n. 26), 40.

[35] 'A Programmatic Document which Strengthens the Political Construction of Our Army', *JFJB* (28 Feb. 1990), trans. in *FBIS* China 90-041, pp. 32-3.

[36] Tai Ming Cheung, 'Political Payoff', *FEER* (5 Apr. 1990), 23-9. Cheung notes that 'Western intelligence agencies estimate that the Chinese defense budget based on Nato [sic] accounting methods would be 100 to 150 per cent above the official Chinese figure'. Also see *Ming Pao Yue Kan (Ming Bao Monthly)*, 286 (Oct. 1989), 3-15, trans. In *JPRS* CAR-90-005 (22 Jan. 1990), pp. 1-17; and *Wen Wei Po* (Hong Kong, 22 Mar. 1990), 2.

[37] The budget was RMB 20.96 bn. in 1987 and RMB 21.53 bn. in 1988. *Military Balance 1988-89* (London, 1989), 147; *Jane's Defense Weekly* (30 Apr. 1988), 819; and *Xinhua* (26 June 1988), trans. in *FBIS* China 88-123, pp. 32-3.

defence spending dropped from 15 per cent of GNP to less than 6 per cent.

It has been widely supposed that this defence budget increase was a reward for the Tiananmen massacre, or a bribe for continued PLA loyalty. If so, it was a miserly one. It is fairly clear how the money will be spent: PLA headquarters has already announced that a substantial part of it will be devoted to improving soldiers' living conditions. This was desperately needed before Tiananmen, and will be very costly, because of long neglect. Over the past decade, much of the real reduction in military spending has been borne by the rank and file. The PLA's severe lack of funds literally impoverished individual soldiers, depriving them of food, lodging, and services. Pay for soldiers and officers was raised for the first time in many years in 1988, but soldiers' pay still lags far below that of factory workers.[38] Individual and collective poverty lowered the prestige of the PLA and hampered recruitment and retention. Units could not conduct proper training because they expended their time and energy on self-sufficiency production and commercial enterprises.

PLA regulations prohibit individuals from engaging in business while encouraging units to do so. The boundary between the two is unclear however, and legal guidance is vague. By mid-1988, discipline and morale were suffering in a climate of semi-official bribery, profiteering, and 'bureaucratic racketeering'. Because of their financial plight, PLA units were vulnerable to local authorities and state enterprises, which extorted illegal taxes and fees for goods, services, and real estate.[39] The 'Draft Law on Protection of Military Installations' of February 1990 was intended, in part, to address this situation.

Another budgetary priority is the shift to internal security forces. More units are being moved to larger cities; riot-control gear and associated equipment are being purchased. Since 1986, the PLA has expended disproportionate resources on selected units designated for 'rapid response' in 'limited war' situations. Some of these

---

[38] *Jane's Defense Weekly* (28 Jan, 1989), 187; and *CD* (27 June 1988), 3, in *FBIS China 88-124*, p. 23.

[39] Harlan W. Jencks, 'Organization and Administration in the PLA in the Year 2000', in Richard Yang, ed., *SCPS PLA Yearbook, 1988/89* (Sun Yat-sen Center for Policy Studies, National Sun Yat-sen University; Kaohsiung, Taiwan, publ. in the US by Lynne Rienner Publishers), 52–4.

units are supposed to be 'high-tech', and are quite expensive.[40] They continue to enjoy priority, because they are also useful for internal security missions. As already noted, rapid-response militia and reserve detachments have been ordered to set up 'contingency systems' in coastal areas and cities, explicitly for both 'limited war' and for internal police missions.[41] As a July 1989 *Liberation Army Daily* article pointed out, 'suppressing class enemies' remains a primary PLA mission.[42]

Minimal improvement in military living conditions, plus expenditures on the expanded PAP and dual-mission (internal security and limited war) rapid-response forces will leave little of the budget increase for anyone else. Naval construction continues modestly — also for 'limited war' in the South China Sea. The air force, most of the ground forces, and even the nuclear forces, are unlikely to see their budgets increase much.[43]

As spring 1990 conscription work began, Shanghai Radio announced that conscripts would undergo stringent examination of their political and educational training. It added darkly that, 'Those who refuse to answer or evade conscription and those citizens who obstruct conscription work will be punished according to . . . regulations'.[44] A circular of 'Central Commission of Political Science and Law', directed that in this year's conscription work

. . . special attention must be given to strictly prevent being inducted into the army those who supported or participated in the Beijing turmoil and counter-revolutionary rebellion; unlawful elements who beat, smash, loot and burn people or things; and those imbued with serious bourgeois liberalized thinking or who harbor dissatisfaction with the [party] and the socialist system.[45]

[40] Ibid. 47–9.

[41] Hangzhou Zhejiang Provincial Service (27 Feb. 1990); and *JFJB* (20 Jan. 1990), 2.

[42] Li Fengho and Li Wenhua, 'Reinterpretation of the Army's Status and Function in a Period of Peace', *JFJB* (14 July 1989), 3.

[43] Three months after the increased budget was announced, the Air Force cancelled the next phase of its biggest and most prized foreign technology contact, the F-811 fighter upgrade by the US Grumman Corporation. While political factors obviously were important, industry observers widely identified the high cost of the programme as a major factor in the cancellation. I would argue that economic cost was the *main* reason. There was great political advantage to keeping the F-811 programme going, as a 'foot in the door' of the American defence establishment in the aftermath of Tiananmen.

[44] Shanghai City Service (7 Feb. 1990), in *FBIS* China 90-043, pp. 38–9.

[45] Quoted in *Tang Tai*, 14 (see n. 9), 8.

The Beijing garrison commander, Lieutenant General Yan Tongmao, was replaced in July 1989. A routine reshuffle of Military Region (MR) commanders, due at the end of 1989, was delayed until April–June 1990, evidently to avoid upsetting an already touchy situation. Never publicly announced, the reshuffle began quietly in April, and was only reported by the Hong Kong press in mid-June.[46] At the time of writing, details are still unclear. Six of the seven MR commanders and five of the seven political commissars were transferred or retired. Three commanders simply rotated to command different MRs. The Beijing MR commander (Lieutenant General Zhou Yibing) and political commissar (General Liu Zhenhua) were replaced. These two, and several other changes, appeared to be reward or retribution for 4 June. Some transfers were said to enhance the power of the 'Yang family gang' led by President Yang Shangkun and General Yang Baibing. On the other hand, some of the changes appeared routine, notably the retirement of such old men as Navy Political Commissar Admiral Li Yaowen (72) and National Defence University Political Commissar General Li Desheng (74).

The Chinese Officer Corps

After ten years of reform, the PLA officer corps was far more professionalized in early 1989 than ever before. It obeyed orders in the expectation that the orders would be legal, and had largely withdrawn from factional politics. Alan P. L. Liu has noted the absence, by all accounts, of PLA involvement in the 'crisis management' of April–June 1989.[47] Once the hard-liners won the power struggle, authority clearly was established at the top and Chinese officers, almost unanimously, obeyed their orders — even though they were not the orders most would have wished.

While the officer corps has a major stake in economic and technical reform, it perceives little or no stake in political or social reform. Quite the contrary. Like professional military officers

[46] 'Deng Xiaoping Gives Yang Baibing Military Power', *Cheng Ming (Contending)* (Hong Kong, June 1990), 14–17; Tai Ming Cheung, 'Stars and Bars', *FEER* (14 June 1990), 32; *China Post* (Taipei, 14 June 1990), 1.

[47] Alan P. L. Liu, 'Aspects of Beijing's Crisis Management: The Tian'anmen Square Demonstration', *Asian Survey*, 30/5 (May 1990), 505–21.

everywhere, most PLA officers want social and political stability. They and their families are a favoured élite, and most want to keep it that way. They only want modernizing change in the economy, industry, science, and technology. Like other Chinese élites over the past century and a half, many do not recognize the inevitable connections between modern political and social forms and modern technical methods.

The overwhelming majority of PLA officers support the Four Basic Principles.[48] In 1989 they disapproved of dissident activity in the streets of their cities. Like military officers elsewhere, they regard social upheaval as dangerous to national security and shameful to national honour. In this, the officer corps probably mirrors the majority of the PRC population, who deeply fear chaos.[49] It was particularly galling to see the leader of the Soviet Union come to Beijing on a day when Tiananmen Square was so filled with demonstrators that he had to enter the Great Hall of the People by the back door. Still worse, the mob hailed Gorbachev, a foreigner, as a hero.

About 17 May 1989, 150 active and retired senior PLA commanders reportedly submitted a letter to Deng Xiaoping and the CMC. They declared that the PLA should not spill the people's blood.[50] Signatories reportedly included Defence Minister Qin Jiwei and Chief of the General Staff Chi Haotian. Others included former Chief of Staff Yang Dezhi, former Defence Minister Zhang Aiping, former Navy Commander Ye Fei, former Logistics Director Hong Xuezhi, and former Commandants of the Higher Military Academy Sun Shilun and Xiao Ke. On 21 May, following declaration of martial law, the two surviving marshals of the PLA, Xu Xiangqian and Nie Rongzhen, published statements calling for civil order, but saying the PLA should not resort to force.[51] Both the letter and the old marshals' statements were explicit rejoinders

---

[48] The Four Basic Principles are (1) uphold the socialist road, (2) uphold Marxism-Leninism-Mao Zedong Thought, (3) uphold the people's democratic dictatorship, and (4) uphold communist party leadership.

[49] On the Chinese aversion to *luan*, see Lucian W. Pye, *The Dynamics of Chinese Politics* (Cambridge, Mass., 1981).

[50] The reputed contents of the letter were broadcast over 'the Tian'anmen Square broadcasting station of the student hunger strikers' on 18 May. That version was summarized in *Zhongguo Tongxun She* (Hong Kong, 18 May 1989), trans. in *FBIS China* (89–095), pp. 38–9.

[51] *Wenhui Bao* (Shanghai, 21 May 1989), 1.

to Deng's 24 April three 'Don't Be Afraid' statements: 'Don't be afraid of domestic reactions, don't be afraid of foreign opinion, and don't be afraid of bloodshed'.[52]

In June 1989, the Western press spread its own wishful thinking that parts of the PLA were 'liberal', that they favoured the demonstrators and agreed with their political views. That was simply not true. There is a vast difference between hesitating to murder people in the streets and agreeing with their political objectives. A majority of PLA officers disapproved of clearing the streets with brute force, because that would escalate the disorder and discredit the army, but they also disapproved of the demonstrations.

The officer corps is far from homogeneous of course. Age, experience, organizational affiliation, and rank form particularly significant divisions. The military reforms of the 1980s regularized PLA command arrangements and personnel assignment to a significant degree, ending practices like multiple office-holding and lifetime tenure, and reducing the importance of personal patronage and connections. Progress was most marked at the lower levels of command. Nearer the top, at and above group army level, 'China's military command arrangements still seem an uneasy mix of personalistic and professional considerations. The closer to the acme of the system, the less command derives from specified rules and norms'.[53]

At the topmost level of military command in the CMC, we still find, as we have for decades, the elder generation of revolutionary leaders. To label them 'military' or 'civilian' is misleading. Deng Xiaoping, Yang Shangkun, Wang Zhen, Chen Yun, and the rest, have been both military and civilian leaders most of their lives. They are revolutionaries, to whom such institutional identifications do not apply. The same is true of Defence Minister Qin Jiwei, who joined the Red Fourth Front Army at the age of 15 in 1929.[54] At the next level down, the heads of the PLA general departments, the same can be said of Yang Baibing, the General Political Department's director. He joined the Red Army in 1938

---

[52] Lucian W Pye, 'Tian'anmen and Chinese Political Culture: The Escalation of Confrontation from Moralizing to Revenge', *Asian Survey*, 30/4 (Apr. 1990), 338.

[53] Pollack, 'Structure' (see n. 33), 31.

[54] Zhao Wei, 'Qin Jiwei: Focal Person in Chinese Military', *Jiushi Niandai (The Nineties)*, 238 (Nov. 1989), 59–61, trans. in *JPRS CAR-90-005* (22 Jan. 1990), pp. 77–81.

and served throughout the liberation war, and subsequently, as a political commissar.[55] Chief of Staff Chi Haotian, on the other hand, joined the Eighth Route Army in June 1944, at the age of 16, and ended the civil war as an assistant squad leader. It was only during the Korean War that he distinguished himself and began his rapid rise through the ranks.[56]

There are still elderly revolutionary leaders in uniform. Of the seventeen officers awarded the rank of full general in September 1988, only Chi Haotian, Chief of the General Logistics Department Zhao Nanqi, and Air Force Commander Wang Hai are in their early 60s. The other 14 are now in their 70s.[57] As noted above, at least three of them, Liu Zhenhua, Li Yaowen, and Li Desheng, were retired in 1989–90. In the next few years, we can expect to see the incapacitations or deaths of many more. We will also see the death or incapacitation of the 'gang of elders' who sit at the unofficial political pinnacle.

Undoubtedly, there is a major power struggle going on in the upper reaches of the party — another 'pre-mortem succession struggle' like the one during Mao's last decade.[58] We simply do not know who, if anyone, among top PLA generals, could discuss a *coup d'état* with another general without fear of betrayal.[59] Presumably, Deng and the 'gang of elders' do not know either. If and when they even suspected such a pair of generals, they would try to remove at least one of them. It is especially hard for foreign observers to guess at such things, because of the success of the 1980s reform in promoting relatively young officers into the high command. We just do not have the biographical data we had on the older revolutionaries.

Another issue, of course, is which generals are allied with which members of the 'gang of elders'. That is somewhat easier to guess

[55] Jin Bo, 'All PLA Commanders in Chief were Political Commissars: Enigma of Yang Baibing's Experience Revealed', *Kuang Chiao Ching (Wide Angle)*, 204 (16 Sept. 1989), 88–9, trans. in JPRS-CAR-90-005 (22 Jan. 1990), 82–4.

[56] Chao Wei, 'Chinese Communist Chief of Staff Chi Haotian and the 27th Army', *Ming Bao Yue Kan*, 286 (Oct. 1989), 16–21, trans. in JPRS-CAR-90-005 (22 Jan. 1990), 69–74.

[57] Chen Ruixia, 'China's Generals are Aging; Succession Question Attracts the Attention of Many', *Kuang Chiao Ching*, 205 (16 Oct. 1989), 22–23, trans. in JPRS-CAR-90-005 (22 Jan. 1990), 68–9.

[58] Lowell Dittmer coined this apt term.

[59] Roderick MacFarquhar raised this question in discussing an earlier version of this paper.

at – and speculating about it is a minor industry in Hong Kong and Taipei. This brings us to the widely remarked on 'Yang family gang'. Recently, a Hong Kong magazine asserted that the whole PLA is now divided between the Yangs and the 'anti-Yangs'.[60] Clearly, President Yang Shangkun (also CMC first vice-chairman) and his half-brother, GPD Director Yang Baibing (also CMC secretary general) are extremely powerful men, with an extensive network of supporters. Yang Baibing is in a particularly powerful position to control PLA personnel actions, and some of the spring 1990 reassignments seemed to strengthen his hand further. Contrary to speculation, however, the 27th Group Army probably is not commanded by a son-in-law, and the Yangs are not related to Chief of Staff Chi Haotian.[61] Chi, CMC Vice-Chairman Liu Huaqing, and especially Defence Minister Qin Jiwei, are generally said to be 'anti-Yangs'.

Below the generals are field-grade officers (majors, lieutenant colonels, colonels, and senior colonels) who entered the PLA in the 1950s and 1960s, and today command battalions, regiments, and divisions. As the 1980s reforms emphasized formal education, and because of increased rotation and reassignment, they are better educated than more senior officers, and their regional identifications are somewhat weaker.

The world over, field-grade officers are the most politically volatile. Most of the PLA aircraft defections over the past decade have been flown by field-grade pilots. On 29 July 1989, a PLA major and his wife defected at Panmunjom, Korea. Field grades defect most often for the same reason they are politically dangerous: they are too junior and too numerous to be totally controlled or co-opted; but senior enough to have access to information and significant military resources, including airplanes, weapons, and personally loyal troops.

Generally, PLA field-grade officers are disciplined and obedient, and want social stability. But they are frustrated by the PRC's

---

[60] 'Deng Xiaoping' (see n. 46), 14–17.

[61] I have seen at least four reputed names for the elusive 'commander Yang' of the 27th Army (Yang She, Yang Jianhua, Yang Shaojun, as well as Yang Baibing), but cannot confirm even the existence of any of them. The 27th was commanded by Qian Guoliang in Sept. 1988. Chi Haotian has explicitly denied any family relationship with the Yangs. His wife is Jiang Qingping, a naval medical officer. (See PLA literature, Aug. 1988.) I am grateful to Ellis L. Melvin for drawing this to my attention.

persistent poverty and backwardness, and resent the pervasive corruption that led to last year's unrest. The post-Tiananmen situation has increased their dissatisfaction for a variety of reasons.

First, and perhaps most important, the prestige of the army was irreparably damaged by the massacre of citizens in the streets of Beijing. The special trust and empathy between the PLA and the people, which persisted through decades of economic and political turmoil, is gone. The officers who must lead the PLA into the future resent that deeply, for China's defensive strategy of last resort—'people's war'—is now problematic. They also resent the suspicion and paranoia their top leaders have directed at them. Further, they resent that after ten years of promises, technical modernization has been further (needlessly) delayed by foreign sanctions and the shifting of limited resources to the police.

In response to this situation and their own dissatisfaction, most field-grade officers will trim their sails to the political winds, as they have before. However, one of the great benefits of the 1980s reforms was a relative absence of political campaigns, which Deng had repeatedly promised would cease. Even more than civilians, soldiers must resent having to resume political play-acting, since they live in a disciplined milieu where participation is stringently enforced.

Many field-grade officers have been frustrated at the slow pace of modernization. The tragic events of 1989 exacerbated that frustration. These 'frustrated modernizers' have much in common with the dissatisfied officers who have taken over the governments of other unstable, corrupt, developing countries. For the first time in PLA history, it is conceivable that a few officers may actually be contemplating *coups d'état*. Military *coup* is against PLA traditions, and is still quite unlikely, but it is now conceivable, as it never was before.

Frustrated Modernizers

Field-grade PLA officers were junior leaders during the Great Proletarian Cultural Revolution, which was a memorable and thoroughly unhappy experience. They remember being pulled away from military duties and thrust into radical politics; and

how the PLA was divided against itself and fell to fighting.[62]
They are now in their late 40s and 50s, and are better educated
than their military superiors. Like the frustrated intellectuals,
bureaucrats, and others who went into the streets last spring, the
PLA's 'frustrated modernizers' have been strongly affected by the
'information revolution'. They know or suspect the truth about
what happened in China and in Eastern Europe in 1989. They are
aware of the outside world, aware of China's backwardness, aware
that things can be better, aware that Marxism-Leninism is a moribund ideology. They understand who was demonstrating in China's
streets and why. While they do not sympathize with taking protest
to the streets, they understand why it happened. They too suffer
from inflation and corruption. But they are also extremely patriotic.
Above all, they want to see a strong, secure, united China take
its rightful leading place in the world.

The 'frustrated modernizers' generally agreed with Zhao Ziyang's
view that the PLA would best serve the state (and the party) by
disengaging from political infighting. They supported, and benefited from, the technical and professional reforms of the 1980s.
As their technical expertise increased, they took less interest in
politics, both because they lacked the time and because it seemed
safe to leave politics to civilians. Party and state leaders consistently
assured them, and everybody else, that reform policies would not
change. Among these men, there was a tremendous increase, from
1978 to 1989, in Huntington's three aspects of military professionalism: professional expertise, a sense of professional responsibility to the state, and an increasing self-awareness of the officer
corps as a corporate entity. Officer corps corporateness is identified
by Perlmutter, Huntington, and most other observers as one of
the critical aspects of civil–military relations.[63]

---

[62] Harlan W. Jencks, *From Muskets to Missiles: Politics and Professionalism in the Chinese Army, 1945–81* (Boulder, Colo., 1982), ch. 4.

[63] Samuel P. Huntington, *The Soldier and the State* (New York, 1957), 13; Perlmutter, *Military and Politics* (see n. 2), p. xv; Jaques van Doorn, 'Political Change and the Control of the Military', in J. van Doorn, ed., *The Military Profession and Military Regimes* (Paris and the Hague, 1968), 22–3. Pollack notes an increased 'felt need for autonomy' among PLA officers by 1989 ('Structure' (see n. 33), 2).

The Authority Crisis

In April–May 1989, while the party leadership was paralysed by internal divisions, the situation in the streets got out of hand. No one acted while the demonstrations were still manageable. The military high command avoided taking sides in the political debate, and apparently hesitated to obey (possibly contradictory) orders from *ad hoc* or irregular sources. To that extent, we saw the results of the professionalizing trend of the 1980s. There were instances of PLA and PAP commanders refusing orders from the supposedly retired 'proletarian revolutionaries of the older generation' who took *de facto* control in late May. A few days before martial law was declared, a rumour had it that a PAP commander in Beijing had refused to suppress the demonstrations because the order was illegal. Lieutenant General Xu of 38th Group Army demurred and then resigned, partly for the same reason. These incidents speak volumes about the 1980s reforms. Raising the issue of legality (i.e. the formal chain of command) would not have occurred to any Chinese a decade ago. It was one of several ways in which senior soldiers tried to keep out of the debate, and out of the political arena, but they were pulled in, and forced to commit themselves.

Fully developed professionalism (military, medical, legal, or whatever) is impossible in a Leninist state. It involves professional autonomy, which implies social–political pluralism, which even Zhao Ziyang rejected. However, I emphasize that the level of military professionalism did increase markedly during the decade of reform. The PLA would not have obeyed as well, nor closed ranks so quickly, in June–July 1989, if it had been as factionalized and regionalized as it was before 1979. Today's civil–military crisis is shaped by that increased relative level of military professionalism. As in the Cultural Revolution, however, the PLA ultimately intervened on behalf of the maximum leader, not the party. Naturally, that cannot be admitted openly, so the official version of 4 June speaks of wavering PLA loyalty to the party and of ideological contamination.

If nothing else, the rhetoric that came with a decade of military reform created an expectation that orders to the military would become regularized, legal commands. There was a sense among many PLA officers that factional, political exploitation of the PLA was a thing of the past.

For some . . . the events surrounding the June 4 Incident created considerable confusion about the command mechanism that shifts the PLA from political participation to an intervening military force.[64]

The military reforms were supposed to remove the PLA from factional politics, but in May–June 1989 that aspect of political institutionalization, like so many others, failed. It is hardly surprising, since it was the two main architects of the military reforms (Deng Xiaoping and Yang Shangkun) who reverted to *ad hoc* authoritarianism during the crisis. The 1980s reforms tried to reconcile irreconcilables: a Leninist vanguard party and regularized procedures, 'absolute party control' and military professionalism.[65] A Marxist-Leninist party is defined by its 'correct line', whereas 'seeking truth from facts' implies tolerance, multiple truths, pluralism, and compromise. In the 1989 crisis, Deng and Yang — who are still Marxist-Leninists — refused to compromise and repudiated regularized procedures.

Jonathan Pollack identifies specific examples of irregular or arbitrary procedures that confused military command and control during the 1989 crisis.[66] They included 'the non-utilization of available procedures' and 'the intrusion of leaders without formal military responsibility (in particular, Premier Li Peng and the leadership of the Beijing Municipal People's Government) into armed forces channels'. Deng Xiaoping, chairman of the CMC, seems not to have participated in key military decisions. Still more striking was 'Deng's need for direct consultations with military region commanders in Wuhan, presumably to assure compliance with directives issued in the name of the CMC' and his 'extraordinary action of redeploying troop units from . . . other military regions' to Beijing and its environs. Martial law authorities relied principally on main force units and strategic reserves, betraying their doubts about the political loyalties and discipline of some Beijing-based PLA and PAP units. Moreover, Zhao Ziyang, supposedly the 'leader' of the CMC,[67] was excluded from decision-

[64] Richard J. Latham, 'China's Party Army Relations after June 1989: A Case of Miles' Law?', unpubl. paper (July 1990), p. 18.

[65] Kenneth Jowett prompted my thoughts on this issue.

[66] The following is drawn from Pollack, 'Structure' (see n. 33), 46–8. I have offered my own detailed analysis of the 1989 crisis in Harlan W. Jencks, 'The Losses in Tian'anmen Square', *Air Force*, 72/11 (Nov. 1989), 62–6; and id., 'The Military in China', *Current History*, 88/539 (Sept. 1989), 265–8, 291–3.

[67] In June 1988, Deng told a Polish delegation that 'the Central Military Commis-

making after 19 May, which seems to have been the basis for several commanders' questions about the legality of orders.

In retrospect, 'confusion' seems to be the single word that best characterizes the Tiananmen tragedy — confusion, both real and perceived, about who commanded the army, and how, at the pinnacle of political power. 'Some party apologists have laid the blame at the feet of individual PLA officers. There is reasonable cause to conclude, however, that the bedrock problem is *how the party commands the gun*.'[68] There was never any question about the PLA's loyalty to what Latham calls the CCP as 'party of policy'. Official post-hoc commentary, by focusing on the 'party-commands-the-gun' issue, has glossed over the dangerously flawed command and control system at the military–political apex. The 'party-in-command theme implies there was an element of confusion, a lack of discipline, or a failure to comply with orders',[69] so the 'legality' of orders may not have been exactly, or solely, the problem. Rather, the problem seems to have been confusion about the command relationship(s) between and among the topmost organs of the party and the PLA.

'Regardless of which group prevailed in the power struggle in . . . 1989, neither the reform group nor the hardliners can be comfortable with the actual or rumoured command relationship between the party and army. At best, it is messy.' We do not know, and quite possibly nobody in China knows, just what is the 'accepted or legal military chain of command at the top of the national command structure'. The most fundamental 'party–army question arising from [the Tiananmen crisis] was "Who in the party controls the army?" rather than "Does the party control the army?" '[70] Closely related questions are 'How is control exercised, and through what channels?'

After the retirement of Deng and the elders from their formal party and state positions to the 'second line', there was a mismatch between actual and formal authority. Deng and the elders retained the former, while the latter lay with Premier Li Peng

---

sion is now under the leadership of Comrade Zhao Ziyang'. *Zhongguo Xinwen She (China News Publishers)* (7 June 1988), trans. in *FBIS* China (8 June 1988), p. 8.

68 Latham, 'Party Army Relations' (see n. 64), 21 (emphasis in original). This section draws heavily on Latham's analysis.

69 Ibid. 3.

70 Ibid. 17.

and Party Secretary Zhao Ziyang. That mismatch inevitably affected national-level military command and control. That would have caused problems even during an external military crisis. In an intra-party factional clash, it must have resulted in confusing and even contradictory orders coming from multiple sources. 'We have no way of knowing how even the best intentioned PLA and CCP leaders understood the political manœuvering in early June [1989].'[71]

Foreign reportage during the 4 June incident was clouded by rumours and reports of opposition to PLA action by old military leaders, disobedience of some officers, claims that troops abandoned their weapons and equipment, armed clashes between 'loyal' and 'disloyal' units. These, and other reports, probably created a good deal of confusion within the top levels of the political leadership as well, adding to their misgivings about PLA loyalty and discipline.[72]

For most of this century, politics in China has been a zero-sum game, and top CCP leaders still think in terms of solving political problems with military force. Some still regard control of the military as necessary not only to protect the party, but to protect individual party leaders and policy positions. Events in Eastern Europe reinforced that belief. Inevitably, military and political power are inextricably mixed at the top of the party. Therefore, even if there are formal rules about the chain of command, in crisis, and even routinely, there is dependence on *guanxi* and factional alliances.[73]

Because of these factors, some analysts argue that the PLA's political role varies with the political situation: It is quiescent in normal political times, but intervenes, or is used to intervene, in times of political conflict.[74]

The logic is reasonable, but glosses over the institutional difficulties the PLA encounters shifting among these disparate situations. The point is

---

[71] Ibid. 17 and 18.

[72] Ibid. 16.

[73] Ibid. 22. Seventeen years ago, William Parrish made essentially the same point in his critique of the 'field army elites thesis'. See William L. Parish, 'Factions in Chinese Military Politics', *China Quarterly* 56 (Oct.–Dec. 1973), 667–99.

[74] Latham, 'Party Army Relations' (see n. 64), 12, cites Eberhard Sandschneider as making this argument in his 'Military and Politics in the PRC', in June Teufel Dreyer, ed., *Chinese Defense and Foreign Policy* (1989), 346–7.

not that the PLA has not played such roles, but that the shifts are neither routine nor easily accomplished, the role changes have been controversial and divisive for the PLA . . . [A]n increasingly professionalized army has a more sharply defined sense of missions. The missions cannot be quickly changed because they are more directly linked to force structure and weapons than to policy. *What the June 4 Incident reveals is that many of the party's leaders were unaware of how force modernization constrains political employment options.*[75]

Despite their reservations about the wisdom of their orders, and about the *ad hoc* authority of the 'gang of elders', the vast majority of PLA officers obeyed. It certainly was not a 'military takeover'. They went into the streets, and did what they were ordered to do. They recognized that a unified, disciplined, national army enforcing bad policy is better than a divided army at war with itself, even for the best of reasons. But many officers resent being cast as the instrument of repression, and being thrust back into factional politics.

PLA officers are no more fooled than anyone else when they are told that reform and openness continue. They are aware of the degree of active and passive popular resistance. They know the party no longer commands the fear and awe which allowed it to crack down so often in the past. Instead of party authority, there is now just power. Worst of all, the 'gang of elders' destroyed the respect and affection the people held for the PLA, even after the abuses of the Cultural Revolution and the less-than-glorious war with Vietnam.

The Future

There is a widespread perception among informed Chinese, and surely too in the officer corps, that the party leadership is in disarray, preoccupied with infighting. Whether by design or owing to confusion, the 'gang of elders' seemed to overreact to events in the streets of Beijing, and then to events in Romania. Such overreaction implies a sense of insecurity. So do the shake-up in the CMC, the purge of the People's Armed Police, the strengthened internal repression, and the Maoist-style indoctrination campaigns.[76]

---

[75] Latham, 'Party Army Relations' (see n. 64), 12 (emphasis added).

[76] In a recent paper, Arthur Ding identifies still another set of ideological contradictions for the PLA. He outlines the arguments used by PRC military thinkers

Many of the old verities about the PLA, and PRC politics in general, no longer apply, for 1989 changed things profoundly. The urban intelligentsia, workers, and commercial classes, with overseas Chinese, have made China's twentieth-century revolutions. Among these informed Chinese, the CCP was terribly discredited, and Marxism-Leninism (to say nothing of Mao Zedong Thought) was discredited all over the world. China's revolutionary fervour has burnt out, replaced by pervasive cynicism.

It is probably premature to write the CCP off, because the rural masses seem to have been fairly indifferent towards the 'democracy movement', and some believe the official story of a 'counter-revolutionary riot'. The party's themes of 'restoring order' and 'suppressing chaos' appeal to the deep-seated Chinese fear of chaos. Still, it is difficult to overstate the impact of the 'information revolution', even in the countryside.

In the aftermath of Tiananmen, even the eight million or so members of the CCP *nomenklatura* seem to be in some disarray. By contrast, the collective cohesion and discipline of the one million or so PLA officers remains solid. The officer corps 'also has material resources, an organizational structure that does not atrophy, weapons, and unmatched technical capability for command'.[77] By default, the officer corps is likely to determine China's future, because it is by far the most unified, disciplined, and authoritative national institution.

As Deng Xiaoping and the 'gang of elders' die off, the succession will be messy, if not chaotic. Led by Deng himself, the elders have destroyed the institutions Deng created to smooth the transition. Moreover, they have removed Zhao Ziyang, the only 'pure civilian' leader to have won a degree of PLA acceptance. So, what will happen when the old men die? In order of likelihood, here are three plausible scenarios:

---

to explain why a global great power war has become unlikely, noting the explicit and implicit divergence from orthodox Marxism-Leninism involved in these factors. The whole notion of global interdependence, for one example, contradicts Lenin's theory of imperialism as the 'highest form of capitalism'. See Arthur S. Ding, 'War in the Year 2000: Beijing's Perspective', a paper presented to the 19th Sino-American Conference on Mainland China, Institute of International Relations, Taipei, Taiwan, 13 June 1990.

[77] Latham, 'Party Army Relations' (see n. 64), 22. On the *nomenklatura*, see John P. Burns, *The Chinese Communist Party's Nomenklatura System* (1989).

1. The PLA as 'Guardian' and 'Kingmaker'

Under this, the most likely scenario, civilian succession would be peaceful, as the officer corps threw its weight behind a civilian candidate for national leadership. One-party rule would continue. In its role as 'guardian', the military high command would insist that destabilizing policies be avoided. PLA commanders want to keep the army unified, and avoid direct political intervention. However, they stepped in and told Mao to stop the radical nonsense in 1967, and might step in again, *in extremis.*[78]

The candidate the PLA supported would have to have enough civilian support to be a viable leader and be minimally acceptable to military interests. He could turn out to be any of a number of men, who might lead the PRC back into a police state or resume the reforms of the 1980s. Much, of course, will depend on individuals and factions. Much depends, too, on the order in which the old men die. If hard-liners like Wang Zhen, Li Xiannian, and Chen Yun die first, Deng Xiaoping and Wan Li might take China in a fairly moderate direction. If Wang Zhen and Chen Yen are the last survivors, they might retreat into neo-Stalinist autarky.

After the elders (especially Deng Xiaoping and Deng Yingzhao) are gone, Li Peng is not likely to survive, much less Jiang Zemin. A possible candidate is Zhao Ziyang. In the absence of a few of the hard-liners, Zhao might be positioned for a come-back. Zhao evidently won a measure of acceptance from the PLA high command in 1988–9, when he became directly involved with military planning issues.[79] In the absence of consensus on a civilian leader, the officer corps might put forward one of its own to lead the country. Some senior officers have substantial support among civilian officials, and could maintain the theory of party leadership.

Such speculation begs a question crucial to any of our three scenarios: who speaks for the officer corps? In the short term, it is the uniformed members of the CMC and the commanders of the general departments and service arms. All work in Beijing, and can consult frequently. As the 'gang of elders' dies off, however, other military men will demand to be heard, including retired leaders and the Military Region and Group Army commanders.

---

[78] I am grateful to Allen Whiting for reminding me of this.
[79] Pollack, 'Structure' (see n. 33), 24.

Moreover, decisions will have to be made about promoting new men into the standing committee of the CMC.

Currently, retirement, selection, promotion, and assignments are controlled by the secretariat of the CMC (which has very little dedicated staff)[80] and by the General Political Department. Yang Baibing directs both. Historically, however, the chief of the general staff has usually dominated the other general departments and their directors. The General Staff Department controls more material resources, and it heads up the operational chain of command, which may be more important than ever in an era of diminished party legitimacy. If intra-military conflict remains confined to bureaucratic infighting, Yang and the GPD have the advantage. If it comes down to moving forces and using troops, the general staff and its chief probably have the edge.

The danger of dissension with the officer corps would increase as the power-broker or 'kingmaker' role evolved towards direct intervention. As the domestic situation worsened, demanding more drastic measures, ever more heated and more widespread conflict would erupt within the officer corps over issues of policy and political power. Field-grade officers, especially the 'frustrated modernizers', would make themselves heard.

2. The Polish Scenario

Under this scenario, in the absence of any viable civilian candidate or because of extreme social disorder, the officer corps would directly intervene to 'restore order'. It would probably, but not necessarily, act in the name of the communist party. Having intervened, the army could install a civilian figure-head, or a military leader who formally retired from the army, like Park Chung Hee in Korea (1961). A uniformed officer could simply take over, as General Jaruzelski did in Poland in 1981. Such a government would probably be quite authoritarian initially. However, moderate reformers might regain influence, using the now familiar argument that only by reform and opening can China gain economic and military power.

This scenario would certainly involve factional conflict within

[80] Ibid. 20.

the officer corps, with more and more officers demanding to participate in any consensus that purported to represent 'the military'. The 'Polish Scenario' could evolve into an irreparable PLA split. 'Frustrated modernizers' would become sufficiently restive to contemplate a *coup d'état*. They might try to pressure their generals into action, or act themselves. A miscarried *coup* attempt could easily split the officer corps and lead to intra-PLA fighting.

3. Regional Breakup

This is the most extreme and least likely, but still conceivable, scenario. It would come about if intra-PLA fighting spread beyond Beijing and lasted longer than a few days. If it did, the PRC itself could split up.

Thanks to the reforms of the 1980s, regional breakup of the PLA is much less likely than it was during Mao's lifetime. The army is more resistant to regionalism than any other institution because of its command–control–communications, logistics, and educational systems, which are all national in scope. Moreover, the reforms of the 1980s, especially periodic officer reassignment, 'homogenized' the PLA considerably, weakening its 'independent kingdoms'. Military power is much less tied up with regional political and economic power than it was at the end of the Cultural Revolution.

Nevertheless, the PLA officer corps could split up under extreme conditions. If it did, the PRC would split into regions, each dominated by a military commander. This could lead to civil war and a new version of 'warlordism'. There might be an extended period of 'one nation, many states'. As during the warlord period (1916–27), one government in Beijing might continue to speak for China internationally. The various military-dominated regions might coexist uneasily, with each evolving its own economic, political, and social system.[81] Some regimes might attempt to remain centralized planned economies. Because they would be smaller and more manageable, they might be somewhat more successful than

---

[81] My thoughts on the 'Regional Breakup' scenario are prompted by Allen Whiting (private correspondence, July 1990) and Roderick MacFarquhar's remarks at the 'Choices for China' Conference sponsored by the World Affairs Council of Northern California, Asilomar, Calif., 28 Apr. 1990.

the PRC has been. Some regions might attempt to work out combinations of socialism and capitalism, while still others might adopt market economics. Some border minority areas might not only discard Marxism-Leninism, but declare independence or even join themselves to entities beyond PRC borders.

Conclusion

Today, the crucial party–army issue for the People's Republic of China is the degree to which civilian politicians can maintain and exercise institutional authority. Even under the best of circumstances, that capacity is now severely limited. In all probability, the PLA officer corps will act as the 'guardian' and 'kingmaker' as Deng Xiaoping and the other elders pass from the scene over the next decade. Today, the unity of the People's Liberation Army is the strongest — perhaps the only — factor holding the PRC together. If the officer corps splits, the country will split, leading to 'one nation, many states' or to civil war.

7. Foreign Policy

GERALD SEGAL

China is more secure now than at any time under communist rule, or indeed at any time in the several hundred years since the coming of Western imperialism to East Asia. Despite the bad press that China earned from the Beijing massacre in 1989, the reality remained a country remarkably free of external threat. But the path to this successful foreign policy was tortuous, including obvious successes and failures. It would be convenient to be able to suggest some pithy principles that govern Chinese foreign and defence policy. While some have attempted to outline such generalizations, it seems increasingly clear that Chinese policy is too complex to fit into such convenient strait-jackets.[1] While Chinese foreign policy may have some broad objectives, for example, defence of territory or furthering international socialism, there is no route map to those ends. What is more, the objectives remain so distant that flexibility in the short term can be justified.

Instead, what can be offered is an analysis of central Chinese concerns. Problems for defence policies have varied over the past forty years.[2] Analysts can at most outline the nature of these problems, and assess the options. In essence, Chinese policy has been concerned with four types of issues: threats to territorial integrity, threats at the frontiers, enhancing economic prosperity, and the search for global influence. Yet the analysis cannot be complete without an understanding of the domestic context of Chinese policy.

Domestic Decision-Making

At one level, the question of who makes Chinese foreign policy is simple — it is the Politburo of the Chinese Communist Party.[3]

[1] Gerald Segal and William Tow, *Chinese Defence Policy* (London, 1984), Gerald Segal, *Defending China* (Oxford, 1985), and id., ed., *Chinese Politics and Foreign Policy Reform* (London, 1990).

[2] Michael Yahuda, *China's Role in World Affairs* (London, 1978), and *China's Foreign Policy after Mao* (London, 1983).

[3] A. Doak Barnett, *The Making of Chinese Foreign Policy* (Boulder, Colo., 1985).

Certainly the Chinese state and party constitutions are perfectly clear on the 'leading role' of the CCP in all areas of policy. Thus an organizational chart of foreign policy-making is simple. Yet, in China, as in the similar party structure in the Soviet Union, the actual foreign policy-making is far more complex.

The complexity is derived from several sources, but three seem most crucial. First, there is no single, comprehensive set of ideals, shared by all Chinese leaders, on how to govern. Debates on policy are of course normal in any state. Second, as the CCP established the People's Republic, political conflict developed, based in part on institutional affiliation.[4] China, the mother of bureaucracy, has not escaped the parochialism of institutional politics. Third, with all these divisions, Chinese leaders also split on the basis of personal factions.[5] Chinese political culture seems especially susceptible to vicious personal factionalism. This problem is made more acute since in the generation that made the revolution, the men in charge tended to hold more than one position, thus confusing lines of power and policy. Does a military professional in charge of a machine-building industry act in the interests of his faction, his ministry, or the military?

Even as the CCP was consolidating power in 1949, its foreign policy was far from clear cut. Some elements of the CCP, perhaps even including Zhou Enlai, did not see an inevitable need to 'lean to the Soviet side' in the cold war. That Mao eventually led China into the Soviet camp is as much to do with China's lack of options, as a positive desire to support the Soviet Union. The central point is that foreign policy options were seriously considered.

Later in the 1950s, when the Soviet model was called into question in China, debates returned. Did China need to rely on Moscow, or could it afford to strike out on a more independent path? The debate was protracted, cutting across almost all sectors of Chinese society. The Soviet model had penetrated so far into Chinese politics that its rejection could not have been anything but difficult. The repudiation of Soviet guidance in internal Chinese politics came first, followed by an interregnum in the early 1960s, and finally an open split on foreign policy in 1963. But all these steps were far from unanimous. In 1966 when party-to-party ties were severed, the

---

[4] Paul Godwin, *China's Defence Establishment* (Boulder, Colo., 1983).
[5] Lucian Pye, *The Dynamics of Chinese Politics* (Cambridge, 1981).

debate flared once again. The factional lines were complex, linking in with the Cultural Revolution and a strategic assessment of the threat posed by the United States in the expanding Vietnam War.

With the winding up of the extreme phases of the Cultural Revolution in 1969, the pressing Soviet threat along the frontier, and the signs of *détente* from the United States, foreign policy again came under debate in China. The purge of Defence Minister Lin Biao in 1971 obviously was more related to domestic politics, but his opposition to the Sino-American *détente* was not unimportant in the formation of the anti-Lin coalition.

Debates simmered through the 1970s as radicals and moderates fought each other in anticipation of the succession to Mao Zedong. Once again, foreign policy was not the *prime* issue at stake, but it was an issue. The extent to which China's door should be open to foreign influences was a hotly debated topic. Even after the fall of the Gang of Four, foreign policy has continued to figure in leadership debates. The recent *détente* with the Soviet Union was at the centre of a strategic debate in the early 1980s. Related issues included concern over the impact of Western 'spiritual pollution' and whether excessive concessions had been made to the United States over Taiwan.

After the events of June 1989, a new series of debates emerged as China questioned its own path of modernization, and the communist party states of Eastern Europe collapsed. Initial tendencies to xenophobia and to blame Westerners for the student protests and the ensuing massacre were soon replaced by a more sensible attempt to return to business as usual with the West. As debates rumbled, the collapse of communism in Eastern Europe made the choice more stark as there was an ever-shrinking socialist world on which to rely. Despite some hesitations, by mid-1990 Chinese leaders recognized there was no alternative to seeking close relations with the West.

Are there any patterns to these debates? It seems not. There are certain themes that recur, although the conclusions reached in the debates are not consistent. For example, there seems to be regular debate on how open China should be to foreign influences.[6] Both the Soviet model and the late 1970s' opening to the West were examples of receptiveness to foreign ideas. Yet the Cultural

---

[6] Yahuda, *Foreign Policy* (see n. 2).

Revolution and the early 1970s are examples of xenophobia and a narrow nationalistic approach. That the open door swings to and fro is clear, but there seems to be no 'natural' place for it to be propped open or slammed shut.

Similarly, there was no consensus on whether to be more concerned with the threat from the north, or with regaining Taiwan and fending off capitalist ideas. Both options had advantages and disadvantages for China. But with the emerging variants in both socialism and capitalism, and the collapse of many communist party regimes in 1989, the choices became far more complex and debates are likely to be altered as a result.

There is also a fairly consistent Chinese concern with trends in international politics and the threats or opportunities posed for China. Yet the implications of this globalism are unclear. Does it lead to an interventionist Chinese policy, spreading foreign aid and offering advice on revolution or how to challenge the superpowers? Or does China retreat inward, calculating that the best way to ensure long-term strength against international problems is first to develop a strong China? And even if the latter option is chosen, is spending on the armed forces a primary part of building strength, or is the military forced to wait for general economic growth before it can get its toys? This 'guns v. butter' argument, as with the others, has no answer. China, like most great powers, seeks both, with the balance regularly shifting.

These, and indeed other, dilemmas of policy are at the root of foreign policy debates. The specific policies adopted result from a complex web of factors. Personal factional lines cut across ideological debates and institutional politics. Different generations may also share the views of some, but not of others. There are those trained under the Soviet model who have a vested interest in Soviet organizational routines, but who may also loathe Russians on a personal level. There are those of the 'lost generation' of the Cultural Revolution trained to reject things foreign, who may feel alienated from a policy that encourages learning from 'advanced Western technology'.

In sum, the domestic dimension of Chinese foreign policy is crucial, for it is constantly affected by debates and natural dilemmas over options. None of these problems will diminish in importance in the near future. Neither will some of the essential realities of Chinese domestic politics that help shape foreign policy. The poverty of China forces Beijing to choose between more limited options than those faced by other great powers.

Foreign Policy Objectives

China, like most great powers, has four types of foreign policy concern. The scope and relevance of all four are often different for each great power. What is more, the relative importance of each aspect has changed in the past forty years, and certainly the policies adopted in each case have not been consistent. While it is impossible to speak of principles of Chinese foreign policy, it is possible to discuss certain problems as being of enduring importance.

Territorial Integrity

China is unique among contemporary great powers in having unresolved problems of territorial integrity. While the Soviet Union has territorial claims against it (from Japan) and Britain has a secessionist movement in Northern Ireland, no great power faces China's problem of territorial claims against neighbouring states. The importance of unfinished national unification cannot be overestimated.

One primary strength of the CCP, in its triumph over the Guomindang, was its credible claim to be able to unite the state and expel foreign influence. The experience of the rape of Qing dynasty China by imperial powers shaped the perspective of those revolutionaries who fought for power after China's 1911 revolution. While the Soviet Union may have been invaded from time to time from Western Europe, the invasions were always short-lived. In China's case, imperial occupation was measured in centuries.

If all this foreign exploitation had been terminated by the Chinese revolution in the twentieth century, then the supersensitivity might have begun to fade. But the implications of foreign occupation are still felt today. China retains a number of problems of incomplete territorial integrity that play a major role in contemporary foreign policy.

First, there is the problem of Taiwan and the associated offshore islands. After 1949 it was plain that the CCP held *de facto* control, but the Guomindang was able to maintain the fiction of its claim in large part because the Chinese civil war was also an international event. With the United States having supported the Guomindang, and the CCP being associated with the communist bloc in the cold war, the division of China coincided with the division of international politics.

The CCP's revolutionary experience was, however, not dependent on its international communist links. Like Tito in Yugoslavia, but on a grander scale, the CCP came to power on its own. Therefore, there was a natural Chinese pride in its special revolution, and its greater relevance to other Third World states. Yet in part the validity of the Chinese claim to international stature depended upon its ability to show that its revolution was not partial, and could overcome all the problems of the colonial legacy. Therefore, the unresolved Taiwan problem appeared all the more galling to the CCP leadership.

The fact that Taiwan was supported by the United States, and the mainland was communist, soon gave a cold war feel to the Taiwan problem. Questions of Chinese territorial integrity seemed overtaken by larger events. Yet until the outbreak of the Korean War in June 1950, globalization of the Taiwan problem was by no means inevitable.

The Korean War and the decision by President Truman to have the United States Seventh Fleet patrol the Taiwan Straits ensured that American involvement in the Chinese civil war would continue. It also meant that the CCP had to put off its planned assault on Taiwan. The process of national unification was then in its final stages with the capture of Tibet and Hainan island in 1950. However, the CCP's limited capability, especially in amphibious operations, could not overcome American military power.

The Korean War not only resulted in a new role for the Seventh Fleet but also necessitated a Chinese military operation. The collapse of the North Korean drive, and the American counter-offensive up to the Yalu river bordering on China, drew a Chinese counter-punch in October 1950.[7] Now the notion of a full-scale invasion of Taiwan was clearly out of the question. PLA arms were being used in direct support of an ally in trouble. It was made even more necessary by the fact that the United States had directly

[7] Allen Whiting, *China Crosses the Yalu* (New York, 1960), and *China's Calculus of Deterrence* (Ann Arbor, Mich., 1975).

intervened in the Chinese civil war and thus constituted China's main foreign threat. The PLA operation in Korea was undoubtedly costly, but the risks of inaction were perceived as greater, both for China's security and for its sense of national pride.

With the winding down of the Korean War, China turned once again to consideration of the territorial problem and Taiwan. The first Taiwan Straits crisis in 1954-5 was in part a Chinese probe to determine the United States and Taiwanese position. China had regained some minor offshore islands since 1949, but such larger islands as Quemoy and Matsu in the Taiwan Straits posed special problems.

The Chinese probe of Taiwan's intentions in the 1954-5 crisis was also a test of American intentions as the United States built up alliances in East Asia. The establishment of the South-East Asian Treaty Organization (SEATO) was clearly behind the Chinese challenge. As a result of this first Taiwan crisis, China learnt that the United States was prepared to prevent the loss of territory to the communists. China also learnt that its forces were unable and, more to the point, unwilling to run great risks to take the offshore islands. Therefore it was even less likely that China could launch an operation against the main island of Taiwan. This recognition of the realities of power was hard for Beijing to acknowledge.

The second Taiwan Straits crisis in 1958 was similar. The United States made it clear that it was not prepared to tolerate Chinese territorial gains, and Taiwan once again proved its ability to make the costs of any Chinese invasion too high. By the late 1950s, and especially with fading Soviet support for Chinese irredentist claims, Beijing was forced to see the Taiwan problem as long-term. This shift of the issue to the back burner did not mean, however, that it ceased to be important.

This long-term strategy required a more subtle approach. It was certainly obvious that non-military means had to be tried. Force of arms remained important, if only as a threat, but could not serve as a useful instrument for reunification. The more the sword was brandished, the further off the political target appeared. Thus the Sino-American *détente* of the 1970s opened up new possibilities for this peaceful long-term strategy.

China sought to isolate Taiwan politically, and starve it of military support. This meant a direct approach to the United States to cut its links to Taiwan. China remained especially sensitive to

American perceptions that Sino-American *détente* meant that Taiwan was no longer important. The Chinese view was that Taiwan was as important as ever, but that the method for its incorporation into the mainland was to be peaceful. This required the ending of United States arms sales and above all a growing sense in Taipei that it had no choice but to deal with Beijing. On both counts Chinese policy largely failed. Taiwan survives, and indeed flourishes, as a pariah but an important trading partner for the West. The United States has reduced but not severed relations with Taiwan. The Taiwan problem has not gone away and remains the key symbol of China's unsatisfied national integrity. It therefore also remains the main problem for Sino-American relations. Major cosmetic deals have already been arranged, but the reality of an independent Taiwan remains as real as ever.

Taiwan and its associated islands are not the only unsolved territorial problem for China. The British and Portuguese colonies of Hong Kong and Macao have still not been reincorporated into China, but agreement with Britain in 1984 provided for the return of Hong Kong in 1997. This remarkable deal was the first time China managed to negotiate the peaceful return of some sovereign territory. It was a triumph for Chinese diplomacy, in a sense regardless of the eventual fate of Hong Kong, but it does have significance in the long term for the Taiwan question.

Just as the Special Economic Zones are seen as examples of how China will manage the translation of capitalism into a socialist state, so Hong Kong is seen as an example to Taiwan of how its future will be managed. China is offering Taiwan greater independence than presently promised to Hong Kong, but the example of Hong Kong's transition remains essential. In the end, China seems willing to sacrifice some economic gain in return for political principle and territorial integrity. Beijing's hard-line response to what it interpreted as subversive support from Hong Kong for protestors inside China in 1989 was a typical example of putting politics in command of economic self-interest. The reaction in Taiwan, which at the same time was widening its own democracy, was to reinforce further the sense of more than one China and encourage those who favoured *de facto* independence. The regime in Beijing could see Taiwan slipping further away and thus the military option was not ruled out.

China does have complete control, however, over how open it is to foreign influence. In the imperial past, before Western attacks, China was largely closed to external influence. But the experience of the Qing dynasty, when the Chinese door was prised open by Western traders, did not encourage many Chinese to believe that relations with the outside were good for China. An opposing view, perhaps more prominent in communist as opposed to nationalist China, emphasized that some positive foreign ideas, like Marxism, could be useful for China. However, the essential point is that China was ambivalent about opening itself up to the outside.

The emphasis on economic development, and compromise on allowing in some 'polluting' influences, is similar to that adopted in the Soviet Union over the past decades. It is also related to China's longer term approach to the question of territorial integrity. The problems of China are now recognized for the difficult and intractable ones that they always have been. Thus the role of brute force and the military option is not stressed. The primary concern is now with long-term economic modernization. The new trend towards pragmatism and lower expectations in Chinese foreign policy is naturally derived from this longer term domestic strategy.

National Defence

Next to regaining Chinese territory, China's main foreign policy objective is to ensure its national defence. Chinese strategies in defence of its territory have often been peculiar, but the need is basic to almost every power. The special aspects of Chinese defence policy are essentially derived from the geographical situation.[8] China is the world's third largest state and has more neighbours than any other state. Thus, there is a basic threat derived from the multiplicity of defence problems, but also an opportunity provided for wide Chinese influence.

The human geography of China, at once the world's most populous country and a poor peasant state, provides for strengths and weaknesses. The population can support massive armed forces and produce a large GDP. Yet the weaknesses are more obvious; the most pressing is the need to feed more than one billion mouths daily and overcome the rural poverty of millions. China is clearly a great power, but it is also a poor power.

---

[8] Segal, *Defending China* (see n. 1).

A more obvious defence dilemma has been the question of whether China should meet threats 'at the gates', or else sit back and allow an enemy to be swallowed in a sea of millions of hostile soldiers. Chinese defence policy has also been of two minds on whether to base defence on poor equipment but rich manpower resources, or else strive to modernize at least parts of the PLA. The bias, until recently, has been on 'man over weapons'.[9]

In forty years China has faced five major crises which raised these dilemmas. The Korean War (1950–3) showed China's willingness to take on a threatening power beyond China's borders. Despite the farce of Chinese 'volunteers', the PLA was engaged in lengthy combat in Korea. In fact, no subsequent PLA engagement was as costly as the Korean War. The PLA fought beyond the gates in defence of both China's national security, and in support of an allied communist regime.

The Korean War is instructive in other important ways. First, it demonstrated China's willingness to run great risks in defence of an ally. To be sure, there were good reasons for China to fear for its own security, but the scale of the reaction indicates that some part of China's calculation was the need to support fraternal regimes. Second, China indicated a willingness to make sacrifices for allies, especially at a time of serious economic need in China itself. Third, the weaknesses of the PLA were shown up by the war. Despite becoming embroiled beyond its gates, the PLA proved to be a blunt instrument. Especially when confronting the modern United States armed forces, the strategy and arms of the PLA were deficient in many respects. Clearly the circumstances of the early 1950s did not allow China to act as confidently as it might have hoped. If the PLA could not succeed in the Korean War on China's borders, plainly it could not have an effective reach further afield.

China's next military engagement in defence of its national security did not come until nearly ten years later, and in the opposite corner of the country. The 1962 punitive war against India began with a Chinese perception of Indian territorial encroachments, and resulted in a Chinese strike into Indian territory.[10] The conclusions from this venture outside China's gates are different from the Korean case. Chinese success was also more clear than in Korea,

---

[9] Ellis Joffe, *The Chinese Army after Mao* (London, 1987).

[10] Whiting, *China's Calculus* (see n. 7), and Neville Maxwell, *India's China War* (London, 1970).

but that was less due to PLA prowess, and more to the pathetic performance of the Indian army.

After the triumph of the PLA, Chinese defence policy acquired a new character in the area. India's long-standing quarrel with Pakistan helped bring China and Pakistan closer together. This tacit alliance developed despite Pakistani links with the United States. It was based overwhelmingly on the notion that 'the enemy of my enemy is my friend'. Chinese aid to Pakistan soon included military transfers and was encouraged during the 1960s by increasing Soviet–Indian alignment and the developing Sino-Soviet split. China thereby showed a willingness to act decisively to support its foreign policy, but even here there were limits.

In both the 1965 and 1971 Indo-Pakistani wars, China was unable to offer any serious support to its ally in Pakistan. To be sure, there were diplomatic noises, but China was outgunned by its Soviet neighbour which matched any Chinese signal with a more credible military threat. Thus Pakistan may have been China's ally, but China proved to be a paper ally in times of crisis. The circumstances that allowed China to defeat India in 1962 were special to the time, and did not mark any change in China's basic weakness in threatening military action in support of its foreign policy.

During the late 1960s, China faced its third defence policy problem. To the east the expanding United States presence in the Vietnam War raised the question of whether China should treat the threat as it had treated the threat in Korea. China made it plain to the United States that it would regard any crossing into North Vietnam as a threat to China. To that extent, Chinese deterrence extended beyond its gates, but was not tested.

However, Chinese deterrence was probed in a peculiar way by extensive United States bombing of North Vietnam. China became involved in the air defence of North Vietnam, firing on American aircraft and suffering casualties. This very mild form of defence beyond the gates was in response to the controlled American threat to China's neighbour. Thus the parallels to the Korean War are close. China proved itself just as willing to engage the source of threat at an early stage and with serious military action.

However, there were important differences from the Korean experience. China's relations with Moscow were more strained in the 1960s, leading to a more independent Chinese military role. China's relations with North Vietnam were also less strong than in the Korean case. Vietnam was more able and willing to act on its own, while receiving aid from its communist allies. Thus China was less able to direct the combat, and the PLA was not called upon to become seriously involved. The Vietnam War was not so much a test of PLA power, as it was of Chinese foreign policy resolve. It should be recalled that China did offer serious aid to Vietnam, and was not asked for more. The military seemed a useful, if limited, instrument of Chinese foreign policy.

The fourth major threat to China's national defence is perhaps the most crucial, despite China having suffered relatively few casualties in combat. The Sino-Soviet clashes of 1969 were in themselves fairly minor, although they were the most important fought by the Soviet Union since 1945. The true significance of these clashes lies in the potential threat they symbolize.[11]

The implications of the combat were felt far beyond the frozen ground on which they took place. China was eventually forced to the negotiating table by Soviet threats. Beijing realized that it had to take its northern neighbour seriously, especially in military terms. China and the Soviet Union were eventually to turn the struggle into a global competition to encircle each other.[12]

China responded with a combination of stratagems. It sought global support for its anti-Soviet campaign, but also concentrated on developing a minimal military capability that could raise the cost of a Soviet invasion. This deterrence by denial hinges not only on a threat to engage in a people's war, but also relies on a certain degree of military modernization. It is notable that there is little place for large-scale outside help in this modernization. For such basic aspects of defence, China must continue to rely on itself. Defence modernization remains a protracted process.[13]

China's weakness when facing the Soviet Union has not led it into entangling alliances. Despite tacit co-operation with the United States, China has no choice but to rely on itself. Thus, when facing superior military power, China chose to take a low key position. When the Soviet Union invaded Afghanistan in December 1979, China expressed concern for a neighbouring state, but could offer no real resistance. China's ambivalence also ensued from

[11] Richard Wich, *Sino-Soviet Crisis Politics* (Cambridge, Mass., 1980).
[12] Gerald Segal, *Sino-Soviet Relations after Mao* (IISS, Adelphi Paper No. 202; London, 1985).
[13] Joffe, *Chinese Army* (see n. 9).

Afghanistan being far from core China, and it having already been conceded as a Soviet sphere of influence.

By the mid-1980s, because of the clear priority of domestic economic development for China, Sino-Soviet *détente* began to ease tension on the Soviet front. The first moves towards Sino-Soviet *détente* were taken by China in the early 1980s. But when Mikhail Gorbachev came to power in 1985, it was the Soviet Union that sped up the pace. By May 1989, only a few months before China's fortieth birthday, China normalized relations with the Soviet Union and thereby completed the last major aspect of its foreign policy reform.

The Chinese no longer officially speak of a Soviet threat. Tensions along the frontier have eased. The Soviet Union will have withdrawn close to 350,000 troops from Asia by the end of 1991, thereby reducing its forces to nearly half the late 1970s peak. China has already cut its armed forces by a million men. The stage was set for formal arms control and confidence-building measures along the Sino-Soviet frontier.[14]

The final threat to Chinese national defence was less pressing than any of the previous four, but still resulted in massive Chinese casualties. The 1979 Chinese attack on Vietnam was an attempt to teach the Soviet Union that its allies could not run amok, especially in China's area of interest. On all counts, the use of Chinese force was unimpressive. While it is true that Vietnam did suffer massive damage in the north and was forced to make some adjustments to its troop deployments, in the end China lacked sufficient military clout to obtain its objectives.

In 1974, when China seized the Xisha islands from South Vietnam, Beijing showed that it could effectively use military force in the area. But the capture of those islands, claimed as Chinese territory, was achieved under special conditions. The enemy was the decrepit South Vietnamese regime, which was fighting North Vietnam. China's swift operation left little room for communist opposition to manifest itself against another communist state taking territory from the United States-supported South Vietnam.

In March 1988 China again took some islands from the Vietnamese in the South China Sea, this time in the Spratly group. In 1988 the enemy was Vietnamese communists, but the recipe for

---

[14] Gerald Segal, ed., *Arms Control in Asia* (London, 1987) and id., 'The Asian Road to Arms Control', *Arms Control Today* (May 1989).

success was the same: superior arms and excellent political timing. With growing Sino-Soviet *détente* Moscow was unwilling to risk losing the bigger prize of improved relations with China, for the sake of keeping Vietnam happy.

In the 1979 war with Vietnam the two ingredients of past and future Chinese success were absent. Chinese action took place after Cambodia was overrun by Vietnamese troops and left China with the more difficult military task of compelling rather than deterring Vietnamese action. What is worse, Vietnam had tacit Soviet support, thereby forcing China to wage a limited war against Vietnam that it could not win. The political objective of 'punishing' Vietnam hinged on a swift military success, and that was precisely what China could not achieve.

The implications of the 1979 war were in part similar to the previous cases. China showed a willingness to use arms to support its national defence, and back up an ally in need. The use of the military instrument was beyond China's borders and entailed some serious sacrifice in men and material. However, in contrast to Korea, Chinese troops performed poorly. In Korea, they adequately defended North Korea, but in 1979 they failed to punish Vietnam. China's Cambodian allies were relegated to a sideshow along the Thai frontier, and China was unable to help them break out.

China's poor showing in 1979 marked the low point in the effectiveness of the use of China's military instrument. The lessons learnt were myriad, including the need for a less hostile view of Soviet power, and the need for thorough defence modernization. Most importantly, China perhaps saw that it was still a great power with not enough punch in the 'power'. The new sense of realism about what China could achieve in foreign policy in general was related to its realistic appreciation of China's military potential. The enduring dilemmas of Chinese defence policy remained. Uncertainty over defence beyond its borders, the question of the pace of military modernization, and the extent to which China needed to compromise with foreign threats, all were as difficult choices as ever. But as long as China remains essentially poor, and a great power with global concerns, these dilemmas will not disappear.

Economic Prosperity

As a continental economy, China has rarely sought economic prosperity by close contact with the outside world. In the past, curiosities were collected from as far afield as Africa, but the success of the Chinese state was defined and obtained back within core China.[15] China was ravaged by foreign powers for several hundred years before the communist revolution, and modern China remained ambiguous about how much to open to the outside world for economic prosperity.

In the 1950s, prosperity and modernity were sought through an alliance with the Soviet Union and adopting the Soviet model. The impact of the Soviet Union on the Chinese economy is impossible to quantify. But given the desperate state of the Chinese economy at the time, even the limited assistance from the Soviet Union was vital for putting China back on its feet. The rapid Chinese growth had a great deal to do with simply taking up the slack of the past, but Soviet aid was vital to the speed and direction of modernization.

When China chose to pursue its own radical economic experiments, such as the Great Leap Forward in the late 1950s, no outsider could be held responsible for the failure. In fact, it was the Soviet Union that warned China that what it was doing was lunacy. The resulting death of some twenty-five million Chinese from famine was entirely China's fault, although it came at a time when China broke with the Soviet Union and Khrushchev withdrew his advisors in 1960. For close to twenty years, China then went it alone in economic development. The result was the occasional spurt of success, followed by radical upheaval and economic failure. The Cultural Revolution was the primary example of the xenophobia and economic madness of domestic Chinese leaders.

With the death of Mao and the pursuit of Deng's reforms from 1978, China showed that it had learnt its lesson. The decision to open China's door to the outside world resulted in a drastic increase in the percentage of Chinese GDP that was related to foreign trade.[16] Foreigners came to China in their millions as tourists and traders. Superficial changes, from advertising hoardings to snazzy

15 S. A. M. Adshead, *China: A History* (London, 1988).
16 Martin Lockett, 'The Economy', in David Goodman, Martin Lockett, and Gerald Segal, *The China Challenge* (RIIA, Chatham House Papers; London, 1986).

hotels, showed just how serious China was about opening its doors. More importantly, foreign technology and expertise was brought in, not always successfully.

Most interestingly of all, China opened vast parts of its coastal territory for Special Economic Zones. The idea was to have certain parts of the economy drag the rest into the twenty-first century. The record was mixed, but there could be little doubt that China was serious about learning from the outside. This was the most sustained period of Chinese cosmopolitanism and it led to the opening of various open doors, including one to the north and the Soviet Union.

Despite the set-backs to economic reforms in the late 1980s and the new hostility from some Western states, China seemed convinced that the door had to remain open. Despite debt problems, China's rank in world exports rose from thirty-second place in 1977 to fourteenth in 1989. The commodity composition of foreign trade had shifted dramatically in favour of manufactured goods and away from primary products. The range of trade partners was far wider and China joined a range of international economic institutions. Despite some real uncertainty about the extent of interdependence it should have with the international economy, the reality was that Chinese prosperity depended on increasing contacts with the international market economy. Unlike reforming East Europeans, China had managed to keep a grip on its level of debt and could even keep trade roughly in balance, despite having such powerful trading neighbours as Japan, South Korea, and Taiwan.

Of course, it is still too early to tell how successful this radical change in Chinese attitudes will be. China also sees the obvious benefits that come from playing a major role in international organizations. Basic features of the Chinese approach, including racism to Africans or distance from any foreigner, remain characteristic of China's handling of the outside world. China is still not happy about its open doors and they still swing and creak on their hinges. But it is hard to see even a more nationalist leadership closing China's doors to anything like the extent it once did. In a more interdependent modern world, and one that is recognized as such nearly everywhere else in the communist world, the idea of closing doors and ignoring the global market economy seems unlikely and fruitless.

Global Influences

The fourth dimension of China's basic foreign policy concerns takes it further afield. The Chinese communists were interested in far-flung international events well before they assumed power in 1949. Even now, although lacking effective 'reach' in some parts of the world, China sees it as necessary to have a fully developed position. The motives for this desire for a global role are several and often overlapping.

At the most basic level, as a large power with many borders, China naturally extends further than any other power except the superpowers. The Chinese certainly see themselves as 'important', if only because one out of every five people in the world is Chinese. What is more, China is a poor peasant state, and unlike the super-powers, can claim to understand the developing world. China's efforts to lead the South against the North are largely based on its self-image as the most important Third World state.

China is not just a Third World state with Third World problems, it is also a state with a guiding ideology. The precepts of that ideo-logy are essentially universal, if only in urging world-wide revolu-tion towards socialism. The extent to which these revolutionary objectives are pursued is, of course, a matter of major debate, even within China. This makes it hard for China to argue that it has the correct answer for other developing states. But the legitimacy of the CCP in China is based in part on its ideology, and the ideology urges an international role. It was precisely that ideology in the 1940s that gave the CCP a global perspective of the place of the Chinese revolution.

Furthermore, the nature of the threats faced by China itself has involved it in international politics. China's major defence policy problems were to be found first with the United States, then the Soviet Union, and now with both together, which has led China to view its own foreign policy problems in global terms. Struggle against the United States and the Soviet Union involves other regions, in large part because the superpowers themselves see their role as international. Although China may know it lacks the long reach to compete with the superpowers in every distant crisis, China appreciates that what happens in those distant parts does affect China.

In the 1980s China even began to show that it had the reach of the superpowers. By supplying arms to both sides of the Iran–Iraq War, China was pursuing a pragmatic policy of making money. But it was also seeking some influence in that it hoped to have proven its friendship in time of need and also its ability to deliver goods on the scale and at the distance required by local states.[17]

Lastly, China has an acute sensitivity to what may happen if it ignores the outside world. The legacy of the imperialist's rape of China taught many Chinese leaders that they cannot ignore the outside world and close China's gates. In the end, a closed China is a weak China. Modern communications, and more effective military power deployed at a distance from the home base, make China potentially more vulnerable than in the nineteenth century. The solution to such weakness is seen in part as learning what is best from the outside, and creating alliances to deflect or reduce external threat.

This concern to avoid new international humiliation involves a basic desire to build up China's internal strength through modernization. But it also seems likely that this desire for a breathing space to develop internally will not result in a new isolationism if modernization should be achieved. Internationalism is not merely a tactic, it is a strategy for the continuing development of China.

Yet there remain serious challenges to internationalism as a guide to Chinese foreign policy. Certainly it defines much of China's longer historical practice. The Confucian and Sino-centric worldview that dominated imperial China's view of the world has, of course, been generally overstated. But it remains true that China was relatively unbothered by the need for alliances or the complex international politics of Europe. While it seems clear that Chinese foreign policy in the twentieth century has broken away from these narrow ethnocentric perspectives, there remains an enduring Chinese perspective of cultural superiority. The jingoistic element has not been entirely absent from Chinese foreign policy in the past forty years.

Other motives for more Chinese isolation are derived from the economic backwardness of China. Some have argued that excessive concern with external relations only saps China's ability to deal with domestic problems. China lacks the basic resources for a global foreign policy. While it might some day seek a more international

---

[17] Anne Gilks and Gerald Segal, *China and the Arms Trade* (London, 1985).

role, in the short term it must concentrate on its own affairs. In a country as poor as China, these arguments can be persuasive.

On balance, there remains a basic dilemma. Does China seek global influence, or does it concentrate more on domestic problems? This is not merely a matter of ideology versus pragmatism, for there are ideological justifications for both isolationism and internationalism, for both a closed and an open door. The dilemma remains unresolved, and China has experienced various different ways of coping with the choices.

In the first phase, after Korea and during the Sino-Soviet honeymoon, China sought as many friends as possible. The drive for international recognition derived from various sources, including a desire to overcome the legacy of pre-revolutionary humiliation, and the need to win friends in order to isolate Taiwan. This presented China with the possibility of direct confrontation with the United States power, but it was a possibility China chose not to pursue. The Bandung phase of the five principles of peaceful coexistence was best served by a low-key emphasis on Chinese demands, and more enhanced by a broad smile and professions of friendship.

This phase had some obvious success. China was not seeking direct aid, or pushing the revolutionary cause very firmly. The minimal desires were therefore more easily satisfied, especially by other Third World states seeking friends in a hostile and polarized Cold War world. China did support some revolutionary movements, but they were mostly close to home, and relatively uncontroversial as the opponents were Western-supported regimes. China certainly lacked any long reach into distant parts of the Third World and so, wisely, minimized this aspect of its ideological objectives. Thus it is not surprising that China's gains in this period were swift and relatively easy. China established a reputation in the Third World as sympathetic, if less useful than the Soviet Union. However, the honeymoon did not last long.

The developing Sino-Soviet split in the late 1950s and the early 1960s brought out the sharper side of Chinese policy. The basic drive was still internationalist, but more radical and assertive. China now had to justify its position not only against the 'imperialist' West, but also against the communist Soviet Union. The relatively simple desire for revolutionary change became clouded when China urged 'true' revolution and not the moderate Soviet version. China seemed more concerned with confronting

Soviet-supported causes than in challenging Western-dominated movements. Most importantly, China's splitting of the revolutionary cause upset many of its former friends in the Third World. While they may have agreed with China's long-term objectives, and felt China was more sympathetic to their problems, they were concerned that Beijing was undermining revolutionary unity. What is more, China lacked the economic clout to support its radical posture, and so left the Third World states and movements with the choice of support from China in words, or arms and aid from Moscow.

It is therefore not surprising that Chinese policy suffered. The campaign for recognition was slowed as some states came to see China as the more revolutionary wing of the communist movement. States that supported India and Yugoslavia in their moderate leadership of the non-aligned were disconcerted at China's 1962 war with India and the sharp attacks on Tito in the struggle with the Soviet Union. This Chinese policy was still internationalist, but it was more radical, leading more to isolation than global influence. From the mid-1960s the trend became more rather than less radical.

In fact, the Cultural Revolution was a time of a virtually non-existent foreign policy. All ambassadors but one were recalled to China, although this did not mean that China ceased to pay any attention to the outside world. While China had a position on most international issues, it was invariably a radical one that did not last far into the 1970s. When China returned to an active foreign policy, after the double shock of the Soviet invasion of Czechoslovakia and the Ussuri river clashes, it found the world less sympathetic.

During the 1970s, as Chinese foreign policy shifted to a perception of the Soviet Union as the main threat, Beijing was disconcerted to find the going somewhat tough. First, after the radical excesses of the Cultural Revolution, China was no longer seen as stable. The purge of Lin Biao and the factional politics of radicals and moderates in the 1970s enhanced this image. Secondly, the failure of the Cultural Revolution took the shine off China's revolutionary appeal. The evident inability of Chinese leaders to cope with the problems of making revolution in a Third World state did not attract those who sought a coherent model for revolution. Thirdly, China still lacked the economic and military power to support these revolutionaries. If China was now seen as being as much of a revolutionary failure as the Soviet Union, then it was best to take aid from the Soviet Union who could at least offer far more material assistance than poor China. Fourthly, China's new sharp anti-Soviet foreign policy often upset many Third World states and movements. Unlike the 1960s when China at least opposed both superpowers equally, in the 1970s it was an often uncomfortable associate of the United States simply because it was at the time taking an anti-Soviet position. Support for conservative regimes in Zaïre, or Chile, did much damage to China's image.

The latest phase of Chinese policy began about 1980 with a series of internal and external policy reassessments. The foreign policy changes towards greater pragmatism and openness had three main dimensions. First, Chinese leaders recognized the failure of many of their past domestic experiments. The judgement on the role of Mao Zedong meant that China could begin to chart a new future. It meant a policy of retaining certain 'Maoist' elements, but also far greater pragmatism in adopting new and even foreign ideas. This was then a major motive for a return to a more internationalist perception, but also one that sought as much to learn as to teach others. It was a return to the Bandung phase, but with less grandiose dreams, and with less need to obtain recognition. Unfortunately, the problems were more protracted ones of developing influence, and developing China's own economy.

Secondly, China abandoned its one-sided anti-Sovietism in favour of a more balanced challenge to both superpowers. This is not to suggest that China saw both superpowers as equal, and in collusion and contention, as in the 1960s. This time, China saw some areas in which the United States' policy was the primary problem, for example, Central America and the Middle East, and others, such as South-East Asia or Afghanistan, where the Soviet Union was the major problem. The great advantage of this new dual-adversary posture was that it afforded China far more flexibility. China abandoned any pretence of an overarching theory of international politics, such as the much discredited Theory of Three Worlds. In its place, China offered vague support for the South in its claims against the North, and urged all states to abide by the Five Principles of Peaceful Coexistence. China's main focus of attention seemed to be in establishing itself as the champion of the South against the North.

Yet China's new concern with the Third World did not go hand in hand with a massive aid programme. Unlike previous phases of involvement in Third World politics, China now recognized more openly the limits to its power. It pleaded poverty like most Third World states, and drew on international monetary arrangements as did many other members of the South. To be sure, some Chinese aid programmes were evident, but the scale was much reduced. What is more, Chinese relations with many Third World states, especially in the OPEC subcategory of the Third World, involved more economic deals and trade that benefited China's own domestic development projects.

China still sees the Third World as important. The old motive of seeking international recognition is no longer present. But the desire to win friends and influence is still relevant. China's renewed concern with international politics focuses on threats posed by both superpowers, and China does see that it can play a role in helping the Third World deflect superpower pressures. Yet China is also far more pragmatic and long-term in its approach than in previous decades. The problems of international divisions in the Third World are now more openly acknowledged by China. Beijing's own limitations in providing aid are also recognized, but unlike in the past, China does not try to make grandiose promises or offer confident advice in lieu of real aid.

Directions of Change

Has Chinese foreign policy been a success in the past forty years? And what of the future and the challenges to China's foreign policy? The answer must be positive, although the Chinese clearly took a circuitous route to their ends. They have fought more major wars than any other great power since 1949 and they certainly have lost more men in combat. They now stand with a bit more territory than where they began. Apart from Tibet, there have been tiny territorial gains in the offshore islands, the South China Sea, and the border with India. Hong Kong and Macao will return in less than a decade's time. Apart from the South China Sea region, there is little prospect of any further Chinese gains.

China is a more prosperous place than it was in 1949, in part because it has learnt from the outside. But the lost time and opportunities have been considerable and momentous. China left most of its doors closed for so long that it is remarkable that China has done quite as well as it has in the past forty years. Comparisons with the newly industrializing countries of East Asia, and especially Taiwan, suggest just how much more China could have done and needs to do in the future.

In broader terms, China's global influence has improved, if less dramatically and obviously. China is now seen as a poor place that is of marginal importance to the prosperity or power of Western states. The dreams of the China market have mostly faded, as have images of China as NATO's sixteenth member. The collapse of the communist world has limited Chinese options and led to a Sino-Soviet *détente* based on pragmatic realities of two neighbours distracted by domestic development. Most of the developing world sees China in less friendly terms, with the possible exception of the Middle East. China has few real friends in Asia and tension with ASEAN states may well increase as the sense of a Soviet and Vietnamese threat fades. Despite the increased number of diplomatic relations, and despite the slogan about 'having friends all over the world', China has fewer real friends than at any point since 1949. Yet China is still more prosperous and secure from external threat than at any point for several hundred years. Although it did not need to take forty years to get to where China is now, at least it has managed to do so. Only the most churlish would not be thankful for large mercies.

8. Taiwan and the Reunification Question

LEE LAI TO

Since the lifting of the ban on family visits to the mainland via third areas in November 1987, Taipei has taken incremental steps to broaden its contacts with Beijing. After the death of Chiang Ching-kuo in January 1988, the KMT government under Lee Teng-hui continued cautiously to allow more contacts between the two sides of the Taiwan Straits. Although there is no official dialogue between the two sides, Taipei's three-no policy had become a misnomer by the end of the 1980s. As analysed elsewhere by the author, the new directions in Taipei's mainland policy were mapped out on the principle that the stability and security of Taiwan and power of the KMT would not be challenged. The contacts with the other side were made as a political offensive to promote the Taiwan experience. Steps were also taken by the KMT to test the water for the recognition of the existence of two separate political entities in the Taiwan Straits, whether in foreign or domestic affairs.[1] Taiwan's potential for independence became much clearer and was borne out by Taipei's reactions to the Tiananmen incident in June 1989 and new developments in Taiwan's reunification policy which followed.

Taipei and the Tiananmen Demonstrations

On the whole, the death of Hu Yaobang and the subsequent student demonstrations did not command prompt attention from the KMT leadership. The response was low-key and cautious. Thus the Central Standing Committee meeting of the KMT held on 26 April 1989 gave only verbal endorsement to the pro-democracy movement of the students, saying that, to support it, Taiwan's

---

[1] For details, see Lee Lai To, 'Taiwan and the Reunification of China', *Pacific Review*, 22, pp. 132-40, and 'The PRC and Taiwan: Moving Toward a More Realistic Relationship', in Robert Scalapino *et al.*, eds., *Asian Security Issues: Regional and Global* (Institute of East Asian Studies, University of California; Berkeley, Calif., 1988), 165-95.

experiences should spread to the mainland.[2] The mass media in Taipei reported the events and some newspapers gave considerable coverage to the turmoil on the mainland, indicating that there was still some empathy between the people of Taiwan and those on the mainland. However, the revelation that Finance Minister Shirley Kuo would be going to Beijing for the 1989 ADB meeting attracted more attention than the student protests. To Taipei, Kuo's Beijing trip was probably much more important and a bold step in seeking a *de facto* recognition of two separate political entities in China and the newly mooted 'one country, two governments' proposal.[3] Although Taipei still protested against the designation of 'Taipei, China' for its delegation at the 1989 ADB meeting, the excitement about Shirley Kuo's trip in Taiwan and the general acceptance of the usefulness of close encounters with Beijing and other countries on such official occasions was an encouragement to the KMT government's planned return to the international community.

As the euphoria created by Taipei's participation in the Beijing ADB meeting began to subside and the situation in China began to get worse for the students, notably with the declaration of martial law in Beijing on 20 May 1989 and possible use of the military against the demonstrators following the defeat of the 'liberals' by the hard-liners in the Chinese leadership after the Sino-Soviet summit in mid-May 1989, relatively more attention to the tension on the mainland began to surface in Taipei.[4] Events in China had already attracted world-wide attention and support, particularly from the West and Hong Kong where there were massive demonstrations in support of the students in the mainland. Still, the response from the KMT was very conservative. It was not prepared to take any concrete action.

After the declaration of martial law in Beijing, the spokesman of the KMT government issued 'A Statement by the Government of the Republic of China on the Movement for Freedom and Democracy in Mainland China' on 21 May 1989, declaring Taipei's steadfast support for the pro-democracy movement and

---

2 *China Times* (Taipei, 27 Apr. 1989).
3 The 'one country, two governments' proposal will be elaborated later in this chapter.
4 The following analysis in this section is drawn from the author's postscript in *The Reunification of China: PRC–Taiwan Relation in Flux* (New York, forthcoming).

condemning the Chinese communists. President Lee Teng-hui and KMT Secretary-General Lee Huan called for meetings examining the situation on the mainland. It seems that, at that time, the KMT was still adopting a wait-and-see position, in spite of all the polemics that Taipei would join hands with mainland compatriots to fight against the CCP and act as the 'rear guard' for the movement on the mainland. However, the general public and non-ruling élites of the KMT, notably the ordinary KMT members of the Legislative Yuan were more forthcoming in demanding the government take action against the CCP. An unprecedented massive demonstration in support of the pro-democracy movement, similar to those in Hong Kong and elsewhere, took place in Taipei on 31 May 1989.

The KMT's cautious posture before the 3–4 June incident, according to Shaw Yu-ming, director-general of the Government Information Office, was attributed to the care taken by Taipei not to give the Chinese communists an excuse to suppress Chinese on the mainland because of Taipei's support for the pro-democracy movement. While there may be some truth in this, it should be noted that the KMT probably had other concerns as well. For one thing, Taipei had its own share of problems from university students. It probably did not want to be seen to be encouraging student agitation on the mainland, nor to be contradicting itself by supporting students on the other side of the Straits while putting the lid on campus democracy at home. In fact, at the time of the pro-democracy movement on the mainland, some students at Taiwan National University clashed with the university authorities on the election of the student union president and 'self-determination' by the students. More than 800 academics from 22 institutes of higher education also petitioned the Legislative Yuan for academic freedom and campus democracy in the drafting of legislation for the universities.

The KMT was also caught in the problems created by the resignation of Premier Yu Kuo-hwa in May. These were not really settled until late May when it became known that Lee Huan would be the succeeding premier and that James Soong would take over Lee Huan's job in the KMT as the new secretary-general. The personnel changes in the government as well as in the party required the KMT leadership to pay considerable attention to ensuring a smooth transition.

Most important of all, the priority of the KMT government lay increasingly clearly in the development of Taiwan and the security of the island. Its concern with the mainland and any related policy was secondary and had to be subsumed under Taipei's primary concern with development and security on the island. This was made abundantly clear by President Lee Teng-hui on the first day of the second plenary session of the Thirteenth Central Committee of the KMT on 3 June 1989. While supporting the KMT's claim that the demands for democracy and freedom on the mainland were the inevitable result of Taipei's gradual and relaxed policy towards the other side of the Straits, and reiterating the KMT's support for the pro-democracy movement, President Lee admitted unequivocally that there was no way for the KMT government to exercise its rule on the mainland for the time being and it would be best for Taipei to be courageous enough to admit this fact and map out practical and pragmatic policies based on its effective rule in its own area of influence. In terms of foreign affairs, there was a *de facto* recognition in Lee's stand that Taiwan could not represent the whole of China, although Lee still talked about one China which must eventually be unified. This sense of realism in Taipei's foreign relations, coupled with Lee's earlier statement that he would visit places like Singapore even if they had formal ties with Beijing, reinforced and denoted a new era of renewed activism and pragmatism under Lee Teng-hui.

It remains to be noted that the KMT's emphasis on self-concern and self-preservation did not prevent it from watching closely the situation on the mainland. In fact, officials of the KMT were summoned by President Lee to an emergency meeting on the morning of 4 June 1989 after news of the 3–4 June crackdown reached Taipei. An emergency press conference was held at 11.30 a.m. on the same morning to allow President Lee to make known Taipei's stand. In addition to his condemnation of the CCP's use of force and his support for the pro-democracy movement, it was interesting to note in the press statement that President Lee also urged the people of Taiwan to 'remain alert to Chinese Communist inclination toward the use of violence and military force, and to be prepared, on the eve of the collapse of the Chinese Communists for any action they might risk taking'. Accordingly, the armed forces on Taiwan were put on alert, indicating again Taipei's security consciousness. Apparently, Lee also felt compelled to make other concrete responses to the events in China. These included, *inter alia*, a propaganda blitz against Beijing, breaking the latter's black-out on news concerning the Tiananmen incident. Direct mail and telecommunications between the two sides were also sanctioned shortly after the Tiananmen incident. By and large, the measures taken by Taipei were designed to take advantage of the situation on the mainland by launching a political offensive against its rival.

Taipei's somewhat belated reactions to developments on the mainland definitely disclosed the harsh realities across the Taiwan Straits. The KMT government did not want and could not really hope to overthrow the CCP, even in times of turmoil on the mainland. What Taipei could do was exploit the chaos to project itself favourably not only on the mainland and at home, but to the Chinese abroad and the international community at large. In addition, the Tiananmen incident was very useful in cooling down the China fever and diluting whatever illusions people on Taiwan might have had about the CCP and its policy towards reunification. The concern of the people on Taiwan for their compatriots on the mainland could also make less credible the claim of the opposition that the Taiwanese were not Chinese.

The limited and cautious reactions of the KMT revealed that pragmatism was in command and that Taipei would like to steer the island into a safe haven for its people in a secluded position off the Chinese coast based on a cool-headed assessment of the political situation. While rhetorically reiterating its interest in having one China, it was much more interested, at least for the time being, to 'pressure' Beijing and persuade the international community to recognize a separate place for Taipei in international affairs. As a result, the Tiananmen incident was used effectively by Taipei, at a time when many countries, especially those in the West, were alienated by the use of force against unarmed citizens on the mainland, to show off its successful development experience and its worth as a member of the international community. With its skilful use of its economic diplomacy, its 'elastic' posture in establishing ties with other countries, and the more favourable international environment in the aftermath of the Tiananmen incident, Taipei could expect to score some successes in its international relations.

The One Country, Two Governments Proposal

As Beijing has always been the stumbling block for Taipei in world affairs, the latter has been forced since the 1970s to opt for 'substantive diplomacy'. Essentially, what this amounts to is the development of bilateral relations in the absence of official ties with other countries. This could be pursued by means of economic, technological, cultural, and even semi-official links with as many countries as possible. And for activities in the international organizations, Taipei, as demonstrated by its acceptance of its new name, 'Chinese Taipei', in the Olympic Committee during the 1980s, would be more flexible in accepting dual membership with Beijing by toning down its insistence on using its official name at least for those international organizations of a socio-economic nature.

As for the more official international organizations, Taipei may take part even if its official name has been changed. This was demonstrated by Taipei's reappearance at the ADB 1988 meeting in Manila, although it protested against the change of its name to 'Taipei, China'. More importantly, Taipei decided to send its Finance Minister, Shirley Kuo, to head the delegation to attend the ADB meeting held in Beijing in 1989. For the first time, the KMT government in Taiwan had a high-ranking official attending a meeting where there was official representation from Beijing. Moreover, the official delegation from Taipei attended a meeting in Beijing and not in a third country. Taipei pointed out that its Finance Minister was in Beijing as Taiwan's representative to the ADB's board of governors and it protested again against the use of 'Taipei, China' in the 1989 meeting. It also emphasized that the delegation attended the meeting sponsored not so much by Beijing but by an international organization in Beijing.[5] Still it was a significant precedent for Taipei's officials to travel to the other side of the Taiwan Straits to attend meetings. In fact, Premier Yu clearly indicated that Taipei would consider attending all official and unofficial meetings under the auspices of international organizations on the mainland according to the 'ADB model'. He further added that, for similar meetings held in Taiwan, delegates from the mainland could attend and that the KMT government would

---

[5] *United Daily* (Taipei, 8 Apr. 1989).

act according to the decisions of the international organizations concerned.[6]

Although Taipei in principle still rejected bilateral relations with Beijing and argued that it would not discuss bilateral relations with Beijing in international meetings held on the mainland, the simultaneous appearance of officials from both sides of the Taiwan Straits at the ADB meeting signalled that the policy of accepting dual representation in international organizations had been advanced a major step by Taipei's 'flexible diplomacy'. The earlier indication by President Lee (in his trip to Singapore) that Taiwan's name was not that important also flagged the KMT government's acceptance of a change of name which did not diminish it into a local government. More importantly, Taipei's use of the 'ADB model' indicated that it would like to test the idea of 'one country, two governments' proposed for the conduct of its international relations. Premier Yu explicitly recognized that such a proposal was worth investigating and asked the Ministry of Foreign Affairs to conduct research for future reference.[7]

The revelation of Taipei's serious consideration of the 'one country, two governments' formula was made at a time when it was known that an official delegation would be attending the ADB meeting in Beijing during 1989. The KMT government must have considered it mature and opportune to do so after a close monitoring of the problems and prospects of its endeavour to make a come-back in international politics. It had taken a very cautious, step-by-step, and yet pragmatic approach in assessing the various ways to overcome its diplomatic isolation and had come to the conclusion that the 'one country, two governments' formula might be worth considering. To be sure, there had been no lack of similar suggestions to the KMT government over the years.[8] However, the disclosure of official investigation and consideration of 'one country, two governments' by Premier Yu was significant.

What this portended was the coexistence of the Taipei and Beijing governments in international affairs. It was in a way a concession on the part of Taipei as it recognized the CCP government as the other part of China, giving up its long-held 'constitutional rule'

[6] *Central Daily News* (Taipei, 8 Apr. 1989).

[7] *China Times* (9 Apr. 1989).

[8] For a survey of the other suggestions, see Lee Lai To, *Reunification* (see n. 4), ch. 4.

over the whole of China. It was also a recognition of the division of China. To underscore the parity of Taipei and Beijing in this arrangement, the proposal was formulated as 'one country, two *equal* governments'. Quite clearly, Taipei wanted to emphasize the point that it would not accept its debasement under 'one country, two systems' as a local government. It seems that Taipei was prepared to fight for some kind of official standing in the international community under the new proposal. As Taipei established mutual unofficial offices with other countries and rejoined some international organizations on the 'Olympic model' it became clear to the KMT government that it would be desirable and inevitable for it to consider the upgrading of its bilateral ties with other countries to more official levels and to explore ways to rejoin more official international organizations. In addition, Taipei devoted attention to thinking of ways and means to prevent those countries and organizations which had diplomatic and official ties with Taiwan from breaking off relations with the KMT government. By using the 'one country, two governments' proposal, Taipei hoped to be able to carve a niche for the area effectively ruled by it in a more official manner on the international stage. The term 'two governments' is far more obvious and formal than earlier suggestions of having 'two seats', a 'multi-system', or 'two administrations', in the creation of two separate political entities in international affairs.[9]

To a certain extent, the 'one country, two governments' proposal to upgrade relations at the official level also coincided with the major objective of the 'dual recognition' proposal, although the latter was more concerned with bilateral relations while the former had much broader implications. Although Taipei has since denied that it was following a policy of 'one country, two governments' officially, it was obvious that a *de facto* 'one country, two governments' approach was followed and that Taipei was determined to act separately in diplomacy while clinging symbolically to the one-China principle. The approach has, to a certain extent, a sense of realism as it acknowledges the division of China. Moreover, as far as the reunification of China is concerned, it emphasized Taipei's lack of interest in talking to the other side about the issue, being

[9] Ibid.

more concerned in the short term with negating its diplomatic isolation.

Major developments in Beijing–Taipei relations since the official consideration of the 'one country, two governments' proposal by the KMT government have also reinforced Taipei's *de facto* recognition of two governments in China. As noted, Finance Minister Shirley Kuo's attendance of the ADB meeting in Beijing was used to test the water for the proposal. After a short spell of tension between the two sides as a result of the Tiananmen incident and Beijing's accusation of Taipei's interference in the turmoil, the people of Taiwan resumed their practical contacts with the other side of the Taiwan Straits. These contacts with the mainland were facilitated by the direct telecommunication links between the two sides of the Taiwan Straits from June 1989. Likewise, trade between the two sides did not seem to be affected adversely, except for a short period after the June crackdown.

As renewed contacts increase and Taipei condones and broadens more measures for such interactions, the KMT government also seems to be prepared to legalize the separateness of the two sides as demonstrated notably by the adoption of the draft of the 'Temporary Stipulations on People's Relations between the Taiwan Area and Mainland Area' by the Mainland Task Force of the Executive Yuan in October 1989. To a large extent, the draft, which covers areas like immigration, residency, employment, marriage, investment and trade, hereditary rights, communications and telecommunications, and other legal matters, recognizes the rule of the CCP government and its laws on the mainland. The concession, however, did not hide the fact that the KMT government was drafting the stipulations as an independent and separate political entity trying to regulate the traffic between the two sides of the Taiwan Straits.

Further steps are known to have been taken by the KMT government in early 1989 to establish mediatory organs to oversee affairs and problems in the interactions between the two sides. No doubt there were already unofficial bodies trying to arbitrate business disputes. However, it seems that the KMT would like to have more encompassing organs at the 'people-to-people' level to handle such matters. This was made abundantly clear when the spokesman of the KMT government, Shaw Yu-ming, said in May 1990 that his government would like to set up a mission in China to promote 'stable and peaceful development' of relations between the two sides of the Taiwan Straits.[10] Although the mission would be considered unofficial, it would receive government funding. In addition, Beijing would be allowed to establish a similar office in Taiwan. The suggestion of having some kind of representative office with governmental backing in each other's territory signifies again the KMT government's desire to be on equal terms with the CCP government. By early August 1990, it was revealed by the newly appointed Premier Hau Pei-tsun that Taipei would set up 'an intermediary organization' later on in the same month to govern its booming unofficial links with the mainland.[11]

However, the most important manifestation of the adherence to the 'one country, two governments' principle came from President Lee Teng-hui when he was sworn in to his first full six-year term in May 1990. President Lee made it known that his government was willing to hold talks with China 'within the one-China frame-work and on a government-to-government basis with the two sides having equal status'.[12] He also offered to end the state of war with China. However, Lee's offer was premised on three conditions. They were that Beijing must renounce the use of force against Taiwan, stop interfering in Taipei's efforts to expand its inter-national relations, and move towards democracy and a free economic system.[13] If these terms were met, according to Lee, Taiwan would completely open up academic, cultural, economic, trade, scientific, and technological exchanges with the mainland and, when 'objective conditions are ripe', Taipei would be able to discuss the issue of the reunification of China 'based on the common will of the Chinese people on both sides of the Taiwan Straits'.[14] It was interesting that Lee did not reiterate Taipei's demand that Beijing should forsake Deng's Four Basic Principles. None the less, it was quite obvious that there was no way that Beijing would accept the three preconditions. Knowing very well that that was the case, President Lee's suggestion gave him the advantage of supporting a popular ideal without having to put it into effect. At very little political cost to his government, Lee seemed to be making a counter-

10 *The Straits Times* (Singapore, 16 May 1990).
11 *The Straits Times* (3 Aug. 1990).
12 *The Straits Times* (17 May 1990).
13 *The Straits Times* (22 May 1990).
14 *Free China Review* (July 1990), 8–9.

proposal to Beijing's suggestion of having a party-to-party dialogue. Lee's proposal also highlighted his determination to preserve the parity of status between Taipei and Beijing in working towards eventual reunification. What Taipei wanted was an environment in which both sides of the Taiwan Straits could compete and coexist peacefully.

The recognition that China has 'one country, two governments' has finally been well accepted and used by President Lee as a basis for Taipei's reunification policy in the 1990s. However, it is clear that the immediate agenda for Lee was not so much the reunification of China, but the strengthening of the KMT's power after its relatively poor performance in the December 1989 elections and the democratization of the political system in Taiwan itself. In fact, Lee had given himself a two-year timetable for fairly radical democratization of the island's politics during 1990 and 1991. This tall order at home will be the major preoccupation of the present KMT administration.

Beijing's 'Principled' Response

After the death of Hu Yaobang, the most significant and immediate development in PRC-Taiwan relations was no doubt the ADB meeting in early May 1989. And, as far as Beijing was concerned, it did not use the occasion to embarrass the delegates from Taipei. In fact, it tried to accommodate the sensitivities of the Taiwan delegation in its immigration procedures, accommodation, and other details for the Taipei delegation on the trip. China would have liked to treat Taipei's presence at the Beijing ADB meeting in a low-key fashion. Its primary concern was to ensure that Taipei could not use the occasion to produce 'two Chinas'. As a result, its principled stand of having a one-China policy and the naming of Taipei as 'Taipei, China' was upheld by the ADB at the 1989 meeting on the insistence of Beijing.

The meeting itself did not really produce any hiccups in Beijing–Taipei relations as China displayed its 'brotherly love' towards Taiwan. Special emphasis was placed on treating the Taiwan delegation as kinsmen from the other side of the Taiwan Straits. At the time of the meeting, the Chinese leadership might have been embarrassed or perturbed by the ongoing student pro-democracy movement which by then had spread throughout the Chinese capital and other parts of China. However, the ADB meeting did not seem to have been disturbed that much, especially compared with the Sino-Soviet summit later in mid-May 1989. Major problems in PRC–Taiwan relations seem to have surfaced only later, when Beijing charged that Taipei was involved in fanning the turmoil on the mainland.[15] In spite of this allegation, it was obvious that Beijing did not want to put too much strain on PRC–Taiwan relations. It still had its overall interest in promoting the reunification of China. In fact, as early as 26 June 1989, Tang Shubei, deputy-director of the Taiwan Affairs Office of the State Council, issued the first statement after the Tiananmen incident on Beijing's unchanged policy towards Taiwan, namely, advocating 'peaceful' reunification and the use of the 'one country, two systems' formula to incorporate Taiwan into China. Subsequently, CCP leaders like the newly elected General-Secretary Jiang Zemin, Li Xiannian, and Wu Xueqian restated Beijing's 'peaceful' strategy to reunify the country.[16]

Beijing was probably quite relieved that the contacts between the two sides, at least at the unofficial level, were not adversely affected for long. Except for a short period after the June Tiananmen incident, the people of Taiwan were quick to resume their practical contacts with the other side of the Taiwan Straits. In fact, in the case of trade between Taiwan and China via Hong Kong, it rose to US $3.4 billion in 1989, a 28 per cent rise over the previous year. An estimated US $1 billion has been poured in from Taiwan for various investment projects on the mainland in recent years.[17] In addition to the small and medium-sized firms, some large corporations in Taipei were also interested enough to prospect for investment opportunities on the mainland. From all indications, it seems that Beijing still values the 'people-to-people' relations not only for its benefit to the goal of the 'Four Modernizations' but also to that of the reunification of China. Its hope is that these can pave the way for direct and official contacts.

In the face of Taipei's drive to upgrade its relations with other countries and its relative success in wooing small countries like Grenada, Liberia, and Belize to have formal ties with the KMT

---

15 For details, see the postscript of Lee Lai To in *Reunification* (see n. 4).

16 See e.g. *China Times* (16 Sept. 1989).

17 *The Straits Times* (25 July 1990).

government, Beijing decided to suspend diplomatic relations with such countries in order to thwart what it considered to be Taipei's attempt 'to bring about "dual recognition" or to create "two Chinas" or "one China, one Taiwan" '.[18] Probably, Beijing's calculation was that it could afford to suspend such links and that the chances were that Taipei would only succeed in tempting those smaller countries which could use the economic help from Taiwan. For the other countries, especially those which had vital strategic and economic interests with China, Beijing's hope would be that they might be less tempted to follow a 'two-China' policy. More important, it was a matter of principle that China had to sever its relations with such small countries under such conditions. If it swallowed its pride and accepted 'dual recognition', it would open a Pandora's box of diplomatic embarrassment for Beijing and give Taipei more breathing space in international affairs. Quite obviously, that would also set precedents which could hamper or at least slow down the process of the reunification of China.

Events later on in 1990 indicated that Beijing was determined to pursue its one-China policy, ending its formal ties with two African states, Lesotho and Guinea-Bissau, when the two resumed or established diplomatic ties with Taipei.[19] In spite of this and its problems with Western countries as a result of their economic sanctions against China after the Tiananmen incident, Beijing did not seem to have been significantly isolated in its foreign relations. In fact, Saudi Arabia established and Indonesia resumed formal ties with Beijing in July and August 1990 respectively. This could be followed by Singapore, Brunei, and South Korea, as far as the Asia-Pacific region is concerned. At a time when Japan and some Western countries have already shown signs of wanting to resume normal activities with Beijing, this would also encourage Beijing to adhere closely to its one-China policy and increase Taiwan's difficulties in international affairs.

As a result of its one-China policy and wish to reincorporate Taipei by the 'one country, two systems' formula, it is not surprising that Beijing would find it difficult to accept the 'one country, two governments' proposal from Taipei. From the outset when the 'one country, two governments' proposal was first officially mooted,

---

[18] See e.g. *BR* (14–20 Aug. 1989), 7.
[19] See *BR* (23–9 Apr. 1990), 6, and (11–17 June 1990), 5.

Beijing had been most negative towards the idea. It categorically denounced it as a scheme which established 'two Chinas' under the name of 'one China'.[20] When President Lee Teng-hui mentioned the proposal again in his inaugural speech in May 1990, Beijing considered his conditions for government-to-government contacts 'impossible'.[21] The response from General-Secretary Jiang Zemin also reiterated Beijing's previous condition of talks 'on a reciprocal basis between the Chinese Communist Party and the Kuomintang'. However, Jiang added that China also attached importance to the role of other parties, social groups, and individuals from all walks of life in realizing the cause of reunification. He ventured to suggest that 'representatives from these parties and people's organizations may also be invited to attend the negotiations'.[22]

Perhaps Jiang and his colleagues in the party were heartened to learn that not everyone in Taipei objected to party-to-party negotiations. Notably, Liang Su-rung, speaker of the Legislative Yuan and other legislators in Taipei were reportedly considering bi-party negotiations as a possible way of establishing official contact between the two sides of the Taiwan Straits when the time was ripe.[23] In view of the influence of the opposition in Taiwanese politics, Beijing was shrewd enough to broaden the proposed negotiations between the CCP and KMT to include the participation of other political forces.

It remains to be said that Beijing seems absolutely set on its master plan of introducing the 'one country, two systems' formula in reunifying China. The plan will be implemented and tested in Hong Kong, as demonstrated vividly by the adoption of the Basic Law of the Hong Kong Special Administrative Region in April 1990 after two rounds of consultation. As such, it is not likely that Beijing would forsake the 'one country, two systems' approach towards reunification until it has gained sufficient experience in realizing the problems involved in the implementation of the Basic Law in Hong Kong. Such experiences will probably be used to improve or even modify the introduction of such an approach in incorporating Macao and Taiwan into China later on.

In the mean time, Beijing is facing probably one of the severest

[20] *BR* (22–8 May 1989), 20.
[21] *BR* (4–10 June 1990), 8.
[22] *BR* (18–24 June 1990), 4.
[23] *The Nineties* (July 1990), 39.

tests of its rule at home and abroad after the Tiananmen incident. On the domestic front, it not only has to meet many of the ongoing developmental problems in its economy, but the perennial challenge of unifying the leadership and people whose views became polarized by the pro-democracy movement in 1989. The uncertainties with regard to the political succession also aggravate the situation. On the foreign front, the international pressure against Beijing after the Tiananmen incident and developments in Eastern Europe and the Soviet Union also put the hard-liners in Beijing on the defensive. In view of these problems, unless there are signs that Taipei is opting for its own independence, Beijing has to live with the existence of two governments in China for the time being and a Taiwan becoming more and more assertive and confident of itself in Chinese politics.

Concluding Remarks

Presently, the KMT government under President Lee is most concerned with problems in democratizing Taiwan. It is trying, among other things, to solicit more ideas and support in its road towards a more democratic society as demonstrated notably by the convening of the National Affairs Conference in June–July 1990. In its relations with the mainland it would like to emphasize peaceful competition. It is, as always, concerned with the security of the island in dealing with Beijing. As a result, one of its major tasks has been to find ways to regulate the surging interactions between the two sides, rather than the reunification of China. Within the KMT government, Lee probably has to build up a consensus before he can make any bold move on the reunification issue, particularly in view of the pluralistic and divergent views on how to deal with the CCP. His immediate concern in Taipei as far as the communists are concerned is to end the 'Temporary Provisions Effective During the Period of Mobilization for the Suppression of the Communist Rebellion' as soon as possible.[24] Taipei's objective remains the launch of a political offensive against the mainland and the promotion of the Taiwan experience to exert its influence in China.

---

[24] According to Lee Teng-hui, he will terminate the Provisions within one year. See *China Times* (23 May 1990).

According to Lee Teng-hui, there will be opportunities for the KMT to go back to the mainland within his six-year term.[25] In the mean time, it is obvious that Taipei is not ready to have reunification talks because of the many urgent issues at home. It also sees no major political benefits for it to engage in such a dialogue at the official level as it is still looked upon as a local government by Beijing. With the dilution of the emotional attachment of some of the people in Taiwan to the mainland and the increasingly open expression of the desire to have a separate and even an independent Taiwan (especially from the opposition), Taiwan's commitment to reunification could also be affected. While reiterating its one-China policy and the territorial integrity of one China as a matter of belief or, perhaps more importantly, out of fear of retribution from Beijing, the KMT government may be tempted to opt for a separate way in the future. Whether it will eventually garner enough courage and strength to go independent under more favourable circumstances, or will accept a nebulous political link with the mainland in some new form under the one-China principle in the future, remains to be seen.

[25] *China Times* (23 May 1990).

9. Hong Kong and China: Economic Interdependence

MICHÈLE LEDÍC

Economic relations between China and Hong Kong are complex, close, and long-standing, and in the 1980s became very close. This was partly a result of China's open-door policy, and partly of outstanding entrepreneurship and robustness on the part of Hong Kong. The purpose of this chapter is to provide a better understanding of Hong Kong's economic interdependence with China in the last decade, and to analyse how relations will develop in the 1990s, in particular after 1997.

This chapter will first compare the size and nature of the two economies, and examines how important they are to each other. Secondly, it examines visible trade flows between China and Hong Kong, including the role of re-exports, and the growing importance of outward processing. Thirdly, the flow of capital is analysed. The movement of long-term capital, in the form of direct investment by China in Hong Kong, and of Hong Kong investment in China, especially in the Special Economic Zones, is another strong indicator of interaction between the two economies. The growth of these relations since 1979, and especially since 1984, when the Sino-British Joint Declaration on Hong Kong was signed, is also discussed.[1]

In the aftermath of the events of June 1989 in China, and the impending transfer of Hong Kong's sovereignty to China in 1997, the growing influence of Beijing on Hong Kong's political and economic life is considered. It will be seen that doubts must now arise about how far the autonomy guaranteed to Hong Kong by the Sino-British Declaration of 1984, and more recently embodied in the Basic Law, will be honoured in practice by China. This in turn raises questions about Hong Kong's future prospects as a financial and business centre.

---

[1] The first version of the present chapter appeared in D. Goodman and G. Segal, eds., *China at Forty: Mid-Life Crisis?* (Oxford, 1989). That version contained an analysis of the implications of Chinese–Hong Kong developments for UK trade. This analysis is not repeated in the present chapter.

The Economies of China and Hong Kong

Hong Kong's Gross Domestic Product (GDP) in 1965, measured in US dollars, was some 3 per cent of China's GDP. Twenty years later it was 12.5 per cent. China's GDP during this period had an average annual growth rate of 7 per cent, while Hong Kong had nearly double this rate of growth, both of these measured in constant US dollars. In the same period, GNP per capita in China grew by 5.2 per cent per annum and in Hong Kong by 6.2 per cent. In 1987 China's GNP per capita was US $290, while Hong Kong's was thirty times higher, at US $8,070.[2]

The two economies differ greatly in the composition of their output, especially in the importance of agriculture and services. Both of these sectors had slower growth rates in China over the period than the industry sector, but in 1987 agriculture still accounted for as much as 31 per cent of GDP, as compared with 49 per cent for industry and 20 per cent for services. The composition of Hong Kong's GDP, on the other hand, is much more like that of an advanced country, with less than 1 per cent of GDP coming from agriculture, 29 per cent from industry, and 70 per cent from services. The service sector has for some time expanded much faster than the rest of the economy.

The trade links between China and Hong Kong are very strong. Between 1978 and 1989 Hong Kong's total trade with China increased, in current prices, by over twelve times, and since 1985 China has been Hong Kong's largest trading partner. At the same time, Hong Kong is China's largest export market, with some 43 per cent of China's total exports going to Hong Kong in 1989. In 1988 Hong Kong displaced Japan as the largest importer into China. Hong Kong is China's largest source of direct foreign investment and joint venture investment. It is an entrepôt of great importance for China's exports, most recently in respect of the indirect trade with South Korea and Taiwan. It is estimated that 30 to 40 per cent of China's foreign exchange receipts are earned through Hong Kong.[3] Remittances sent from Hong Kong to relatives in

---

[2] *World Bank Development Report 1989* (Oxford, 1989).

[3] 'Hong Kong Works', talk given by Mr K. Y. Yeung, Director of Industry, Hong Kong Government, at a seminar held in London on 7 Sept. 1987. Also 'Hong Kong in Transition', speech given by Sir David Wilson, Governor of Hong Kong, at Chatham House, London, on 21 Mar. 1988.

China are a valuable source of income for China.

Chinese investments in Hong Kong are large and growing, especially by CITIC (China International Trust and Investment Corporation) Hong Kong. In the manufacturing sector, they have overtaken British investments, and are now exceeded only by those of America and Japan. Chinese interests control fifteen banks in Hong Kong, as well as an estimated 3,000 to 4,000 companies, of which less than one-third are officially authorized by China.[4]

Foreign Trade of China and Hong Kong

Exports are of growing importance for China, increasing from 7.4 per cent of national income in 1980 to about 13 per cent in 1989. These figures compare with 14 per cent for Japan, 22 per cent for the UK, and a very high figure of 104 per cent for Hong Kong in 1989.

There has recently been a substantial change in the composition of China's trade, and its exports in particular (Fig. 9.1, exports). Manufactured goods in 1985 accounted for 49 per cent of total exports, but by 1989 had reached 71 per cent of the total. The value of manufactured exports, in current US dollars, had increased by 1989 to nearly 2.8 times the 1985 level.[5]

Exports of primary goods, which include oil, declined by some 20 per cent (in current US dollars) between 1985 and 1986, when the oil price collapsed. However, overall exports increased by over 11 per cent. Many observers had predicted a sharp decline in export performance in 1986, due to the oil price collapse, especially as China's oil and oil-product exports accounted for 28.5 per cent of the total value of exports in 1985. Foreign exchange earnings from these were indeed halved to some US $3.8 billion in 1986, in comparison with the year before. They accounted for only 12.3 per cent of total exports, while in volume terms they were 6.3 per cent lower. Textile and clothing exports, on the other hand, rose by nearly 30 per cent in value terms, between 1985 and 1986, to US $8.3 billion, in

---

[4] *Financial Times*, Survey 'Hong Kong', 8 Nov. 1989, 'Slow Beginning to the Anti-Corruption Drive'.
[5] The RMB/US$ exchange rate changed from 2.9 in 1985 to 3.2 in June 1986 and 3.72 in Dec. 1986. It remained at that level until Dec. 1989, when it was devalued to 4.72. Since 1987 Chinese customs statistics have been published in US$ only. The HK$/US$ exchange rate has been fixed at 7.8 since 1983.

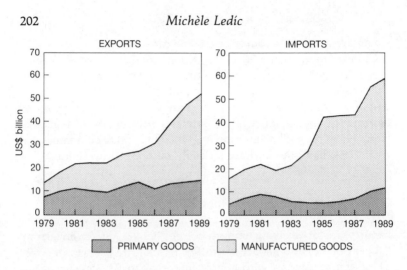

Fig 9.1 *China: commodity composition of trade*

spite of being subject to protectionism under the Multi-Fibre Arrangement.[6]

Few countries could have emerged from the 1986 oil crisis with such a quick and effective response. China rapidly switched its exports from mainly primary to mainly manufactured goods, notably to textiles and clothing. Oil exports stayed at about the 1986 level, in US dollars, from 1987 to 1989, but textile and clothing exports rose steadily from US $6.5 billion in 1985 to US $14.7 billion in 1989, when they accounted for 28 per cent by value of total exports. Increased exports of other manufactured goods also, combined with import controls, enabled the trade deficit to be reduced from nearly US $15 billion in 1985, to US $6.7 billion in 1989. Import controls, following an explosion of manufactured goods imports in 1985, account for the fact that manufactured goods imports, while still amounting to 80 per cent or more of imports in value terms, rose only by some 13 per cent between 1985 and 1989, while primary good imports rose by 130 per cent (Fig. 9.1, imports).

Hong Kong and Japan are the most important partners in China's foreign trade. Together they accounted for 59 per cent of its exports

---

[6] For a detailed analysis of Chinese textiles and clothing export performance see: Z. A. Silberston (in collaboration with M. Ledic), *The Future of the Multi-Fibre Arrangement* (HMSO; London, 1989), chap. 7, 'China', pp. 71–83.

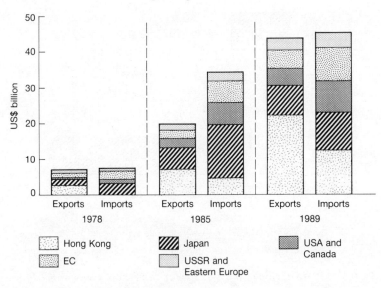

Fig 9.2 *China's top trading partners*

and 39 per cent of its imports in 1989. However, in bilateral terms, the trends were very different. China's imports from Japan fell by 30 per cent in value between 1985 and 1989, while its exports increased by 37 per cent. Trade with Hong Kong took a different direction, with imports increasing during this period over two and a half times and exports by over three times (Fig. 9.2). Hong Kong is now especially dominant as an export market for China.

Trade figures that are not shown separately in Chinese statistics, but are given in detail for Hong Kong, are those of re-exports. Re-exports are classified by both country of destination and country of origin. Hong Kong's total re-exports consist of re-exports not to China; re-exports to China of Chinese goods; and re-exports to China of non-Chinese goods. In 1988 re-exports outstripped Hong Kong's own total domestic exports for the first time. Total domestic exports consist of domestic exports to China, and domestic exports not to China.

Re-exports are of rapidly growing importance to Hong Kong: in 1985 they accounted for 45 per cent of total exports, but had risen to over 60 per cent by 1989. Re-exports in 1989 amounted to HK $346.4 billion, while domestic exports amounted to HK $224.1

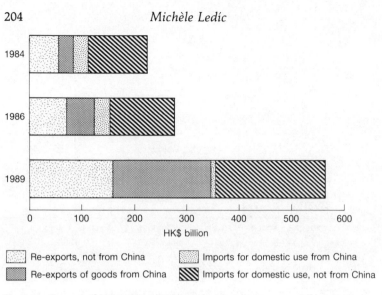

Fig 9.3 *Source of Hong Kong imports for domestic use and for re-exports*

billion (see Fig. 9.4). By source of imports (Fig. 9.3), 96 per cent of
Hong Kong's imports for domestic use in 1989 came from countries
other than China, while 46 per cent of imports for re-export came
from non-Chinese sources. Of total re-exports in 1989, HK $103.5
billion went to China (Fig. 9.4), and HK $188.3 billion came from
China (see Fig. 9.3). China was therefore involved in Hong Kong
re-exports amounting to HK $292 billion, or over 84 per cent of the
total, either as a market or as a source of supply.

With the introduction of more stringent import controls in China
after 1985, re-exports from Hong Kong to China fell in 1986.
However, with import controls still in operation in China, re-
exports from Hong Kong to China rose two and a half times in value
terms between 1986 and 1989, accounting in the latter year for 30
per cent of Hong Kong's re-exports. Of total Hong Kong re-exports
going to China of US $103.5, HK $12.1 billion were of Chinese
origin, and may have been subject to further processing in Hong
Kong (Fig. 9.4).

Hong Kong's domestic exports to China more than doubled
between 1986 and 1989. As a result, China's total imports from
Hong Kong (including re-exports into China) more than doubled

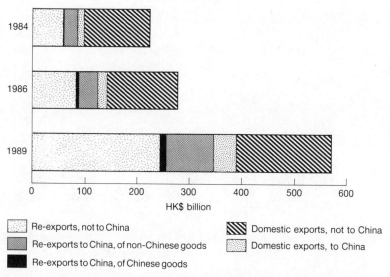

Re-exports, not to China

Re-exports to China, of non-Chinese goods

Re-exports to China, of Chinese goods

Domestic exports, not to China

Domestic exports, to China

Fig 9.4   *Destination of Hong Kong total (domestic and re-exports)*

also. Since China's total imports from all countries between 1986 and 1989 rose by 38 per cent only, it follows that Hong Kong now accounts for a considerably larger share of Chinese imports than previously (see Fig. 9.2).

This surge in trade between Hong Kong and China has been partly due to Hong Kong's highly developed infrastructure, its communication facilities, and its international nature. To some extent, it has been due to its role as an entrepôt in the booming indirect trade of China with Taiwan and South Korea, with neither of whom has China diplomatic relations (Fig. 9.5). By 1989 imports via Hong Kong from Taiwan had reached US $2.9 billion, and trade with South Korea was evenly balanced, but a large deficit persisted with Taiwan. In spite of the lack of diplomatic relations, however, there was — according to South Korean statistics — sizeable direct trade between China and South Korea.

Much of the mutual growth in trade during the last few years can be explained by increased outward processing activities in China, on behalf of firms in Hong Kong. Large-scale outward processing is a relatively new phenomenon, dating back to 1984, and is now very active. An increasing number of simple but

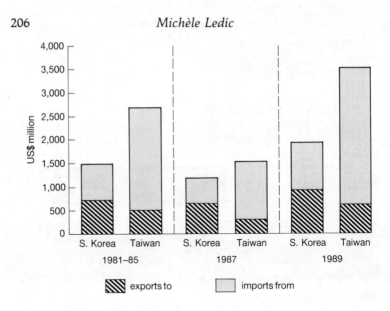

Fig 9.5 *China's trade with South Korea and Taiwan via Hong Kong*

labour-intensive processes, previously carried out in Hong Kong, have been moved to China, mainly to the nearby Guangdong province, to take advantage of lower production costs, especially those of labour costs.

Most of the products are assembled in China and then sent back to Hong Kong as finished goods, or as semi-finished goods needing further processing, possibly thereby qualifying for Hong Kong origin (particularly important for the US market). Products for which the qualifying manufacturing processes are carried out in China would be regarded as of Chinese origin. Even when goods from China are subject to value-added manufacturing processes in Hong Kong, they may not qualify for Hong Kong origin, and might be regarded as re-exports from China.

A sample survey has recently been conducted by the Hong Kong government of Hong Kong's trade with China of an outward processing nature.[7] Its findings are summarized in Table 9.1. For the purposes of the survey, exports to China for outward processing

---

[7] Hong Kong government, *Hong Kong External Trade 1989*, p. 7, tables K and L, and *Hong Kong 1990*.

Table 9.1. *Hong Kong: Estimated Values of Outward Processing Trade (OPT) with China in 1989* (HK$ billion)

	Total trade	Estimated trade	% of OPT
Imports from China	196.7	114.3	58.1
Exports to China	146.8	77.8	53.0
o.w. Domestic exports	43.3	32.9	76.0
Re-exports	103.5	45.1	43.6

Source: Hong Kong government, *Hong Kong External Trade 1989*.

refer to the exporting of raw materials and semi-manufactures, for or through Hong Kong to China for processing, with a contractual arrangement for subsequently re-importing the processed goods into Hong Kong. Imports from China, related to outward processing, refer to the importing of goods from China, of which all or part of their raw materials or semi-manufactures are, under contractual arrangement, exported from or through Hong Kong to China for processing.

Some 58 per cent of all Hong Kong's imports from China in 1989 were related to outward processing, as were 53 per cent of all Hong Kong's exports to China. The figure was especially high, at 76 per cent, for Hong Kong's domestic exports to China. Since nearly all imports from China into Hong Kong are re-exported (96 per cent in 1989), it follows that some 60 per cent of Hong Kong's re-exports of Chinese goods are the result of outward processing. It is also evident from the figures that the bulk of Hong Kong's domestic exports to China are of raw materials or semi-manufactures, to be subject to outward processing in China, and subsequently re-imported into Hong Kong.

While the majority of Hong Kong manufacturers have set up arrangements in China in order to manufacture for export, some have done this in the hope of gaining easier access to China's domestic market. Some estimates quote a figure of more than 10,000 factories in Guangdong province, either processing for Hong Kong companies or in co-operative ventures with them, and employing between two and three million workers. Hong Kong's manufacturing labour force is now just over 800,000. It can therefore be argued that Hong Kong's effective labour force has been more than trebled as a result of this co-operation with China.

The commodity composition of trade between the two countries has been much affected by outward processing. Most Hong Kong toy and electronics manufacturers, and a large number of textile and garment companies, have their manufacturing carried out in Guangdong. The volume of textiles and clothing manufactured for Hong Kong firms in China would probably rise substantially if the Multi-Fibre Arrangement (which imposes quotas for exports by individual countries) were to be brought to an end.

Overall trade statistics for Hong Kong reveal that, in 1989, 18 per cent of Hong Kong's domestic exports to China, and 23 per cent of its re-exports to China, were of textiles and clothing, amounting to HK $31.5 billion. In the same year, 36 per cent of Hong Kong's imports from China were of textiles and clothing, amounting to HK $38.5 billion. Outward processing activity accounted for a high proportion of this trade, with yarns and fabrics from or via Hong Kong being made up into fabrics or clothing in China, for export by China through Hong Kong, or for use in Hong Kong. It is estimated that approximately 60 per cent of China's entire exports of textiles and clothing in 1989 went through Hong Kong.

Another very important category in trade between Hong Kong and China is telecommunications equipment. This accounted for 15 per cent of Hong Kong's domestic exports to China in 1989, and for as much as 60 per cent of its re-exports, amounting to HK $68.4 billion in all. Imports from China into Hong Kong of these items accounted for 3 per cent only of Hong Kong's total imports from China, and amounted to HK $5.1 billion. The relative size of these figures (taking into account also direct exports from China in this category) suggests that outward processing was comparatively unimportant, as compared with imports for retention within China.

Exports of other goods from Hong Kong to China are spread over a wide range of items. The same is true of imports into Hong Kong from China, although here toys, games, and baby carriages (which have been a rapidly rising category for re-export by Hong Kong), and food and live animals, are also important.

Investment in China

Apart from trade, two-way investment constitutes an important part of the economic relationship between China and Hong Kong.

Available data on foreign investment in China show that between 1978 and 1989 foreign investment contracted was in the region of US $33 billion.[8] Of this, some 70 per cent came from Hong Kong and Macao. In the Special Economic Zones Hong Kong's share was nearer 80 per cent. Japan was responsible for about 12 per cent and the USA for 10 per cent of contracted foreign investment during the period. According to some estimates, two-thirds of the Hong Kong total originated with Hong Kong and Chinese companies in the territory, and one-third was routed and financed through foreign-owned Hong Kong representative offices.

It is well known that realized foreign investment in China is much below the contracted figure. It has been estimated that not much more than one-third of contracted investment has in fact been realized. Because of the problems involved with such factors as the repatriation of foreign exchange and ever-changing legislation and policy towards foreign investment, contracted investment itself fell after 1985: in that year contracted foreign investment was US $6.3 billion, but it was not much more than half this in 1986 and 1987. There was however some recovery in 1988 and 1989, to US $5.3 billion and US $5.6 billion respectively, as foreign confidence grew before the events of June 1989.

Foreign direct investment has not fully met the objectives fixed by the Chinese authorities, which were primarily to encourage the foundation of high-tech industries, and to develop basic resources, such as energy. In the period 1980 to 1987, for example, nearly half of utilized direct foreign investment was in the tertiary sector, such as hotels and recreational facilities. Only about 10 per cent was in energy and resources, and some 40 per cent in productive projects. In 1988 the situation improved, from the Chinese point of view, with nearly 60 per cent of all direct foreign investment utilized in that year going into productive projects.

Much of Hong Kong's investment in the Special Economic Zones has been connected with the desire to create favourable conditions for outward processing. A large number of industrial co-operation projects have been concluded between Hong Kong and China. Many have not involved substantial investment in fixed assets, but have used the existing labour force and local industrial

---

[8] MOFERT (Ministry of Foreign Economic Relations and Trade) and State Statistical Bureau Communiqué, 20 Feb. 1990.

premises, and have provided some plant and machinery, as well as training.

Apart from investment in China's industrial and services sectors, Hong Kong capital is also involved in the development of infrastructure in China, particularly in energy-related investment. The Daya Bay nuclear power plant is one of the best known cases, being a joint venture between the Hong Kong Nuclear Investment Company and the Guangdong Nuclear Investment Company.

The prospects for future foreign investment in China suffered a severe blow following the events of June 1989, and many foreign businessmen withdrew from contact and from making new commitments in China. Hong Kong businessmen, among others, have been prompted to consider investing elsewhere. Makers of toys, for example, have been exploring the possibility of investing in Thailand, with Malaysia and Indonesia as other alternatives.[9]

A particularly severe set-back for China was the suspension of loans from the World Bank. At the time of the June events, seven World Bank projects with US $780 million were in the pipeline. If approved, the Bank would have loaned China US $2.2 billion in 1988-9 and US $2.5 billion in 1989-90. Instead, the figure for 1989-90 will be less than US $500 million. By June 1990 only three new loans, totalling US $140 million, had been approved by the bank's executive board, for emergency earthquake relief, agricultural development, and vocational and educational development.[10] Loans from Japan and the European Community have also been suspended. However, Japan announced in mid-1990 that it would probably go ahead with the US $5.5 billion aid loan, which was suspended after international pressure in June 1989.

Despite the apparent hazards, some businessmen have been returning to China. More than 1,000 Taiwanese companies, for example, had put US $1.1 billion into China by the end of 1989. Taiwanese investment in China in 1990 is said to have exceeded that of the USA and Japan, accounting for more than 60 per cent of all recent foreign investment.[11]

---

[9] *FEER* (25 Jan. 1990), 'Hong Kong Manufacturers See Strong Sales', also *Financial Times* (6 June 1990), 'Hong Kong Toys Make Game Recovery'.

[10] *FEER* (6 July 1989), 'Put on Hold'; *FEER* (7 June 1990), 'No More Favours'.

[11] *Financial Times* (6 June 1990), 'Taiwan in Two Minds on Trade with China'. M. Ledic, 'Foreign Economic Relations', in G. Segal, ed., *Chinese Politics and Foreign Policy Reform* (London, 1990), 230-55.

Investment in Hong Kong

Overall foreign investment in Hong Kong's service sectors, especially banking and finance, has always been strong, but foreign investment in Hong Kong's manufacturing industries has accounted in the past for a relatively small proportion of the private sector share of gross domestic fixed capital formation. However, data on inward investment in the manufacturing sector, in respect of projects facilitated by the Industry Department, show a steady rise since 1984.[12]

At the end of 1988 the number of Hong Kong manufacturing companies reporting an overseas investment interest was 605. The value of total overseas investment at original cost at the same date was HK $26.2 billion, more than double the figure recorded in 1984. The value of gross additions to fixed assets in 1988 was nearly 50 per cent higher than in 1987, although no doubt most of the finance for this came from ploughed-back profits.

The USA was the leading source country, contributing 34 per cent of the total value of investment (Fig. 9.6). It was followed by Japan (27 per cent), China (11 per cent), and the UK (9 per cent). Britain had ranked third in 1984, but was overtaken by China in 1986. Over 60 per cent of foreign investment in 1988 was concentrated in four industries: electronics (36 per cent), textiles and clothing (11 per cent), electrical products (9 per cent), and chemical products (8 per cent).

Chinese investment in Hong Kong manufacturing industry only reached significant proportions in the 1980s. In 1988, forty-nine Chinese investments were identified. Of these 78 per cent were joint-ventures, in contrast to American and Japanese investments, which were mostly wholly owned. Chinese investments were spread across a number of industries, with chemical products and electronics the most important areas, followed by textiles and clothing.

Apart from ownership of manufacturing industry, Chinese interests control fifteen banks in Hong Kong and numerous other companies. CITIC, for example, bought 12.5 per cent of Cathay Pacific Airways in 1987, and China has participated in the consortium building a second cross-harbour tunnel. In March 1990

---

[12] Hong Kong Government Industry Department, *Overseas Investment in Hong Kong's Manufacturing Industries 1989* (Hong Kong, 1990).

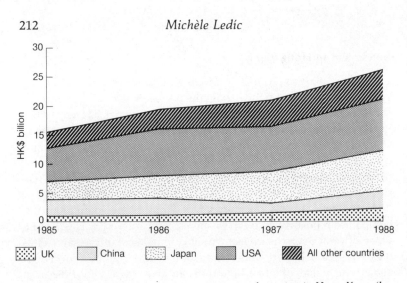

Fig 9.6 *Stock of overseas investment in manufacturing in Hong Kong (by source country).*

CITIC took a 20 per cent share in Hong Kong Telecommunications, and has also taken a 38 per cent stake in Dragonair.[13]

It has been suggested that in 1987 there were well over 500 sizeable companies in Hong Kong with PRC interests, the highest numbers being in trade and industrial promotion, shipping, transportation and tourism, manufacturing, and banking and finance.[14] The same source ranks total Chinese investment in Hong Kong first with HK $80 billion, followed by the USA, with HK $40 billion, Japan (HK $30 billion), South-East Asia (HK $25 billion), and Europe (HK $20 billion). By contrast, Hong Kong investment in China is put at HK $45 billion, well below Chinese investment in Hong Kong. Recent estimates, as previously mentioned, put the total number of Chinese companies of all sizes in Hong Kong at some 4,000.[15]

Japan has been another recent large-scale investor in Hong Kong (as has been Taiwan). For example, some nine Japanese financial

[13] *Financial Times*, Survey 'Hong Kong', 8 Nov. 1989, 'Capitalist-Style Operation is Surprisingly Buoyant'; *FEER* (11 Jan. 1990), 'The Cadres Bargains' (see also 25 Jan. 1990, pp. 62–3, and 15 Feb. 1990, p. 86); *Financial Times* (2 Apr. 1990), 'Chinese Dragon Builds its Hong Kong Treasure Hoard'.

[14] Ching H. Shao, 'Chinese Investment In Hong Kong', Hong Kong, 12 Sept. 1988 (stockbroker's circular).

[15] See n. 4.

institutions established themselves in 1989–90, including four large life assurance companies. Another important area for Japanese investors has been property. They are thought to have invested up to HK $5 billion a year in Hong Kong in 1987–9.[16]

Hong Kong and China: Current Issues

China embarked on an austerity programme which started in September 1988, and was reinforced in November 1989. The initial programme was not a consequence of the events of June 1989, but these events strengthened the Chinese will to maintain the programme.

The austerity programme was embarked upon to curb excess demand in the economy and to bring down inflation. It was also intended to correct structural imbalance — a euphemism for trying to reassert central control over an economy that had developed a great deal of regional and enterprise initiative. The programme involved cutting the money supply, reducing the growth rates of consumption and of investments in hotels, and restraining the growth of government spending. At the industry level, attempts were made to reassert central control, and resources were directed towards heavy industry and the development of basic raw materials.

Measures to manage demand were successful in damping down the economy, and the rate of inflation was brought down from 30 per cent to some 6.5 per cent in early 1990. The rate of growth of output slowed down, especially in the second half of 1989, and retail sales fell in real terms. At the industrial level, in order to emphasize the central plan, some powers previously delegated to provinces and enterprises were taken back by Beijing. Resources were concentrated more heavily in state-owned enterprises.

These measures brought about large-scale unemployment. Industries especially affected have been construction and township and rural enterprises. Workers from these industries are said to be touring the country in search of jobs. Estimates of the numbers unemployed have been put at several tens of millions. In December 1989 the renminbi was devalued by 21.2 per cent, reducing its

---

[16] *The Economist* (12 Sept. 1987), p. 12; *FEER* (7 Apr. 1988), 49–86. *Financial Times*, Survey 'Hong Kong', 12 June 1990, 'Outsiders See Brighter Future'.

value from RMB 3.72 to 4.72 to the US dollar. This was a delayed response to China's deteriorating external position, and was particularly intended to curb imports.

The overall demand measures taken by Beijing may be relaxed if the economy slows down, and this has already been done to some extent, but the industrial measures are likely to hamper the dynamic growth of the Chinese economy, especially if they are maintained for a number of years. The climate is also likely to be unfavourable to foreign investment in China. This is partly because of the slowing down of the economy, and partly because official attitudes have now become less favourable to foreign investment, especially in the service sector, than previously. There is also continued concern, among traders and investors, about the political stability of China, following the June 1989 events, and the continued hard line of the Chinese leadership. Leaders in the coastal provinces, however, will certainly press for a continuation of industrial growth, and of the foreign investment associated with this. Cautious foreign investment interest in these provinces (including interest from Hong Kong) is therefore likely.

Many joint ventures in China encountered difficulties in 1989–90, owing to the downturn in tourism in China, and the recession caused by the austerity measures brought in by the Chinese government. Several joint ventures, including the largest property joint venture – the China World Trade Centre in Beijing – were planning to reschedule their loans.[17]

From the point of view of Hong Kong, its exports to China for China's domestic use are likely to be affected, unless there is some relaxation in Chinese macro-economic policy. Current outward processing activity between China and Hong Kong may not be greatly affected in the short run, although joint ventures may have greater difficulty in obtaining export quotas (in products such as textiles and clothing, subject to the Multi-Fibre Arrangement), and also Chinese raw materials.

In Hong Kong itself, Chinese investment is being consolidated. The Chinese government has plans to shut many of its companies operating in Hong Kong, especially those involved in property and the stock market. This is partly because of the stock market

---

[17] *Financial Times*, (2 Nov. 1989), 'Chinese Joint Ventures Delay Loan Repayments'; *FEER* (26 Apr. 1990). 'Ill Started Ventures'.

crash of October 1987, but in addition the Chinese government has been planning to curb the activities of the very large number of companies set up in Hong Kong by mainland provinces and corporations in recent years. Many of these are believed to have taken part in corrupt trading on behalf of their mainland owners.[18] Large enterprises, however, especially those with state backing, such as CITIC, have continued to be active.

There was a substantial withdrawal of funds from the Bank of China group after the Tiananmen Square events. They are said to have lost 10 per cent of their deposits within a few days. By mid-1990, however, the group had more than made up the lost deposits, although its market share had been reduced.[19]

An important recent development has been an attempt by the Chinese authorities to influence investment projects in Hong Kong, on the grounds that they will only become fully operational after 1997, when China assumes sovereignty over Hong Kong. This has been most evident in the proposed HK $127 billion airport and container port project, on which China ordered an urgent report in April 1990. This was possibly because of fears that the projects would not be viable after 1997, and China would be left with some liability. China's attitude has forced the Hong Kong government to abandon its earlier insistence that there was no need to consult Beijing, because the territory was currently under British sovereignty, and had been promised a high degree of autonomy in economic and other matters after 1997.[20]

Future Economic Relations between Hong Kong and China

The Sino-British Joint Declaration, which was ratified in 1985, guarantees the continuation of Hong Kong's present rights and freedoms for a period of fifty years after 1997. Hong Kong will retain its capitalist system, its freely convertible currency, its status as a free port, and its own customs territory. It will conduct its own

---

[18] *Financial Times* (20 Nov. 1989), 'China to Shut Many of its Hong Kong Companies'.

[19] *Financial Times*, Survey 'Hong Kong', 8 Nov. 1989, 'Windfall for Local and Foreign Banks' and *Financial Times* (1 May 1990), 'Chinese Banks Recoup Deposits'.

[20] *Financial Times* (4 Apr. 1990), 'Peking Acts to Influence 10 bn Hong Kong Projects'.

economic and cultural relations, and continue to participate in international organizations. The Basic Law, embodying these principles, was approved by the Chinese authorities in April 1990.

The Basic Law does not however embody as much protection for Hong Kong's freedom and democracy as had been hoped for in the colony. No doubt widespread protests in Hong Kong, following the Tiananmen Square events, together with the hard line pursued by the Chinese leadership, contributed to this. In addition, Beijing has attacked other developments concerned with civil rights, such as the proposed Bill of Rights in Hong Kong, and the British government's passports' package affecting a total of 50,000 Hong Kong families in all.

Morale generally in Hong Kong has fallen sharply since June 1989. The Hong Kong Bank has suggested that one consequence has been that the outflow of portfolio capital rose tenfold, to HK $24 billion in 1989–90,[21] although they later qualified this,[22] and the Hong Kong government denies that the available evidence demonstrates any net capital outflow. More important, the 'brain drain' from Hong Kong has undoubtedly become worse, running at a rate of some 1,000 per week in 1990. Resignations from the civil service have increased, although this has partly been due to the tight labour market, which has caused the government to plan to bring in 15,000 foreign workers to ease the labour shortage.[23]

Some important companies have moved their domicile from Hong Kong in recent years, starting with Jardine Matheson, the leading local 'Hong', which went to Bermuda in 1984. Since then, some ninety companies (30 per cent of the total listed on the local stock exchanges) have moved, or are planning to move, their domiciles, mostly to Bermuda.[24] The Hong Kong Bank is discussing a merger with Britain's Midland Bank, partly because of the domicile question,[25] although the bank's interest in Europe predates recent

---

[21] 'Capital Flows in Hong Kong', Economic Report, Hong Kong Bank, Apr. 1990.
[22] *South China Morning Post, Business Post* (6 Sept. 1990), 'Missing Dollars "a Statistical Mistake" '.
[23] See 'Developments in the Labour Market', *Hong Kong Bank Economic Report*, (Oct. 1989); *Financial Times* (3 May 1990), 'Hong Kong Companies to Bring in 15,000 Workers'; *South China Morning Post, Business Post* (26 Jun. 1990), 'Chamber Throws Weight behind Scheme to Import Workers'.
[24] *Financial Times* (2 May 1990), 'Jardine's Enters the Lists against Hong Kong Share Watch Dog'; *Financial Times* (17 May 1990), 'Steady Nerves on the Flight to Bermuda'.
[25] *Financial Times* (9 May 1990), 'Problems for the Bank'.

concerns about the domicile question.

Nevertheless, influential groups in Hong Kong are anxious to avoid confrontation with China. Among these are the Group of 89, which contains most top entrepreneurs and businessmen in the colony. They are forming a political party which is not in favour of speeding up plans for direct elections in Hong Kong, and wants to focus on economic and other policies, aimed at maintaining Hong Kong's stability and economic success.

This objective was given a boost in June 1990, when President Bush decided to extend China's most-favoured-nation status in the US market, against Congressional opposition. If this had not been done, Hong Kong entrepreneurs with investments in China would have seen much of their exports from China wiped out by the effect of high US tariffs. Hong Kong's shipping, property, and banking sectors would also have been severely affected.[26]

In a survey of manufacturing industry, conducted between June and September 1989, over 60 per cent of companies considered the manufacturing investment climate in Hong Kong to be favourable. This is probably still the view of foreign investors, but it is not necessarily shared by local entrepreneurs. There is little doubt that those Hong Kong entrepreneurs who remain based in Hong Kong will be looking increasingly, in future years, for investment outside China, in Asian and other countries — possibly including the countries of Eastern Europe.

However, given the close links at present between China and Hong Kong, and the likely strengthening of these links, in spite of the events of June 1989, it seems probable that 1997 itself will not be of great economic significance for either China or Hong Kong. Anticipation of 1997, together with strong economic forces in both China and Hong Kong, are bringing the two economies closer together. It seems likely also that Hong Kong's great importance to China as an entrepôt, as a financial centre, and as a window to the rest of the world, will help to ensure Hong Kong's future economic independence, despite (as far as can be foreseen) political pressures to the contrary.

The longer term economic future of Hong Kong must, however, be in doubt. The uncertainty brought about by June 1989, and also

[26] *FEER* (30 May 1990), 'US Legislators Link Freedom to China's MFN Trade Privileges'.

by the ending of British sovereignty, might lead to considerable changes within Hong Kong, and especially in its style of government. Domestic confidence, as evidenced, for example, by the brain drain, might be weakened further. There is a real danger also that the international community will lose faith in Hong Kong's independent future, especially as a financial centre. Whoever governs Hong Kong in the 1990s needs to make sure above all that a stable and healthy financial environment continues to exist. China, more than most countries, has a considerable interest in Hong Kong's financial environment: as a large international trader, as an importer of capital from Hong Kong, and as the owner of a substantial stake in banks and financial institutions in Hong Kong.

If financial stability cannot be achieved, other centres, such as Singapore, will gradually take over Hong Kong's role as a financial centre, and also some of its entrepôt activities. The future economic well-being of Hong Kong after 1997 was always in some doubt. Now these doubts must be stronger. In the end, a great deal will depend on what happens in mainland China. This is impossible to predict, as recent events have shown.

Index